HOW TO SWAP FORD MODULAR ENGINES
INTO MUSTANGS, TORINOS AND MORE

David Stribling

CarTech®

CarTech®, Inc.
838 Lake Street South
Forest Lake, MN 55025
Phone: 651-277-1200 or 800-551-4754
Fax: 651-277-1203
www.cartechbooks.com

© 2017 by David Stribling

All rights reserved. No part of this publication may be reproduced or utilized in any form or by any means, electronic or mechanical, including photocopying, recording, or by any information storage and retrieval system, without prior permission from the Publisher. All text, photographs, and artwork are the property of the Author unless otherwise noted or credited.

The information in this work is true and complete to the best of our knowledge. However, all information is presented without any guarantee on the part of the Author or Publisher, who also disclaim any liability incurred in connection with the use of the information and any implied warranties of merchantability or fitness for a particular purpose. Readers are responsible for taking suitable and appropriate safety measures when performing any of the operations or activities described in this work.

All trademarks, trade names, model names and numbers, and other product designations referred to herein are the property of their respective owners and are used solely for identification purposes. This work is a publication of CarTech, Inc., and has not been licensed, approved, sponsored, or endorsed by any other person or entity. The Publisher is not associated with any product, service, or vendor mentioned in this book, and does not endorse the products or services of any vendor mentioned in this book.

Edit by Paul Johnson
Layout by Monica Seiberlich

ISBN 978-1-61325-578-0
Item No. SA381P

Library of Congress Cataloging-in-Publication Data Available

Written, edited, and designed in the U.S.A.
Printed in the U.S.A.

Title Page:
This pro street 1967 coupe is being fitted with the still popular 2003–2004 Cobra Terminator engine. It doesn't require drive-by-wire or control of variable cam timing and there are plenty of aftermarket power adders to make the Terminator a good choice for a swap. This car will be fitted with the T-56 6-speed and Cobra independent rear suspension. The car has received a mini tub in the back and all four fenders have been flared 1½ inches.

Back Cover Photos

Top:
Fitting a modular engine into 1967–1970 Mustangs and Cougars requires modifications to the towers or a suspension system that eliminates the towers to make room for the wider engines. This 4.6 SOHC is installed in a 1970 Mustang.

Middle Left:
Suspension upgrades include this custom fitment of the 1999–2004 Mustang SN-95 MacPherson strut front suspension. No geomertry is changed and an early Mustang can ride as well as the newer versions.

Middle Right:
For unique installs, I provide a step-by-step method to fabricate your own motor mounts that can rotate 90 degrees to a chassis or crossmember.

Bottom:
Transmission mounts for early Mustangs and later Fox bodies are readily available for a conversion. This crossmember allows for 6 inches of movement in three axes for early Mustang applications.

CONTENTS

Acknowledgments 4
Introduction 5

Chapter 1: Modular Engines: A Brief History 10
Performance History 11
Swap Spotlight: The Mustang in Black............................ 13

Chapter 2: Modular Engine Features and Identification 16
Assembly Plant 17
Engine Identification.. 17
Vehicle VIN 18
Engine Tags.. 19
Engine Block Displacement 20
Cylinder Heads... 20
Crankshafts.. 20
Intakes.. 22
Summary 22
Transmissions.. 23
Ford Crate Engines 25
Aftermarket Parts... 26
Swap Spotlight: The Mustang Evolution 27

Chapter 3: Installing the Modular Engine in a Project Car 29
Engine Dimensions and Weights 30
Frame versus Unibody... 30
Front Suspension Systems 30
Guidelines for Selecting the Right Suspension 31
Early Mustang Suspension 34
Mustang II Suspension 35
Strut Suspensions... 36
Fox-Body Mustangs and Thunderbirds.......................... 37
Other Designs.. 37
Engine Mounts 37
Isolators.. 38
Oiling System 39
Steering System... 44
Power Brakes... 45
Swap Spotlight: One Bad Kat.. 47

Chapter 4: Powertrain Control Modules and Wiring........... 49
Factory Systems Overview... 49
Ford Wiring and Connectors 51
PATS.. 51
Throttle-by-Wire.. 51
Returnless Fuel System... 51
Variable Camshaft Timing (VCT and TI-VCT).................. 52
Ford PCM Communication 52
Reading Error Codes 52
Scan Tools and Data Loggers 53
Programmers.. 54
Factory Wiring Notes 55
Ford Performance Power Parts Control Pack................ 59
Aftermarket Computer Systems...................................... 59
Spotlight Build: 1967 Pro/Street Cobra Mustang Coupe ... 61

Chapter 5: Intakes and Induction 64
Factory Intake Manifold Considerations........................ 67
Intake Manifold 68
Throttle Body 73

Intake Air Temperature Sensor 74
Mass Airflow Meter 74
Manifold Absolute Pressure Sensor............................... 76
Intake Tubing and Filters... 76
Swap Spotlight: Double Trouble..................................... 78

Chapter 6: Fuel Systems 80
Returnless versus Mechanical Return Line Fuel Systems........... 80
Aftermarket Fuel-Bypass Regulators 81
Single versus Dual Fuel Pumps...................................... 82
Aftermarket Fuel Pumps 82
Fuel Pump Voltage Boosters 83
Fuel Injectors and Rails 83
Fuel Filters 85
Fuel Tanks.. 86
Hoses and Fittings 87
EVAP System.. 87
Drive-by-Wire Gas Pedal 87
Swap Spotlight: Factory Five Cobra 90

Chapter 7: Cooling, Ignition and Engine Systems......... 93
Cooling System 93
Sensors... 100
Pulleys... 100
Alternators and Upgrades 100
Air Conditioning... 102
Instrumentation.. 103
Swap Spotlight: 1952 International Pickup.................. 104

Chapter 8: Transmission and Drivetrain 107
Factory Manual Transmissions 108
Aftermarket Manual Transmissions.............................. 110
Factory Automatic Transmissions 111
Aftermarket Automatic Transmissions 111
Transmission Crossmembers and Designs 111
Aftermarket Controllers... 114
Shifters.. 114
Flywheels, Clutches and Pilot Bearings 115
Bellhousing and Adapters... 116
Clutch Actuation 117
Driveshafts... 118
Swap Spotlight: Coyote Swap into a Fox-Body Mustang......... 123

Chapter 9: Exhaust System 125
Factory Exhaust Manifolds 125
Aftermarket Exhaust Manifolds and Headers 127
Conversion Headers and Header Components 129
Catalytic Converters 129
Oxygen Sensors... 131
Cat-Back Exhaust... 131
Swap Spotlight: 1968 Torino 132

Chapter 10: Startup Tips for Success.......................... 134
Swap Spotlight: 1976 Ford F-100.................................. 138

Glossary... 140
Source Guide 142

Acknowledgments

Although it is true that a book like this doesn't happen by the efforts of one individual, I need to acknowledge that the efforts of the contributors have, in most cases, gone above and beyond just handing out a photo or two. Good personal and business relationships helped to make this book happen.

First, to my mother, Carole Stribling, who doesn't know too much about the technical aspects of car building but knows how to correct some of my Midwest grammar atrocities. To Bruce Faucett, former Application Engineer for Allison Transmission and former NHRA drag racer and current SCCA transplant, I can't thank you enough for your help in sorting out my structure and pointing out my horrible overuse of pronouns. You both have earned my gratitude for your long hours of assistance.

Other key players in this project are Jim Smart, Ron Dickerson, Blake Hartman, and Alexandros Varvounis. Jim Smart helped me gather much needed photos from his immense archives. Ron Dickerson and Blake Hartman allowed me to photograph their collections of eye candy. And Alexandros Varvounis sent photos to a complete stranger. I really appreciate it!

To the people who went above and beyond at my never ending email requests, Andrew Casselberry at Ford Performance Parts; Mark Luton at Modular Motorsports Racing; Eric Vengroff with Sean Hyland Motorsport; Harold Miller at Trick Flow; Mike Roth and MR2 Performance; Brent White and Chase Tenney at Brenspeed; Dennis Devitt at Etter Ford; and Marcia Sledge, Mike Melvin, and Curtis White at Autozone.

For the builders, owners, and business contacts of the projects featured in the book: Robert Emery, Brett Behrens, Chris Donaldson, Skyler Hardy, Gordon Trotson, David Lindsey, Craig Wood and Jeremy Keller, Ryan Korek, Waylon Inman, and Jose Mujia. Thank you for the pictures of your amazing rides.

None of this would have been possible were it not for a customer and a friend, Doug Allen, who saw my vision of putting new and old technologies together to build the MIB car all those years ago. Thank you for your support of my dreams. Special thanks to Mark Houlahan for thinking of me and giving me the column at *Mustang Monthly* and supporting me.

Thanks goes to my children, Caleb and Kayla Surber, Kara and Jordan Stribling. You make the long hours worth it. And thank you to Jesus Christ, who has saved me where stamped steel and petroleum products cannot.

INTRODUCTION

The first 25 years of the Ford modular engine family are now in the books, and the conversion craze has only been a part of that history for the past few years. Why has it taken so long for the conversion to catch on and become a genuine option to older, pushrod technology?

When Ford introduced the modular engine platform in 1991, it was a quantum leap forward in V-8 technology and shared almost nothing in common with the traditional pushrod Windsor V-8 small-block. Unlike the GM Gen II and III platform, this was a brand-new engine. It would take some time to build up a following and a database of knowledge before the aftermarket would really embrace the new platform. Until it was introduced in the Mustang in 1996, it didn't get much traction as a performance engine and was considered a big car and truck engine.

The modular engine was unlike anything else Ford had produced. They did build an SOHC version of the 427 back in the 1960s, but that was a conversion of an existing platform, and the modular engine shared very little with any of the 1960s technology. The GM Gen II (1992–1997) and Gen III and IV (LS platform 1997–up) were big jumps in technology over the original small-block Chevrolet, but they were still essentially pushrod V-8s with the original bore spacing, inner infrastructure, and two valves per cylinder setup from the small-block Chevy. The LS platform had a feel that was familiar, even with its distributorless ignition and different head design. The aftermarket grabbed hold of the LS platform and products came out at a feverish pace. In 2003, Chrysler introduced its 5.7-liter Hemi engine, which was also based on a pushrod platform. Both the GM and Chrysler engines offered the aftermarket a two-valve pushrod engine that used a lot of the data that they had acquired and applied it almost immediately to the new engines. Fitting the GM and Chrysler engines was also familiar because the engines shared a similar footprint to their older counterparts.

The new modular engine didn't intimidate the aftermarket, but the aftermarket was cautious. Although performance was there from the beginning, the Ford aftermarket had to build a brand-new database, and most of what they had learned about the Ford small-block Windsor wasn't going to crossover to the new platform. In a very short time we went from pushrods, distributors, and lifters, to overhead cams, coil packs, and valve-lash adjusters. It was going to take some time and some really good builders to begin a new database to work with the new platform.

Although the Ford modular engine was successful in the racing world, it did suffer some setbacks in certain race venues, such as NASCAR. NASCAR specified a pushrod, carbureted V-8 platform, so Ford Performance continued to invest a large amount into the Windsor small-block program. The LS platform, with its similarity to the original small-block Chevy, had some items approved for the NASCAR circuit, but the overhead-cam Ford was shut out.

Another issue with the modular engine has been Ford taking quantum leaps every couple of years, sending the aftermarket arena back for more data collection. After the introduction of the two-valve engine, Ford released the four-valve DOHC engine. Then Ford brought out the Terminator engines in 2003 and changed everything again. In 2005, the three-valve replaced some of the two-valves, and the aftermarket designers were back to the drawing board. In 2011, the Coyote hit the market and the playing field changed again, and in 2015 the 5.2 was introduced. Although the GM LS engine made similar improvements to its platform, the platform itself didn't change a whole lot. With the Ford engine, these were huge jumps in technology, and the aftermarket spent a lot of time playing catch up. It was good, but it required time to gather information and apply it.

Ford Performance Parts also continued to provide great products, and also raised the bar every couple of years. We got amazing engines, including the Cammer, the Aluminator,

INTRODUCTION

The Ford modular engine produces impressive power, and it makes an excellent powerplant to swap into 1967–1973 Mustangs and many other Ford and non-Ford vehicles.

and the Cobra Jet. It was Ford Performance that finally gave us the one piece that would set the ball rolling for mass use of these engines in more custom cars: the Ford Control Pack computer system.

Because the modular engine is very dependent on its computer controls to run effectively, it did intimidate a lot of builders who preferred the pushrod platform to the new overhead-cam engine. Pushrod EFI conversions continued to flourish, while the modular engine conversions tended to be novelty items, more than practical options. Most of the aftermarket computer systems were designed for all-out racing, not as options for street-driven vehicles (and not legal in some states due to emissions). Ford's Control Packs changed that, as builders found that the simplified controls meant real use for these engines in their conversions.

Industry tech upgrades also played a part for all the major manufacturers. During the run of the modular engine we have seen improvements in ignition (going from coil packs to individual coils), throttle-by-wire (no more cable controls), and variable valve timing (moving the camshaft to improve emissions and performance). Every new technology required new data to make it viable for conversion projects.

Engine dimensions play a role in placing the modular engine in the engine compartment. The footprint of the LS platform is similar to its earlier cousin's; the overhead-cam engines are considerably wider than the original small-block Ford. Although the big-block Ford had been stuffed into small street rods for years, the size and perceived complexity of the modular engine put off some builders in favor of the older engines.

The modular engine conversion became a genuine alternative with the introduction of the Coyote engine in 2011. It wasn't so much about the Coyote engine as it was all of the pieces coming together. In Ford, we had a magnificent engine in the Coyote four-valve, putting out more than 400 hp without breaking a sweat. We'd had the control computers in place for several years, the aftermarket was rolling along with a good database, real conversion products were starting to hit the market, and this engine was winning. Winning big. It was time for this engine, which had been around for 20 years, to come out of the shadows and be a viable option to other conversions.

Whereas most conversions are done for the horsepower gains, the modular engine conversion offers the builder much more than an eye-popping set of hemi heads under the hood. These engines are capable of tremendous power while being amazingly efficient and easy to maintain. The control systems are excellent, and when done properly, require less maintenance than their earlier cousins. More and more components are being introduced to install these engines in different chassis, and the number of vendors supplying products will continue to grow now that the conversion is seen as something more than a novelty idea. The modular engine conversion can provide amazing looks, big horsepower, fuel efficiency, and trouble-free operation, all in one package.

Why a Modular Engine Swap?

The best reason for upgrading to a modular engine is that it is an incredibly efficient, low-friction engine that lends itself to both performance and reliability. Builders have been pushing limits with the modular engines that they couldn't try with the old pushrod engines. Because of the nature of the overhead-cam technologies, it has been banned from some "heads up" engine builds against its rivals in other brands.

Now in its second quarter of a century, the modular engine provides a balance between efficiency, horsepower, and reliability not found in pushrod engines. The bugs are worked out and it is rolling right along. The modern computer controls help you get every ounce of performance and efficiency out of these engines.

I admit it: The main reason most enthusiasts perform a modular engine swap is the WOW! factor. That's it. There is nothing like opening the hood of your car and seeing those overhead-cam covers sitting down in the engine bay. But the modular engine provides so much more than looks.

Reasons for a Modular Engine Swap

Reasons to consider a modular engine swap for your next project extend far beyond the eye candy looks of the engine in your engine bay.

Overhead Camshafts

The Ford flathead had its camshaft in the same basic location as most overhead-valve engines, and moving the valves over the top of the cylinder heads improved the fuel and airflow as well as improved the combustion process. Pushrod engines still relied on valve lifters and pushrods to transfer camshaft motion to a set of rocker arms that pushed the valve in the opposite direction of the camshaft lobe lift. This means a lot of valvetrain inertia loss and energy loss through mechanical transfer. The overhead cams in the modular engine eliminate a large amount of this valvetrain loss by eliminating items such as the lifters (though they use a hydraulic slack adjuster to maintain valve lash) and reducing the size of the springs; the valvetrain is virtually maintenance free.

Low-Friction Design

Ever look at a new engine and wonder how they can run a thin, 5W-20 weight oil? Computer design and tighter tolerances mean you can run lighter-weight oils, which means it takes less energy to spin an oil pump, which means less lost power and better efficiency.

No Distributor/Engine Timing

Instead of a distributor, the modular engine features a computer that controls engine ignition with a greater range of fire. The computer can adjust the trigger and fire the spark plugs when it is optimal, rather than when a mechanically rotating electric circuit gets into position under the distributor cap. The new engines can even adjust the position of the camshaft relative to the crankshaft via a system called VCT (Variable Camshaft Timing) or TI-VCT (Twin Independent Variable Camshaft Timing). By retarding or advancing the camshaft timing, performance is optimized and the emissions can be reduced, eliminating some emission equipment for the drivetrain.

Durable Bottom End

The skirted block has a cross-bolted main cap system, similar to the big-block Ford FE 427's. The head bolts extend down into the block webbing, providing additional

The last U.S.-built Ford pushrod V-8 was a 5.0 small-block and was installed in the 2001 Ford Explorer. It came with a low-friction roller valvetrain, multi-port fuel injection, and distributorless ignition. It was still no match for the efficiency of the overhead cam modular engine, and the 39-year reign of the small-block Ford came to an end.

INTRODUCTION

strength. The results were evident as Ford pushed 15 pounds of boost through the stock engine in a 2013–14 GT500, and the performance world is pushing the envelope further.

The modular engine is an extremely reliable platform. The last-generation of the pushrod 5.0 V-8 was reliable as well and featured electronic ignitions and fuel injection. Installing a pushrod Ford small-block in your car is a popular swap that's been done extensively for years, and the parts are available to make it a much cheaper option than a modular engine swap. But with the modular engine you get a pound-for-pound more efficient engine and drivetrain combination.

Modern Diagnostic Support

The latest computer systems can tell you exactly what is going on inside the engine, and aftermarket tuning and programmers make these engines scream at the same time they are efficient.

One last thing to consider is that the last factory pushrod engines came out in 2001. Some new auto mechanics may have never worked on a pushrod Ford, tuned a carb, or even owned a timing light!

What You Need to Know

Before jumping into a modular engine project, some important guidelines and points need to be considered. Some outside services may be needed to assist in completing the project, and you need to understand your own skill set before beginning. My hope is that by buying this book that is just what you are doing. Perhaps you are looking at purchasing someone else's project and need to find out if it is worth finishing. Knowledge is king, the more you know up front the more success you will have in the end.

If you are looking for high horsepower, a traditional pushrod engine can make more horsepower for less money than a modular engine. It's simple math: four cams instead of one, and the cams are more than just four times the price. While the modular engine can make a huge amount of power, and in some cases exceed the capabilities of older engines, it does come at a price. Fuel injection is more expensive than a carburetor, but fuel injection is much more versatile. Unlike installing a small-block in your favorite 1949 Mercury, it may not be possible to phone up your favorite parts supplier and order engine mounts. It is going to take more planning than most Ford builds, and more than some other company swaps that are old pushrod technology repackaged and re-badged.

Fabrication

Even if parts are available, many times fabrication to make these engines fit into specific chassis may be necessary. For example, some older Ford chassis have large shock towers that conflict with the wider engines, requiring them to be trimmed and re-welded. If you do not have the ability to make modifications, partner with a good fabricator before the project starts.

Tuning and Computer Data

As stated in Chapters 4 and 10, programming the computer is a critical part of making any modern engine perform to its peak. Unless you have a large base knowledge of fuel curves, air-fuel ratios, and oxygen sensor data, the best course of action is to find a reputable tuner and work with them during the project build. This is especially true if you will be making extensive modifications or installing custom components on the engine. It is critical to work with a tuner throughout the build.

Getting Started

Every time I get an inquiry about a modular engine swap, the first question I always ask is: what do you want to do with the car when you are done? Is your purpose for building this car reliability, racing and handling, horsepower, or a full-blown show car? An honest definition of what you want at the end is important to keep your project on target. If you are looking for a good daily driver that looks dynamite (on a modest budget), a high-horsepower supercharged Shelby 5.8 GT500 swap may not be the best choice.

Three Little Questions

Before you buy that half-done project or dream of that magazine car you just saw, decide what the true goal of this vehicle will be. It will help you answer these three questions:

1. Which engine and transmission are you going to use?
2. Which front suspension are you going to use?
3. Which electronics package are you going to use?

Once you have answered these three questions, a vast majority of the parts required to complete your project start showing themselves. Choosing your engine helps you determine the electronics package, choosing the electronics package helps you determine items such as the fuel system,

INTRODUCTION

and settling on the front suspension helps you decide on engine mounts and auxiliary equipment such as radiators and cooling.

Engine and Transmission

You need to select the best modular engine and transmission for your project, so you need to refer to Chapter 2 to make the best choice. Although I address some performance parts in this book, they are in reference to getting your project up and running and not a guide on how to build a monster engine. For that I am going to direct you to my bookshelf and some of the books I rely on: *How to Build Max Performance 4.6-Liter Ford Engines* by Sean Hyland, *4.6 and 5.4 Ford Engines: How to Rebuild* by George Reid, and *Ford 5.0 Coyote Engines: How to Build Max-Performance* by Jim Smart.

Back to my first question: what is the intent of this build? A four-cam 5.4-liter engine is wider and taller than a two-cam 4.6 engine, so it will cost more time and money to drop that engine into a confined space. If over-the-top horsepower is desired, let's look at the taller and wider 5.4, 5.8, or perhaps a V-10 6.8. But if you want something a little more budget and daily-driving oriented, look at the engine that best fits your budget. The 4.6 and 5.0 Coyote have the same base dimensions and can make large amounts of horsepower in the smaller block.

Transmission selection also plays a part in building your project. As transmissions add additional gears, they also add size, and this can conflict with the transmission tunnels on some chassis. Electronic controls are the norm on all modern transmissions, and that may affect the control package you choose. The quick answer here is, if the big 6-speed you want to install doesn't fit, there are alternatives that will work to keep the project rolling. (See Chapter 8 for more information on transmission packages.)

Front Suspension

The front suspension (Chapter 3) helps in the selection of items such as engine mounts and cooling packages. The reason this is important is, the front suspension on many builds determines where the engine is going to sit in the engine bay, and which engine and transmission mounts need to be purchased to install the engine. For example, an early Mustang application can use the original suspension or can convert to a Mustang II front suspension, but both options require different engine mounts, oil pans, and transmission mounts. The shock towers can be removed with the MII suspension, while the original suspension may need to be trimmed back to fit the wider four-cam engines.

Once the front suspension has been selected, many of the other component requirements fall into place. Engine placement may also answer questions on items such as the cooling (how close is the engine to the radiator), oil pans (front sump, rear sump), and the steering itself (header clearance). Not all front suspensions have been designed with modular engines in mind, and you may have to fabricate to make it work together.

Electronics

After you decide on the engine and suspension, you need to decide on the electronics package. An old drag racer's saying applies: You can have all the right parts, but if you can't tune the engine, they are worthless. That saying is taken to the next level with the computer controls on your modern engine. Although it is possible to run the modular engine with a carburetor and distributor, most applications involve the modern engine controls and computer. In the old days, you ordered a cam kit, a carburetor, an intake, and a set of headers; set your points; adjusted the carburetor; and you were set. Today's engines get their power and efficiency from properly tuning the engine, and proper tuning requires a database of information to find out which combinations work best, and how they will work with the intended use of the vehicle. If a computer will be part of the conversion build, working directly with a good tuner is essential, especially if additional mods will be made to the engine for performance.

Chapter 4 is all about the different changes Ford made to the computers and wiring, and your engine choice is influential in determining which computer system works best for your project. Some engines work well with factory systems, some do not. The choice of computer system also helps with choosing items such as the fuel system (returnless or mechanical return line) and engine systems such as drive-by-wire and variable-cam timing. (Chapter 10 details final tuning of the engine package and working with the tuner and the dyno.)

Once you have the engine, front suspension, and electronics package selected, you can then fill in all the other components that will make your build a success.

CHAPTER 1

MODULAR ENGINES: A BRIEF HISTORY

In 1991 Ford introduced its overhead camshaft V-8 in the Lincoln Town Car and labeled it the modular engine. The label came from the method of producing the engine, not the fact that parts are easily interchanged between engine configurations. Eventually it was installed in the full-size Ford Crown Victoria, Mercury Grand Marquis, and the 1994 Ford Thunderbird as the old Windsor small-block V-8 was being phased out. The last year for the pushrod V-8 in a Mustang was 1995. The 1996 Mustang GT was fitted with a two-valve SOHC modular and the Cobra was equipped with a four-valve DOHC version of the 4.6-liter engine. The first Ford trucks equipped with a modular engine came in 1996, and in 1997 Ford introduced the V-10 6.8-liter engine for truck and van applications.

Ford installed its very last production pushrod V-8 gas engine for the American market in the 2001 Ford Explorer, and the following year the final pushrod V-8 engine was sold in Australia. The versatility of the Ford modular engine allowed it to replace three different pushrod engines: the small-block 5.0- and 5.8-liter Windsor small-blocks and the 385 (429/460) series big-block. It will soon become the second-longest-production Ford V-8 engine behind the small-block.

The modular engine was marketed under the name "Intech" V-8 for Lincoln applications and "Triton" for the Ford truck line.

It is important to note that the modular engine does not derive its

On the left is the granddaddy of the first generation of Muscle, the 1970 Boss 429, and on the right is the highest horsepower factory modular engine to date, the 2014 Shelby GT500 Track Pack. The tale of the tape shows how far we have come in 45 years. The Boss 429 puts out a realistic 420–450 hp, and the Shelby an amazing 662 hp. The Boss bolts to 0–60 mph in 7.1 seconds; the Shelby 3.7 seconds. Top speed for the Boss 429 was more than 130 mph, and the Shelby was the first factory Mustang to eclipse 200 mph. MPG for the Boss is 8 to 12 mpg (if you're lucky); the Shelby produces 15 to 24 mpg. Vehicles provided by the Dickerson Collection.

MODULAR ENGINES: A BRIEF HISTORY

The very first Ford modular engine was installed in the 1991 Lincoln Continental. The first engines depended on a lot of borrowed pieces from pushrod V-8s such as the EEC-IV computer and the non-electronic AOD transmissions. The modular engine really started to work well with the introduction of the EEC-V computer system in 1994.

The first tall-deck block installed in the Mustang came in the limited-edition 2000 Ford Cobra R. These 5.4 4V engines used exclusive custom cast and machined heads and special intakes to generate 385-hp naturally aspirated. Only 300 Cobra Rs were produced in 2000. Vehicle courtesy the Dickerson Collection.

name from the ability to swap and bolt different parts from different engines onto a common platform. It gets its name from the manufacturing process in which different manufacturing cells can be pulled and installed, and the plant can be quickly re-arranged to build a different engine configuration. In fact, the modular engine is far from "modular." As you learn in Chapter 2, the modular engine is anything but adaptable, with changes happening between the two different primary plants that build them in the same model year. Gone are the days of Ford making a dozen different and exotic cylinder heads to bolt on a 427 medium-riser block; it is difficult to swap components with the modular engines. If you want to purchase a supercharger for a modular engine, the supplier will have a myriad of questions for you before they sell you one, to make sure you get the right equipment.

Performance History

As of this writing, the modular engine has been around for 25 years and will soon become the second-longest-running V-8 engine series in Ford production history, surpassing the big-block 385 series engine. Only the small-block Windsor has had a longer life span. In addition, 8 of the top-10 fastest production Fords of all time are modular-engine powered (the original FE-powered GT40 and the new Eco-Boost GT40 are the only exceptions).

Due to its robust bottom end, the modular engine could support more cylinder pressure when boosted with turbos or superchargers, and higher compression ratios in naturally aspirated form. It was also the first factory supercharged V-8 because the E-Bird Thunderbird of the 1950s (Shelby offered a supercharger option for the 1966 GT350). The first supercharged modular engines were 5.4-liter 2V lightning engines 1999–2004, followed by the 4.6-liter 4V 2003–2004 Mustang Cobras. The modular engine responds well to supercharging, and the highest horsepower factory Ford ever produced was the 2013–2014 Shelby GT500, which put out a mind-blowing 662 hp out of a CAFE-regulated engine.

Ford V-8 Engine Production History

Engine Family	Years in Production	Start/End
Y-Block	10 years	1954–1964
Cleveland/Modified	12 years	1970–1982
FE Big-Block	18 years	1958–1976
Flathead	21 years	1932–1953
Modular	**26 years+**	**1991–**
385 Big-Block	29 years	1968–1997
Windsor Small-Block	39 years	1962–2001

Ford re-entered the supercar market with the modular-powered 2005–2006 GT. These cars were capable of 0–60 in 3.4 seconds and a top speed of 205 mph. Vehicle provided by Blake Hartman.

With current CAFE regulations, manufacturers are free to build higher horsepower in trucks than they are with cars. The first modular engines to be supercharged from the factory were the Lightning trucks in the 1990s. This 2014 Raptor features the largest displacement V-8 modular platform available, the 6.2 SOHC.

The supercharged 5.4 installed in the Ford GT is custom built and puts out 550 hp stock. If you look closely you can see the dual fuel injectors fitted to these special engines. By overdriving the supercharger (pulley change) and a program upgrade these engines are capable of well more than 800 hp. Vehicle provided by Blake Hartman.

The 2013–2014 Shelby GT500 is equipped with the most powerful engine ever installed in a factory-built Ford, 662 hp and 631 ft-lbs of torque. Along with its 200-mph top end, it is fully capable of driving around in city traffic without overheating or being finicky.

Swap Spotlight: The Mustang in Black

For the first 10 years of the modular engine, the conversions to other vehicles were primarily novelties used in high-end cars and not considered practical for common use vehicles. The technology was different, more expensive, and at the time, the performance and mileage differences between the modular engine and the latest pushrod engines were not significantly different. Most of the conversion parts had to be fabricated because parts to install the new engines just didn't exist. And even though we had EFI computers since the 1980s, most owners found the conversion intimidating.

Mustang in Black (MIB) was built in conjunction with *Mustang Monthly* and *Mustang and Fords* magazine, and it was more than just an engine swap. It was built to prove that the newer technology could be adapted to the earlier cars, and could be used in a practical way, rather than just as a novelty. MIB was built to show that the same performance, convenience, and controls built into new cars could be applied to older-model cars and be a practical alternative to a pushrod conversion. Most engine swaps at that time concerned themselves only with the engine and somehow making it run. MIB incorporates all the drivetrain improvements from a 1999 Ford Mustang Cobra into a 1968 Mustang chassis. The Mustang in Black represents the full range of why you would want to choose a modular engine swap. It has plenty of power, starts with the hit of the key, gets great gas mileage if you keep your foot out of it, and you can take it to any Ford dealer in the country and the dealership can talk to it.

The project goal was summed up in a single statement: "This is what SVT would have built had they been around in 1968." To that end, the goal was not to make a Shelby clone, an unreasonable super car, or a car that was chromed out for show. Instead, the builders took a practical approach to the build, to which one paint rep stated, "Its understated appearance is what puts it over the top."

The Mustang in Black (MIB) was built by the author and was featured in Mustang Monthly *and* Mustang and Fords *magazine back in the mid-2000s. Not only was the 1968 chassis fitted with a 99 Cobra engine, but the complete drivetrain and electronics package were incorporated to demonstrate the new technology would work in the older chassis.*

The 320-hp 4.6 DOHC engine was fitted to the 1968 engine bay and fits under the stock hood. In addition the suspension was installed in the chassis. Rather than apply a lot of chrome and polish, the designers decided to go for a look that would say, "This is how SVT would have built it had it been around in 1968." One journalist said it best: "What makes this car over the top is its understatement."

The donor vehicle for the project was a 1999 Mustang Cobra convertible that had been wrecked but was a complete, driving vehicle. The goal was to use as many of the systems from the donor vehicle as possible, and graft them into the 1968 Mustang fastback chassis. Most of the parts on MIB have a Ford part number on them. The car's powerplant is a naturally aspirated 32-valve DOHC V-8 that makes 320 hp. No modifications were needed to the engine and the only aftermarket improvement to the engine was the inclusion of the K&N Cobra air filter, which fit the 1968 chassis perfectly. Other than the air filter, every original system is as it was when the car left the Ford assembly plant.

The original Tremec T-45 5-speed transmission and clutch assembly were used, as they were low mileage and still in good shape. The first clutch system used the original fork and throwout bearing mated to a Ron Morris Performance cable clutch conversion, which used the sheath in the cable assembly to pull the clutch forward. This was later replaced with a hydraulic throwout bearing and clutch master cylinder. With the placement of the engine in the engine compartment, only a minor trim of about an inch was necessary at the front of the transmission shifter hole to make the Tremec fit. With the addition of the 1968 console, an offset shifter handle was used and the modification was completely hidden.

When deciding on the suspension, the builders avoided using the original suspension or a conversion to an aftermarket Mustang II. They wanted this car to perform and ride like a new car, so the front MacPherson Strut suspension was used and the rear was adapted to run the new-for-1999 Cobra independent rear suspension. Rather than cutting the suspension to work in the chassis, the chassis was designed to bolt the new components in as original, so none of the Ford geometry was changed in the conversion. This also means that any type of aftermarket improvements made to the SN-95 Mustang suspension would bolt up to the 1968 Mustang. The only changes to the front suspension were

The complete factory K-member and front MacPherson strut suspension were grafted to the original 1968 chassis via a new set of frame rails and major surgery. The donor car was a convertible, and the original 1999 Cobra convertible under-chassis brace was modified to tie into the factory 1968 Mustang torque boxes and thus provide additional chassis stiffening.

the addition of Hotchkis caster/camber plates, a set of Koni Sport struts, and the front coils were cut down by one coil. The remainder is all Ford. The only change to the independent rear suspension was a set of Koni adjustable coil-over shocks and Hypercoil springs.

The original 1999 hydroboost braking system was nearly a bolt-in solution and all the original hoses were used. Because the original computer and all four original ABS wheels were still in place, the Bosch ABS unit was also used and functions in the car. Brakes are all stock 1999 Cobra, 13 inches up front and 11 inches in the rear.

The computer system is the stock EEC-V Cobra computer with only a change to bypass the PATS system and the upgrade of the K&N filter. The use of the factory computer and wiring harness allowed the use of the electronic speed control and factory traction control defeat circuit (cleverly hidden in the 1968 reverse lockout pull in the shifter handle).

The stock Cobra exhaust was stretched to match the longer 1968 chassis, and the outlets were custom bent to match the original GT exhaust cutouts. The car retains the sound of the 1999 Cobra.

The 1968 chassis was then fitted with every available option in 1968: deluxe interior and exterior, tilt-away steering, upper and lower consoles, fold-down rear seat, and air conditioning. The modern A/C components were combined with the original underdash components, and the speed control circuit was grafted to an original 1968 speed/turn signal stalk and underdash control switch.

Components not taken from the original donor car include the Alpine stereo and remote CD player (the original AM radio is still in the car; the Alpine deck is hidden in the center console and operated by remote), aftermarket power windows and locks designed for the early Mustang chassis, and a custom-made speedometer from an AutoMeter 160-mph digital unit with a stock-style Mustang face. The original (and rare) 1968 deluxe seats with headrests were eventually replaced with matching black and charcoal high-back seats from a 2003 Mach I.

The car is painted in BASF Glasurit paint, with a custom C stripe that matches the charcoal on the Bullitt rims purchased from the Roush factory from some of its conversion cars. No Shelby styling cues on this car, rather it is full Mustang. While the running horse is still installed in the grille, the corral was removed and a pair of Hella Black Magic fog lights are installed in the grille (attached to a stock 1968 fog light switch).

MIB can be taken to any Ford dealer and serviced: during the final build stage, the car was taken to the dealer for a DTC (diagnostic test code) cooling fan test, and the scanner detected a problem with an oxygen sensor that happened to be unplugged!

The builders of MIB succeeded in showing the world that *all* the technology from the newer cars could be incorporated into a conversion project, not just the engine. The editor of *Mustang Monthly* described the ride simply: "The senses struggle with conflict because the view from behind the steering wheel is all vintage, yet mashing the 1968 accelerator pedal results in the smooth, powerful rush that comes only from a modern four-valve modular engine."

As a result, in 2009 *Mustang Monthly* selected MIB as one of its 45 Most Significant Mustangs of All Time.

In keeping with the "factory" look, the stamped-steel shock towers from the SN-95 Cobra were incorporated into the 1968 chassis. Because the 1999 chassis is wider, the towers are inset similar to the 1969–1970 Boss 429s. The front suspension was not altered, so the factory geometry remains. Hotchkis caster/camber plates were installed.

The stock 1999 Cobra fuel pump was fitted into a replacement 1968 Mustang fuel tank. In 1999 Ford went to a returnless fuel system, and by mounting the pump into the stock tank the engineers were able to take advantage of the returnless design.

A custom, fully adjustable transmission mount was designed to allow 6 inches of movement in three axis. With this mount and with the front strut system, no tunnel trimming was necessary with this T-45 transmission. A 1-inch cut was trimmed out for the shifter location, but the shifter still works with the 1968 stock console. The factory Cobra H-pipe was used with the stock oxygen sensors.

Some of the GTs and Cobras of the SN-95 era were equipped with a hydroboost power brake assist. The hydroboost was nearly a bolt-in with this install and allowed for the wide 4V engine to fit in the 1968 chassis. Other than matching the mounting holes to the firewall, the hydroboost system works with the original 1968 Mustang non–power brake pedal pin location.

CHAPTER 2

MODULAR ENGINE FEATURES AND IDENTIFICATION

The Ford modular engine has a long, varied, and unique history that has spanned more than 25 years, with many component, year, and factory of manufacture differences. With this storied and distinguished history, you need to recognize that all modular engines were not created equal. The only thing these engines really have in common is that they are all overhead camshaft V-8s (or V-10s). They come in three base varieties: the Single Overhead Camshaft (SOHC) produced with either two or three valves and the Double Overhead Camshaft (DOHC). Three block heights were used: the smaller displacements (4.6, 5.0, and 5.2), the large displacements (5.4, 5.8, and 6.8 V-10), and the "midsize" deck height of the 6.2. After that the similarities start to fade.

The two-valve version of the SOHC started out in Ford big cars and was then used in Ford trucks. It was delayed in the new Mustang platform until 1996 and a GT version was used up until 2005. Both 4.6 and 5.4 SOHC versions were installed in Ford trucks up until 2005. The 4.6 and 5.4 2V continued its run in big cars and trucks up through 2014. The 6.2 F-150 Raptor and truck engine uses SOHC heads on the taller block. The three-valve version was introduced in 2005 and was used in the Mustang GT through 2010. The 4.6 3V was dropped in 2010, but the 5.4 3V continued in some trucks until 2015.

The first DOHC engines were installed in Lincolns way back in

Ford Performance Parts offers both a production and modified version of the 5.0 Coyote engine. The M-6007-M50A is rated at 435 hp and 400 ft-lbs of torque. It has an aluminum block and DOHC heads, forged steel crank and rods, and features 11:1 compression. It shares the same mounting pattern as earlier modular engines so it transplants well. (Photo Courtesy Ford Performance Parts)

1993. The 4V became the basis for all the performance-based modular engines. The First Mustang Cobras got the 4V engine in 1996. A 5.4 version of the DOHC was built for some big Lincoln Navigators, the 2000 Cobra R, and the 2007–2010 GT500s. In 2011, Ford introduced the now famous "Coyote" 5.0 4V, which replaced most of the 3V applications in trucks and replaced all the 4.6 and 5.4 engines in all the Mustangs. The Boss 302 and Cobra Jet performance versions are based on the Coyote, and the Coyote platform is also the basis for the 2013–2014 Shelby GT500 5.8 engines, which use the taller engine block with improved heads. The Coyote is also the foundation for the new 5.2 flat plane crank Shelby engine. For big truck application, Ford made a V-10 that uses modular engine technology. The displacement is 6.8 and it came in 2V and 3V SOHC configurations. It was used in trucks and vans up through 2015.

Later three- and four-valve engines produce far more horsepower and torque than earlier two-valve engines. The later two-valve engines produce much more horsepower than the earlier engines. Keep this in mind when you're sourcing an engine for your project car.

This chapter gives you a brief history of the modular engine, and it highlights the major differences among engines in the series. I do not have the space to cover all differences because that would require a book all its own, and it would be obsolete once it was written. Because Ford frequently makes changes to this platform, fitment and components often change. And what is true today may very well not be true tomorrow.

This chapter provides a comprehensive guide to the range of modular engines and should help you to identify what you have. And whether you are well-versed in modular performance or a complete novice, remember this one rule: You need to know the engine package you have; it not only determines the suitability for a particular engine swap to a chassis, but with all the changes and inflexibility this knowledge keeps you from making a very expensive mistake.

You would think that an engine labeled "modular" would easily interchange within the engine family and that the parts would interchange between platforms with ease. But nothing is further from the truth. As you will discover, the modular engine family has tremendous variety among parts and little commonality. The "truth" is that unless you are knowledgeable about these engines, very little interchanges. These engines were assembled in different plants, and parts were built differently at the various locations. These engines are matched components to a specific platform. In part because they do not interchange well, Ford put out several Technical Service Bulletins (T.S.B.) to assist mechanics in working on these engines. It is important to know what you have. If you plan on doing performance upgrades, it is important to partner with people who are versed in these engines and read the books recommended in Chapter 1.

Assembly Plant

Ford manufactured the modular engine at the Windsor, Ontario; Romeo, Michigan; and Essex, Ontario, factories. All of these plants have different specifications or blueprints and, as a result, the modular engines built at the various factories are often different. To give you an idea of how complex these engines are, here are just a few of the many changes between the Romeo and Windsor SOHC engines:

- Valvecover bolts: Romeo blocks use 11 bolts to hold the passenger-side valvecover; Windsor blocks use 14.
- Main caps: Romeo early blocks use a smaller main bearing than Windsors. The Romeo uses a single thrust washer; the Windsor uses two thrust washers. Early Romeo blocks used a jack screw between the main cap and side skirt; Windsors used a dowel system. In 1999 Ford began eliminating the jack screw system in favor of interference-fit main caps on some blocks.
- Crankshafts: Windsor blocks use six bolts to hold the flywheel or flexplate to the crankshaft. Romeo can be either 6- or 8-bolt depending on application. Most performance engines use the 8-bolt crank.
- Connecting rods: Windsor pistons use a floating pin; the Romeo is a press fit pin.
- Camshaft sprockets: Windsor is a press on; Romeo uses a bolt and spacer.

As you can see, it can be difficult to interchange parts between assembly plants.

Engine Identification

If you are not purchasing a crate engine or buying from a known source, it's important to be able to identify what engine you are contemplating. Ford has not been particularly consistent in its means of identifying the modular engines through the years, and what works with some engines doesn't work with others. An engine cobbled together by someone unfamiliar with the platform can end up an expensive boat anchor. In the end, if you can't identify the engine, walk away from the deal.

Vehicle VIN

If you are looking at a complete donor vehicle for your swap project, two pieces of information from the Vehicle Identification Number (VIN) help you figure out what you have and what you need. The first is the 8th digit of the VIN that specifies the engine installed in the vehicle. The second is the 10th digit that denotes the model year of the vehicle (not the year it was built). The VIN is

If you are looking at a complete donor car or are shopping for a used engine, the vehicle VIN sticker in the door tells you a lot about the engine and drivetrain. The 8th digit of the VIN is the engine, and on this 2010 Mustang it is an "H," which is a 4.6 3V engine rated at 315 hp. The 10th digit tells the year of manufacture, here an "A," which stands for 2010 (note the car build date noted in the upper left-hand corner is 09/09). The transmission is denoted under TR as "K," which denotes a Tremec TR-3650 5-speed.

Modular Engine ID for Cars				
8th digit of VIN	Displacement	Fuel type	H/P	Years
Vehicle Type: Car				
F	5.0 DOHC	Gasoline	406–420	2011–2015
H	4.6 SOHC 3V	Gasoline	300–315	2005–2010
H	5.4 DOHC C/R	Gasoline	385	2000
R	4.6 DOHC R/A	Gasoline	305	2002–2004
S	5.4 DOHC GT	Gasoline	550	2004–2006
S	5.4 DOHC S/C	Gasoline	500–550	2006–2012
U	5.0 DOHC B	Gasoline	444	2012–2013
V	4.6 DOHC	Gasoline	260–305	1993–2004
V	4.6 SOHC FF	Flex Fuel	224–239	2006–2011
W	4.6 SOHC R	Gasoline	190–239	1991–2011
X	4.6 SOHC W	Gasoline	225	1996–2006
Y	4.6 DOHC S/C	Gasoline	390	2002–2004
Z	5.8 DOHC S/C	Gasoline	650–662	2013–2014
6	4.6 SOHC W	Gasoline	225	1996–1997
9	4.6 SOHC	CNG	175–220	1996–2004

Modular Engine ID for Trucks				
8th digit of VIN	Displacement	Fuel type	H/P	Years
Vehicle Type: Truck				
A	5.4 DOHC W	Gasoline	295–300	2000–2003
B	6.8 SOHC W	NGV/LPV	295–305	2000
D	6.8 SOHC 3V	Gas–GFP	362–457	2013–2015
F	5.0 DOHC	Gasoline	360	2011–2014
H	4.6 DOHC	Gasoline	300	2003–2005
L	5.4 SOHC W	Gasoline	235–260	1997–2014
M	5.4 SOHC W	CNG	195–260	1997–2004
P	6.8 SOHC 3V	Gasoline	357–457	2013–2015
R	5.4 DOHC R	Gasoline	295–300	2001–2004
S	6.8 SOHC W	Gasoline	265–310	1997–2015
V	5.4 SOHC FF	Flex Fuel	310–320	2006–2010
W	4.6 SOHC R	Gasoline	190–248	1997–2014
Y	6.8 SOHC 3V	Gasoline	305–362	2005–2015
Z	5.4 SOHC W	Gas–GFP	260	1998–2004
3	5.4 SOHC S/C	Gasoline	340–380	2000–2004
5	5.4 SOHC 3V	Gasoline	300	2005–2010
5	5.4 SOHC E	Gasoline	300	2004
5	5.4 SOHC 3V	FFV	300–320	2009–2014
6	4.6 SOHC W	Gasoline	190–231	1997–2003
6	6.2 SOHC	Gasoline	383	2010–2015
6	6.2 SOHC RA	Gasoline	411	2011–2014
8	4.6 SOHC 3V	Gasoline	292	2006–2010

These charts list the engine codes for modular engines 1991–2015. The key is as follows: SOHC = single overhead camshaft; DOHC = dual overhead camshaft; 3V = three valves per cylinder; C/R = 2000 Cobra R; R/A = Mach I Ram Air; GT = Ford GT supercar; S/C = Supercharged; B = Boss; FF = Flex Fuel; R = Romeo engine plant; W = Windsor engine plant; E = Essex engine plant; RA = F150 Raptor; CNG = compressed natural gas; NGV = natural gas vehicle; LPV = liquid petroleum vehicle; GFP = gaseous fuel prep

MODULAR ENGINE FEATURES AND IDENTIFICATION

Model Year Designation in VIN

10th digit VIN	Model Year	10th Digit VIN	Model Year	10th Digit VIN	Model Year
N	1991	Y	2000	9	2009
M	1992	1	2001	A	2010
P	1993	2	2002	B	2011
R	1994	3	2003	C	2012
S	1995	4	2004	D	2013
T	1996	5	2005	E	2014
V	1997	6	2006	F	2015
W	1998	7	2007	G	2016
X	1999	8	2008		

This breakdown shows the year digit, which is in the 10th position of the VIN. Ford used a letter at the end of the 1990s, switched to numbers for the 2000s, and then back to the beginning of the alphabet for the next decade.

The 10th digit designates the year the engine was manufactured. Because of the many running changes in the plants, this may be helpful to you and your engine builder when searching out performance or replacement parts if needed.

Engine Tags

The next level of engine ID is the engine tag. The engine tag includes information on engine calibration, date of manufacture, and assembly plant. Ford's method of identifying engines varied in style and location. Some of them are stickers, others ink. It is possible that they can be switched or fade over time, so the identification of an engine can become difficult. Here are some of the ways to identify an engine.

found on the plate under the front windshield on the driver's side of the dashboard, or on the door sticker.

The sequence of engine codes for modular engines from 1991 to 2015 was not consistent with letters and numbers, and used the same designators in different years. In some cases, within the same year the code could be for either a 6-cylinder or a modular engine, depending on the vehicle. The horsepower ratings also varied over the course of the engine series build, so it is provided here as a range. Finally, a W-code engine in a Crown Victoria and a Ford F-150 may have come from the same plant (Romeo, Michigan), but have different components mounted on it, such as intake and exhaust manifolds.

Ford used primarily vinyl stickers to denote its engines through the modular engine years. The calibration code 2G839AA denotes this engine as a 2003 Cobra supercharged engine. The build date is noted as August 13, 2002, and it was built at the Romeo Engine Plant (REP). This sticker is located on the passenger-side valvecover at the bottom middle of the cover. A similar sticker is located on the driver-side valvecover, but only has the engine calibration code, date of manufacture, and a large bar code.

Modular Engine Specifications

Displacement	Bore mm (cu. in.)	Stroke mm (cu. in.)	total volume cc (cu. in.)	Journal size mm (cu. in.)	Rod Journal mm (cu. in.)	Deck height mm (cu in.)
4.6L	90.2 (3.56)	90 (3.54)	4601 (281)	67.49 (2.66)	52.98 (2.09)	227 (8.94)
5.0L	92.2 (3.63)	92.7 (3.65)	4951 (302)	67.49 (2.66)	52.88 (2.08)	227 (8.94)
5.0L Cammer	94.0 (3.70)	90 (3.54)	4992 (305)	67.49 (2.66)	52.98 (2.09)	227 (8.94)
5.2L	94.0 (3.70)	93 (3.67)	5163 (315)	67.49 (2.66)	-	227 (8.94)
5.4L	90.2 (3.56)	105.8 (4.17)	5408 (330)	67.49 (2.66)	52.98 (2.09)	256 (10.08)
5.8L	93.5 (3.68)	105.8 (4.17)	5812 (355)	67.49 (2.66)	52.98 (2.09)	255.7 (10.07)
6.2L	102.0 (4.02)	95.0 (3.74)	6210 (379)	67.49 (2.66)	52.98 (2.09)	239 (9.41)
6.8L	90.2 (3.56)	105.8 (4.17)	6760 (413)	67.49 (2.66)	52.98 (2.09)	256 (10.08)

Ford has stayed fairly consistent with the base specifications of these engines, with only a few custom setups.

CHAPTER 2

Engine Block Displacement

Although at least a half dozen displacements exist for the modular engine, the base dimensions are one of the more constant parts of these engines. All the engines share the same bore spacing at 100 mm (3.937 inches), except for the 6.2 engine. The two standard block deck heights are the taller 5.4 and 6.8 V-10 at 256 mm (10.079 inches), and for all of the smaller engines, 227 mm (8.937 inches). The 5.8 was slightly shorter at 225.7 mm (10.0673 inches).

But there are variations within variations. The 6.2 Boss SOHC shares many of the engine features of a typical modular engine, but it has a wider bore spacing at 115 mm (4.53 inches) and a unique deck height at 239 mm (9.41 inches). This allows for bigger volumes than the standard modular engine platforms. The Triton 6.8 V-10 is dimensionally a 5.4 engine with two extra cylinders.

Ford has had dozens of blocks over the years, made either from aluminum or iron. Five plants have made blocks for the modular engine: Romeo, Windsor, Essex, Teksid (Italy), and Cleveland, which manufactured the Boss. Between these engines not much interchanges. Some high-performance builders favor certain blocks, but in general all the blocks are very good, strong pieces. What you have will probably work fine.

Cylinder Heads

All modular engine cylinder heads are made from aluminum and come in three basic configurations: a single overhead cam (SOHC) with two valves per cylinder, an SOHC with three valves per cylinder (two intake, one exhaust), and a dual overhead cam (DOHC) with four valves per cylinder. Ford has changed the intake ports and exhaust configuration frequently through the years, making it difficult to swap cylinder heads on these engines. Ford made some improvements in 1999 and introduced the PI head, which stood for "Performance Improved," not "Police Interceptor" as older engines were designated. Early heads are referred to as NPI or Non-Performance Improved. Early 4V heads had dual ports, which was changed to a single port in 1999. SOHC and Coyote engines have round exhaust ports, and Cobra and other 4V heads were oval.

Crankshafts

Crankshafts come in 6-bolt and 8-bolt configurations. The 6-bolt crankshafts were made at the Windsor plant, and the 6- and 8-bolts cranks were used at Romeo. Some special crankshafts were made, such as the forged-steel crank first used in the 2003 supercharged Cobra engines. A lot of performance parts, such as flywheels and clutches, favor the 8-bolt crankshaft.

In 2016 Ford introduced the new flat plane crankshaft for the 5.2 Voodoo engine. The firing order is different from all the other modular engines and gives the engine a unique sound.

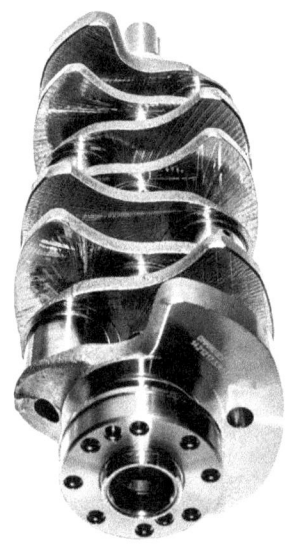

All modular engine heads are made from aluminum. The oval exhaust port on this head identifies it as a pre-Coyote 4V DOHC head. Note the added chain to run the second cam, the center-mounted spark plug, and the use of cam followers and valve-lash adjusters.

Ford turned the performance world on its head with the 2016 5.2 flat plane crankshaft. The flat plane crank allows the engine to fire left right bank evenly, different than normal V-8 engines. This allows for better exhaust scavenging than traditional V-8s. Weight savings is due to not having additional counterweights. Firing order on most modular engines is 1-5-4-8-6-3-7-2, and the 5.2 is 1-5-4-8-3-7-2-6. (Photo Courtesy Ford Performance Parts)

MODULAR ENGINE FEATURES AND IDENTIFICATION

Valvecover ID

The type of valvecover on a modular engine provides a quick identification. In this brief sidebar, the various styles of valvecovers are shown and described to provide a quick and easy indication of the particular engine. To verify the year, factory of origin, and type of modular engine, refer to the engine ID tag. ■

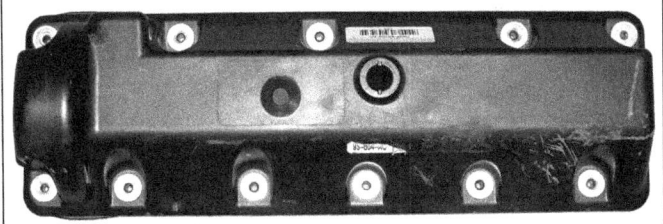

The 4.6 Romeo two-valve valvecover is a composite cover and has 11 bolts holding it to the head. Like all modular valvecovers it cannot be swapped left to right due to the timing chain and gear bulge in the front of the cover.

The 4.6 Windsor-built 2V engines have a 14-bolt valvecover that cannot be interchanged with Romeo 2V valvecovers. (Photo Courtesy Jim Smart)

This typical early four-cam valvecover is painted black on this Shelby 5.4 engine. The silver center plate covers the four coil packs mounted over each cylinder. Earlier coil pack engines had a similar cover over the spark plugs and wires. The coil pack wiring exits the back of the cover.

The 4.6 and 5.4 3V engines featured scalloped valvecovers to help with the relocation of the coils. The VCT (variable cam timing) system mounts in the front of the cover. These covers came in 10-bolt and 14-bolt designs.

The Coyote 4V engines have a much shallower valvecover and the wiring exits up and over the top of the cover to be hidden by the intake cover. The dual TC-VCT plugs can be seen in the front of the cover. The coil cover is aluminum and interchangeable.

HOW TO SWAP FORD MODULAR ENGINES INTO MUSTANGS, TORINOS AND MORE

CHAPTER 2

Most crankshafts are cast nodular iron and have six or eight bolts to hold the flywheel/flexplate, depending on application and plant. Most performance aftermarket companies design parts for the stronger eight-bolt crankshaft design. When Ford came out with the 2003 Cobra, it opted for a forged steel crank to handle the supercharged engine. Forged steel cranks then started making their way into other production engines.

Intakes

The intakes vary depending on application. Triton or Ford truck intakes tend to be taller with smaller, longer runners, whereas cars such as the Ford Mustang have the shortest intakes for clearance.

One of the early problems with the intake was a cracking condition with the new nylon designed intake manifold. The intake would crack along the front coolant crossover and the fitting ports would pull out.

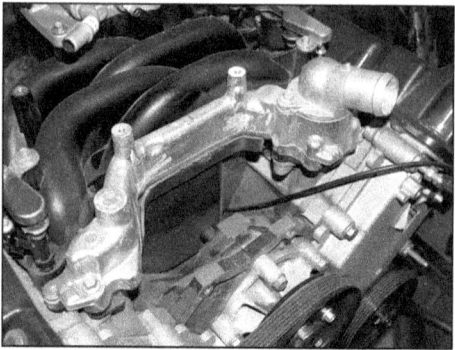

Ford solved the problem with these 4.6 intakes by changing the design to include an aluminum crossover tube in 2002. This remained on the 4.6 production engines through the end. The design for later engines was improved and the intakes became all composite again.

Ford used multiple intake port designs on the modular engine, so swapping among different engines is very difficult. Ford had a factory recall late in the 1990s when a problem occurred with the all-nylon intake manifolds; the fix was an aluminum coolant crossover, which carried on

On the back of this GT engine, this servo arm device is called the Intake Manifold Runner Control Module and sometimes it is referred to as the Charge Motion Control Valve. It shuts off part of the intake runners at low RPM on some engines to help with low-end torque. Performance builders have developed eliminator kits to remove this part for performance builds, as it can rob power in high-performance engines.

through production in the early 2000s.

With the early engines, Ford found that by adding a dual intake runner design and by shutting off runners at low RPM and idle, it could eliminate some of the low-end torque issues with the intake. Starting with some of the mid- to late-1990s Lincolns, Ford began using a dual port intake system, and this evolved into the Charge Motion Control Valve (CMCV) and/or the Intake Manifold Runner Control (IMRC) systems, depending on which year and engine you have. They both do basically the same thing: At low RPM it closes one of the runners to allow for better low-end torque.

Summary

So, which engine is right for your project? It depends on the goals for the project vehicle. The 4.6 SOHC 2V is plentiful and has the smallest dimensions for fitting in the engine bay, but because it is not at the high-end horsepower range, not a lot of new engineering takes place to develop parts for the older platform. As engines such as the Coyote continue to grow in popularity, aftermarket parts will become more difficult to obtain for the 2V as the sources dry up. In fact, while I was writing this book parts that were available became unavailable as they were replaced with parts for the newer platforms.

The older engine combinations may be easier to work with on items such as computers and wiring. The Ford computer controls sold through Ford Performance Parts made a big change on the ease of installing the newer engines, but they are only for use in the later throttle-by-wire setups.

The most popular conversion so far seems to be the Coyote platform.

MODULAR ENGINE FEATURES AND IDENTIFICATION

Available since 2011, plenty of used engines are now available, and Ford Performance Parts sells some amazing crate engines. Ford-sponsored PCM computer controls also helps with this platform's popularity. Surprisingly, the 2003–2004 Cobra Terminator conversion remains a popular conversion engine. Plenty of horsepower, a rugged cast-iron block, and no throttle-by-wire, it was the epitome of cable-throttle engines, and Terminator engines have retained their value because of this.

If the project budget is on the lower side, an SOHC or older DOHC can be used and performance added as needed. Engine platforms such as the Cobra DOHC, Raptor 6.2, Lightning trucks, and Shelbys provide a good foundation with proven horsepower and the ability to go even higher. But the initial cost of these engines will be higher.

If eye candy is what you are looking for, there is nothing more impressive than opening the hood and seeing those DOHC valvecovers staring at you. But the 4.6 SOHC can be dressed out to impress as well. Superchargers, turbochargers, and nitrous are available for all the platforms and most certainly dress up any engine compartment.

The modular engine that fits your project goals, engine compartment, and budget is the right one for you. Read on to gain the expertise to select the right one.

Transmissions

Selecting a suitable transmission for your modular engine and swap project is a little simpler, even though Ford used a variety of automatics and manuals. Except for in the first few years, most of the automatics were electronically controlled, making it fairly straightforward to choose a transmission to tie in to your electronics package selection. In 1999, Ford upgraded from mechanical speedometer cables to an electronic pickup, so older-style gauges don't work with the new VSS signals on most modular engine transmissions.

All but two modular engines have the same bellhousing bolt pattern. The exceptions are: the very first blocks that were mated to the non-electronic AOD transmissions, which had a small-block Ford pattern, and the 1995–2002 Lincoln Continental, which was a front-wheel-drive, front-sump engine with a different pattern for the transaxle (and carried PN F6OE). The 4.6- and 5.4-bolt patterns are the same.

The vehicle VIN tag tells you which type of transmission was installed in your vehicle, and it's usually listed under "TR" on the tag. Earlier cars carried a five-digit code; the first two digits of the number tell you what type of transmission was installed in the vehicle. Later, Ford went to a single-letter code for transmission identification.

Listing each type of transmission is difficult. Much like with the original Ford Toploader, there are variances in the cases and the input/output shafts, depending on the car or truck the drivetrain was installed in. Transmissions can be grouped together, and Ford mated the modular engine to an array of automatics and manuals. Following is a list of transmissions (with the exception of some heavy-duty trucks). I discuss more about fitting transmissions in Chapter 8.

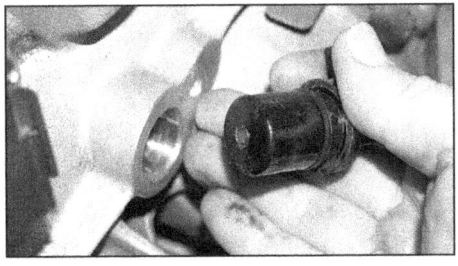

In the late 1990s, Ford discontinued the old-style mechanical speedometer gear in favor of an electronic pickup called the Variable Speed Sensor, or VSS. A spoke wheel passes through a magnetic field and the computer counts the triggers and calculates the speed of the vehicle. Calibrating the speedometer is a snap any time you change gears or tire size. The downfall may come in some older street rods that still use a mechanical speedometer, but there are ways around it. Aftermarket transmissions are available in mechanical or electronic versions.

The modular bellhousing pattern (right) is similar but different than the small-block Ford pattern. The most significant change is that the center two mounting bolts now run through the transmission dowel alignment pins rather than just above them. Note the size of the mini starter and its position on the bellhousing. The modular also has an extra bolt on the driver's side for a seven-bolt pattern.

CHAPTER 2

Automatics

Most modular engine applications use an automatic transmission. Except for the transaxle found in the Lincoln Continental, all are robust transmissions derived from earlier transmissions. As the transmissions added gears, their size increased as well. The earlier 4-speed overdrive transmissions may not be in fashion, but they have the advantage of robust design, and the aftermarket has developed them to handle huge horsepower loads. Another advantage of earlier transmissions is that they fit into tighter transmission tunnels, making them easier to install than the latter units. (See Chapter 8 for specific information on all of these transmissions.)

AOD/AODE: This is a 4-speed automatic with overdrive. Released in 1980, the first automatics were vacuum-operated and fully actuated. The stock overdrive transmission is rated at 300 hp and 275 ft-lbs of torque. The "E," or electronic, versions were released in 1992, and the PCM controlled the shifting duties on these transmissions. The AODE has stronger internals than the vacuum-operated AOD. The AOD was installed in the first few years before the AODE arrived in 1994. The AODE was used for a couple of years until it was replaced by the 4R70 series transmissions. The AODE was also used in the 1994–1995 Mustang GTs. An AODE is a much better option than the AOD, and certainly if the transmission came with the modular engine.

4R70W/4R70E/4R75E/4R75W: The 4R series of overdrives was an upgrade of the AOD platform. The "4" stands for four forward gears, the "R" stands for rear drive, and the "W" stands for a wider gear ratio. The "E" version designates throttle-by-wire technology. The 4R series transmissions began replacing the AOD transmissions about 1994 and were used up through 2011 in large cars such as the Ford Crown Victoria.

E4OD/4R100: This heavy-duty 4-speed overdrive incorporates some of the older C6 automatic internals, but this new-generation transmission was installed in bigger vehicles and trucks. While the 4R70W was used with the smaller 4.6 blocks, the E4OD was used behind the 5.4 and applications where additional torque was needed. These transmissions were used in Ford trucks and vans 1996–2004.

5R Series: Primarily the 5R55S, this is a 5-speed automatic used to replace the 4-speed. A 5R100 version was used in Super Duty trucks and was different from the 5R55 series because it was derived from and replaced the heavy-duty 4R100 4-speed automatics. This light-duty transmission had been around a couple of years until it was fitted into the 2005–2010 Mustangs, and the 5R100 replaced the 4R100 in 2005–2010.

6H and 6R Series: The 6HP26 was developed by ZF and was used behind some 2005–2008 Lincoln Navigators. The 6R80 and other 6R series 6-speed automatics were developed from the ZF transmission and built under license by Ford. The 6R series replaced the 5R series in 2011. The 6R140 series replaced the 5R100 in Ford heavy trucks and vans in 2011.

Manuals

Manual transmissions are found in the Mustang and Ford trucks, but keep in mind that the shifter location on these transmissions dictates the use or application of the transmissions. Ford mounts the truck engine up and under the chassis cab, so the shifter position is typically midpoint on the housing. Mustang transmissions are generally found at the end of the tailshaft or even remote behind the shaft. The earlier manual transmissions were a bit weaker and went through some warranty issues, and the latest versions tend to have issues with the shifting. The T-56 series, while bigger and bulkier than the earlier transmissions, is very robust and is still favored by the aftermarket community. It can also be found in both clutch fork and hydraulic throw-out bearing versions from Ford. (See Chapter 8 for more information.)

Tremec 5-speeds: Starting with the 1996 Mustang GT, Ford began using the Tremec T-45 5-speed, which was upgraded to the TR-3650 in 2001 and was used up through 2010s. The T-45 suffered from shifting issues and the 3650 corrected some of those problems. Ford issued numerous service bulletins to remedy the shifting problems on the 1996–2000 transmission. These primarily focused on fifth/reverse gear forks, which were jamming and breaking, so upgraded forks were offered to resolve this problem.

Tremec 6-speeds: The T-56 was first installed in the 2000 Cobra R, and then the 2003–2004 Terminator Cobra. It's a stout transmission that's also been installed in the Corvette Z06, Dodge Viper, and Aston Martin Vanquish. This transmission can handle a lot of torque. These transmissions can transmit up to about 700 hp, which is suitable for most high-performance street cars. These were fitted with a unique fork placement and used a cable clutch. The T-6060 was derived from the T-56, shares some of the same internals as the T-56, and uses a hydraulic throw-out bearing instead of a clutch fork. The T-6060 was used in the Shelby GT500 2007–2014.

MODULAR ENGINE FEATURES AND IDENTIFICATION

MT82 6-speed: The Ford/Getrag co-developed MT82 6-speed became the standard transmission in 2011, replacing both Tremec manuals for use in the Mustang in 2011.

M5OD 5-speed: The Mazda-built 5-speed was installed in a wide range of Mazda and Ford cars and trucks. Two models were offered: the light-duty R1 and medium duty R2. R1 transmissions were slotted into the Ford Ranger, Explorer, Aerostar, and Bronco II. R2 versions have been used in the F-150, Econoline Van, full-size Bronco, and the Cougar/Thunderbird with the supercharged V-6. This transmission is suitable for most applications up to about 450 hp.

ZF Series 6-speed: The S6-650 ZF manual transmission is used in Super Duty trucks and vans 1999–2010. The manual was dropped in the United States in 2011. In addition, GM installed the ZF6 transmission in the 1989–1996 Corvette. The S6-650 is rated to transmit 650 ft-lbs of torque, so they are tough enough for many specialized and high-performance applications. It is important to be sure that the transmission you select matches your application and engine output.

Ford Crate Engines

Although Ford has been offering the modular engines through its racing parts programs for some time, it wasn't until the fifth-generation Mustangs (2005–2014) that it began looking at bundling its performance engines with control systems to install in other types of vehicles such as street rods.

Ford Performance offers both production versions and special-built versions of its engines. Which one fits your project depends on your horsepower needs and budget. Here are a few of Ford's nonproduction engines from the past few years.

The Aluminator

The Aluminator started out as an all-aluminum version of the famed 2003–2004 4.6 Cobra Terminator supercharged engine, which came from the factory with a cast-iron block. The current iteration of the moniker is an all-aluminum 5.0 GT engine beefed up to handle more than 500 hp.

5.0 Cammer

This was the first 5.0 engine based on a punched out 4.6 DOHC Cobra engine. It was capable of horsepower ratings over 400 and torque of 365 ft-lbs or more. The engine features a Ford Performance 356 alloy aluminum block, high-flow cylinder heads, and 12-mm-lift camshafts. It's also equipped with 11:1 compression; variable geometry, magnesium long/short runner intake; power steering pump; alternator; and air-conditioning compressor.

Ford Performance Parts has marketed several different engine variations under the "Aluminator" name, capitalizing on the versatility and lightweight of the all aluminum architecture. The M-6007-A50XS put out more than 500 hp naturally aspirated and benefits from all the development of Ford's Cobra Jet racing program. It comes with CNC ported cylinder heads, a dual 65-mm throttle body and a slew of high-end Ford racing extras. (Photo Courtesy Ford Performance Parts)

One way to identify the Ford Performance Parts Coyote engines is by the bar code sticker mounted to the back of the driver-side block just below the cylinder head. (Photo Courtesy Ford Performance Parts)

The Ford "Cammer" engine started out as a 4.6 DOHC engine that was re-sleeved and bored out and used in Ford FR500C, Grand Am Cup and Koni Sprots Car Challenge cars, among others. Output was in the mid-400 hp range and a punched out 5.3 version in 2010 made more than 665 hp in a GT for the FIA GT1 World Championship. (Photo Courtesy Ford Performance Parts)

CHAPTER 2

You'll notice the missing emissions systems on this specially prepared Boss 302. The engine is installed in one of the Ford Performance Boss 302S race cars specially prepped by Watson Engineering in Taylor, MI. There were only 50 units built and this engine dyno'd at 520 hp at the crank. The car was provided by Blake Hartman.

Boss 302

The Boss 302 modular is a beefed-up 5.0 Coyote platform pushing 444 hp installed in the 2012–2013 Boss 302 Mustang. It features high-strength components and goodies such as CNC-machined ports, forged connecting rods, forged-steel cranks, and forged pistons. The Boss engine is the basis for many of Ford's racing-sealed engines, and it's offered in stroked version up to 5.3 in short-block form. It produces 420 hp at 6,500 rpm and 390 ft-lbs of torque at 4,250 rpm. Until Ford offers the 5.2-liter GT350 engine in crate form, this is one of the best modular Ford crate engines you can buy.

Aftermarket Parts

The aftermarket has been cautious when it comes to the production of hard parts such as blocks and heads. Most of the aftermarket crate engines are based on production Ford components. Just when you think Ford has settled into a stable new platform, it goes and improves it again. The Coyote is a good foundation for modular engine builds, but then Ford changed things again when it came out with the flat plane crank 5.2 Shelby GT350 engine, which will probably keep the aftermarket world jumping once again, which will mean a new round of aftermarket components to support the new design.

Modular Motorsports Racing now has its GEN-X Coyote blocks available for the extreme engine builds. Machine from a billet of 6061-T6 aluminum, the blocks are available in short and tall deck heights. Engine displacements up to 6.5 are possible, and these monster engines can reliably produce 1,800 to 3,500 hp. (Photo Courtesy Modular Motorsports Racing)

Sean Hyland Motorsport was the first to come out with an aftermarket racing block for the short 4.6 and tall 5.4 deck height engines. SHM poured all its experience in producing a block that can be punched out to 6.0 and can withstand a mind blowing 2500 hp. It accepts all modular engine cylinder head configurations. Note the extra material cast around the cross bolt main holes. (Photo Courtesy Sean Hyland Motorsports)

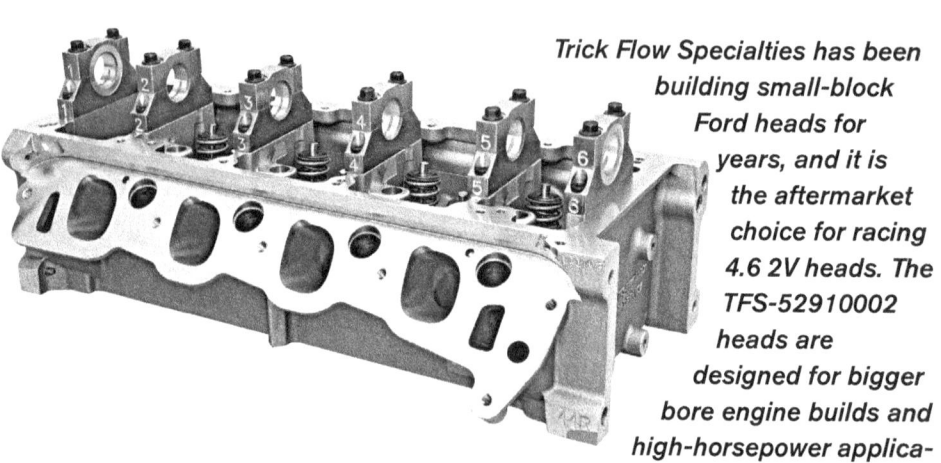

Trick Flow Specialties has been building small-block Ford heads for years, and it is the aftermarket choice for racing 4.6 2V heads. The TFS-52910002 heads are designed for bigger bore engine builds and high-horsepower applications. It works with performance-improved (PI) intake manifolds, CNC-ported combustion chambers and patented replaceable cam bearing journals. TFS heads accept either the Romeo or Windsor valvecovers and most Ford front covers and accessories. (Photo Courtesy Trick Flow Specialties)

Swap Spotlight: The Mustang Evolution

Leading the list of over-the-top modular engine conversions is Brett Behrens' 1978 Mustang II. Brett is a longtime Ford guy who wanted to build something unique, and this beautiful Mustang II is the result. Fitted with a 396-hp 6.8 Triton V-10 modular engine, the second-generation Mustang required extensive fabrication.

Automotive illustrator Ben Hermance designed the Mustang II. He drew the concept car with the corners widened to fit the driveline, and the build gurus at A-Team Racing in Bend, Oregon, made the designs into reality. Fitting 413 cubic inches into a space barely big enough for a small-block 302 was going to require some major stretching and pulling.

The base frame for this project was the tried and true suspension engineering of a 2008 Corvette, which not only allowed for adequate braking, but with the rear-mounted transmission, gave a close to 50/50 weight ratio. The Mustang's frame was stretched 12 inches to complement suspension geometry and retain an eye-pleasing bodyline that didn't take away from the original lines of the Mustang II. Gordon Aram and the group at A-Team started by building a custom frame made from 1⅝-inch DOM steel tubing, and made use of the Corvette front engine cradle and independent rear suspension mounts in the design.

The engine started out as a stock 2005 6.8 V-10, and the team added a custom-made steel-tube intake manifold to which an Accufab 90-mm throttle body was attached. The Iskenderian camshafts were custom reground and 50-psi injectors were installed. A stock Ford computer was re-flashed and installed. The result is a torque monster producing 396 hp and 475 ft-lbs of torque at the rear wheels.

The engine was mated to the torque tube via a custom-made bellhousing, which connects to the rear-mounted Tremec T-6060 6-speed transmission and Corvette independent rear suspension. Custom pieces made for the engine include the valvecovers, intake, and oil pan. The headers were also custom-made and connected to a 3-inch exhaust system that uses Magnaflow mufflers. The exhaust exits from the back via a central exhaust port.

Stopping the stretch MII is the original six-piston front and four-piston rear brakes from the Corvette. The car rides on a set of Forgeline Grip Equipped Laguna rims done in satin black and Toyo tires. The weight of the entire build is equivalent to that of the original Dodge Viper, well under the Corvette and definitely in supercar territory.

Even though the car had to be stretched, the original roofline was not altered and refinements to the body are all custom done in metal. Fender flares from a 2005 Mustang were used to give the body a wide-body treatment, and the fenders were stretched slightly outward. To clear the tall manifold, a 1971 Mustang NASA-style hood center was added, which is functional. The side scoops are also functional, and the rear was originally adorned with a pair of 1970s Celica taillights that fit the pattern and look more like a classic Mustang tribar taillight. The rear spoiler was increased, and the front air dam was modeled after the one found on the 2012 Boss Mustang. The car was covered in 2014 Ford Kona Blue to complement the satin black highlights.

Mustang Evolution is not quite an accurate name for this car. "Re-Evolution" may be more accurate. After the 2015 SEMA show in Las Vegas, a slight mishap occurred with the car on the return trip to Oregon. Brett decided that perhaps it was time to make some improvements while the car was down for repair. The re-works to the reworks was handled by Mayhem Customs of Portland, Oregon, which includes a revamping of the taillight area, smoother side scoops, and other minor tweaks to an already amazing bodyline. The big changes are happening under the

Brett Behrens of Bend, Oregon, has taken two things usually not associated with ultra-high end performance and blended them together to make his own version of the Ford supercar. This 1978 Mustang II is fitted with a 6.8-liter V-10, a torque monster putting out 396 hp, and 475 ft-lbs of tire roasting torque. (Photo Courtesy Brett Behrens)

Suspension and drivetrain were transplanted from a wrecked 2008 Corvette. A full tube chassis was built around the suspension underpinnings, and the V-10 engine was installed. The Mustang II would have to be stretched a full 12 inches to mate with the new wheelbase. (Photo Courtesy Brett Behrens)

hood, where the tube intake is being replaced with a custom-made stack injection manifold and full Holley computer controls. Torque numbers should be off the charts.

Don't think you can afford an over-the-top build like this? Brett Behrens thinks you can. Brett started up Specialty Car Solutions (specialtycarsolutions.com) and is working with top builders in the country to make your over-the-top fantasy ride a reality. Brett drew his inspiration from the little Mustang that was forgotten by the rest of the custom world and made a true giant killer. Your ride can be a reality, too.

The chassis is taking shape, and this shot shows the Tremec T-6060 transmission used in the transaxle position of the Corvette designed suspension. This configuration would give a close to 50/50 weight balance to the much bigger V-10 engine. (Photo Courtesy Brett Behrens)

With the much lower stance of the new chassis, the tunnel was all custom fabricated. Note how far back the V-10 sits in the firewall of this shot. A full roll cage was also incorporated into the design. (Photo Courtesy Brett Behrens)

With the exception of the factory nose, all the outer fabrication is metal. The ram air hood is from a 1971–1973 Mach I, the wheel lip openings are from a 2005 Mustang, and the custom nose was designed after the late-model Boss 302. You can see the stretch done in the fenders and hood, but the original roofline remains untouched. (Photo Courtesy Brett Behrens)

Here is the original configuration for the V-10 showing the custom tube intake and reversed throttle body design. Not much exists for the V-10 dress up, so the intake, valvecovers, oil pan and headers all had to be custom fabricated. (Photo Courtesy Brett Behrens)

The factory V-10 computer was used and reprogrammed to bypass the PATS. Wiring was tucked behind the apron panels for a cleaner engine compartment. Note the angled corvette-style radiator. Forgeline Laguna rims were selected along with Toyo tires. (Photo Courtesy Brett Behrens)

This is an original custom tube intake and Accufab throttle body mounted under the tubes. This system is being replaced with a custom stack injection setup with Holley computer controls to increase the horsepower level. (Photo Courtesy PDXcarculture.com)

CHAPTER 3

INSTALLING THE MODULAR ENGINE IN A PROJECT CAR

One of the biggest intimidation factors for fitting the modular engine is the size of the engine compared to all but the big-block applications of the past. The engine is fairly wide compared to pushrod applications, which can present challenges for engine installation. The way Ford has designed the engine mounting can also be a challenge with an earlier engine bay. In some applications, the front suspension determines how the engine is mounted in the engine bay, and items such as superchargers may force the position of the engine toward the firewall in early first-generation Mustangs. Items such as a brake booster can interfere with the wider DOHC heads. The alternator location on some engines is down low and can conflict with the frame rails of some vehicles. In this chapter I discuss the items you need to address to physically make the modular engine fit in the engine bay.

Your engine must fit your car, and so I'm going to talk about the things you need to do to fit it in the engine compartment. The modular engine is generally wider and taller than traditional pushrod engines, so fitting the engine in some chassis can be a challenge. You may need to make changes to your suspension system to fit the engine in your project. Items such as oil pans, steering systems, and braking systems can also interfere with the engine mounting. This section may be covered in detail in other chapters, but you need to consider these items before you get the engine in the engine bay.

A front view showing the serpentine belt system on the modular engine. The 1970 Boss 302 engine isn't dressed out but you can tell accessory fitting on the modular engine needs to be considered. This supercharged engine has a single belt running everything; some supercharged applications use a separate belt to run the supercharger, making the front end even longer.

CHAPTER 3

Ford V-8 Dimensions and Weights				
Modular Engine	Length	Width	Height	Weight
4.6 SOHC	28	25.625	26	500
4.6 DOHC	28	30	29.875	460-680
5.0 VI-TCT	26	28	27	430
Pushrod Engine				
302	27	18.75	20.75	460
351	27	21	23.75	525
460	32	26	26	720

Some of the more common dimensions and weights of the modular engine compared to the earlier pushrod Ford V-8s. These numbers vary greatly, depending on options and materials.

Engine Dimensions and Weights

One of the reasons people avoid modular conversions is the belief that the engines are much heavier than traditional pushrod engines because they are bigger in some dimensions. Weights and dimensions vary depending on engine size, accessories, and component material. Items such as aluminum versus iron blocks and superchargers lead to great variability. The above chart is provided as a comparison of the 4.6 and Coyote engines to traditional pushrod engines.

Frame versus Unibody

Most small performance cars are unibody construction or constructed with a unitized frame, and this means the sheet-metal panels of the body are welded together to form a functional frame and the structural rigidity of the vehicle. Trucks, full-size vehicles, and most older GM and Chrysler products gain most of their body strength from a traditional ladder frame, and the body simply mounts on top of the frame. It is much easier to modify a full-frame car than a unibody because cutting away the structural metal (like a shock tower) severely affects the integrity of the body strength.

In general, Ford used frames on midsize and larger vehicles and trucks, and these cars had fairly large engine compartments, so the physical dimensions of the modular engine don't come into play as severely as with the smaller cars. Vehicles such as Mustangs, Fairlanes, Falcons, Mavericks, and later T-birds used a unibody construction, so making room in the engine bay may be necessary. The biggest hurdle to getting the modular engine in these cars is the bulging shock towers. They severely limit the ability to install these engines. Most of these vehicles must be modified to accept an entirely different suspension.

Front Suspension Systems

Most classic Ford passenger car suspensions are a double A-arm design with a coil spring and shock absorber. On smaller Ford vehicles, the shock is typically mounted on the upper control arm and to the frame in the bulging shock tower. This takes up vital space within the engine compartment that is necessary for the engine and wider wheels. On intermediate- and full-size vehicles, Ford mounts the shock to the lower control arm and then to a mount point near the frame. This frees space in the engine compartment and helps with the efficiency of the shock system. The closer the lower shock mount is to the lower control arm ball joint, the more efficient it is in transferring movement to the shock.

In 1969, Ford introduced the Pinto and incorporated a compact suspension system into it that was later installed in the 1974–1978 Ford Mustang IIs, which shared the same platform as the Pinto. This suspension system uses an uneven-length double A-arm design with the shock and spring mount between the two control arms, unlike the earlier Ford with a shock tower that mounted the shock above the upper control arm. This allows for a compact suspension, which has become popular in the street rod world because it can be adapted to many different frames. And because the suspension sits low under the frame, it allows for larger engines to fit into engine bays not originally equipped for them. The suspension also makes use of a rack-and-pinion steering system, which works better than the older worm and sector gears. The aftermarket has developed this suspension system for nearly every kind of

The shock is mounted at the top of the upper control arm on this typical, early Ford unibody suspension. This is not the most efficient way to mount the shock, but the big problem is the shock tower that protrudes into the engine bay. Full-size Ford cars and trucks mounted the shock between the two control arms.

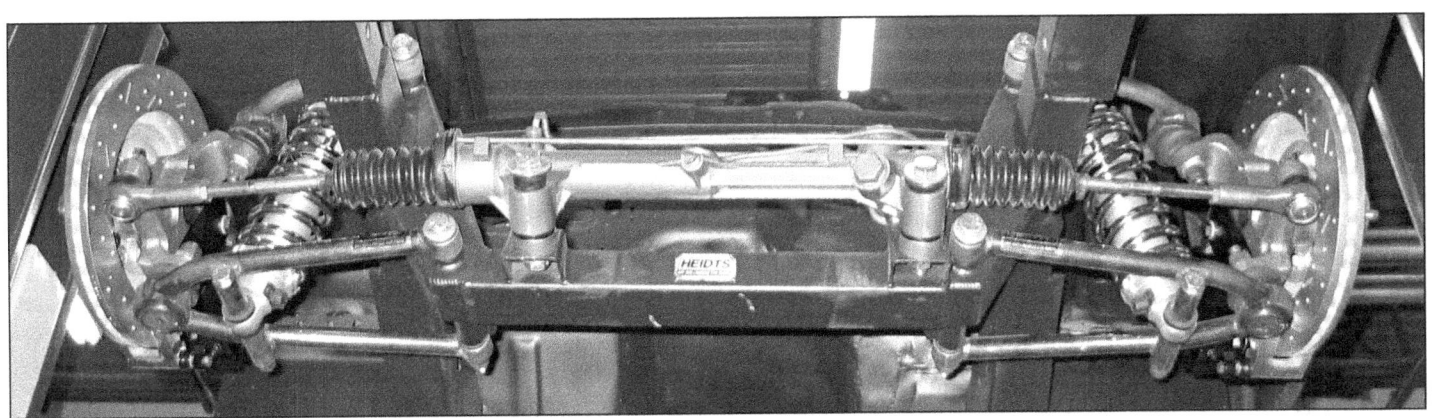

The Mustang II suspension has been adapted to nearly everything due to its compact, simple design. This Heidt's unit is mounted in a 1968 Mustang and being prepped for a 4.6 3V engine. It has been upgraded with power rack, tubular control arms, coil-over shocks, and vented/slotted rotors. If the street rod world hasn't adapted it to your particular chassis yet, Heidts probably can. (Photo Courtesy Mark Houlahan)

chassis, from street rods to unibodies, and with that has come tubular suspensions, coil-over shocks, and large brake conversions.

In 1979, Ford began installing MacPherson strut suspension systems in some of its vehicles and, as a result, the upper control arm was eliminated and the suspension simplified. Most current systems are still strut designs with a reverse-mount lower control arm.

You need to carefully choose the suspension system for your car and modular engine drivetrain. Even if a different suspension system fits in your car, it doesn't necessarily make it the best option. Most aftermarket systems are designed for the original architecture, and sometimes that changes the way the original designers intended the suspension to function. For example, the shocks are usually mounted at an angle defined by the arc curve of the suspension and how it travels. The angle of the shock also affects its efficiency, and the more severe the angle of the shock, the less efficient it becomes. If you fit a new suspension system and change the shock angle, the system may not work as well as the original system it is replacing. Just because it fits doesn't mean it is better.

If you are building your car for any kind of performance driving, particularly with competition in mind, your first question for the manufacturer of choice is, "Who's winning with your stuff?" If you plan on taking your car to the track, use what people who are winning use on their cars. Time and again I hear about people installing the latest fad suspensions on their cars only to find that it doesn't actually work any better than what they just removed.

At this point you may be asking, which system is best for my conversion? There is no single answer because there is no conversion for all applications and you need to realize that suspension systems are designed to work within specific parameters and at different costs. A road racing suspension may not be great for a car driven daily, and a suspension that is made for compact installation may not handle as well as the original system.

Guidelines for Selecting the Right Suspension

1. What is the overall intended use for the vehicle? As I mentioned in the introduction, the application or use of the vehicle determines the needed suspension. Example: If you plan on using the car for drag racing, an independent rear suspension is not the best choice. On the other hand, if you install a race suspension on a street car, it will have a harsher ride and be less fun to drive. You need to determine the type of use before selecting a suspension system.

2. What is available for your project? Mustang II suspensions are available for many different chassis and are probably a universal choice for most builds. The Mustang II suspension is often a great choice for many street cars, but it may not be the best choice depending on your answer to question number 1.

3. How readily available are parts? Exotic systems such as Jaguar rear axles can be expensive and parts for it may be hard to find locally; a system designed from parts available at your local parts store may be a better alternative. For example, the Ford Cobra

Swapping the Modular Engine into 1967–1970 Mustangs and Cougars

If you want to retain the original front suspension in your early Ford Mustang or Mercury Cougar, here are the steps you need to take to physically mount the engine into the chassis. These procedures crossover to some other unibody cars, but some of the parts may need custom fabrication. Note that if you have a supercharged engine, you need to move the mounting point of the engine farther back toward the firewall to help clear the supercharger snout (unless you are cutting a big hole in your hood). Our test subject is a 1970 Mach I being fitted with a 2011 Ford 4.6 Police Interceptor engine and automatic transmission. ■

The narrowest measurement between the shock towers on this 1969 Mustang is just under 25 inches. With the 4.6 2V engine just over 25½ inches, you need to make some room for the engine and the exhaust.

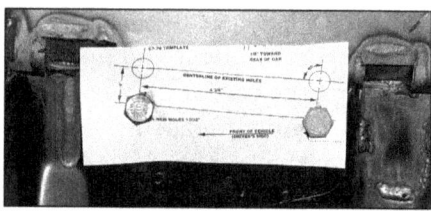

Before cutting the towers, you need to lower the upper control arm mounts. Shelby American discovered in the 1960s that if it dropped the mount points of the upper control arms it could reduce body roll. As an added benefit, this modification moves the control arms away from the exhaust outlets and manifolds so it's easier to fit the modular engine. The template for lowering the A-arms can be found in numerous places on the Internet and is available from Tony Branda. Notice that the plate that's already installed in this car drops lower than the original mount point for the upper control arms.

Your cut needs to be at least 1/4 inch away from the opening of the upper bolt hole for the shock mount cap and shock tower brace. From there, you can cut straight down or you can follow a general slant parallel to the spring. Some aftermarket cutback towers have a more severe cutback for maximum space. Remove all the front suspension components prior to cutting the towers.

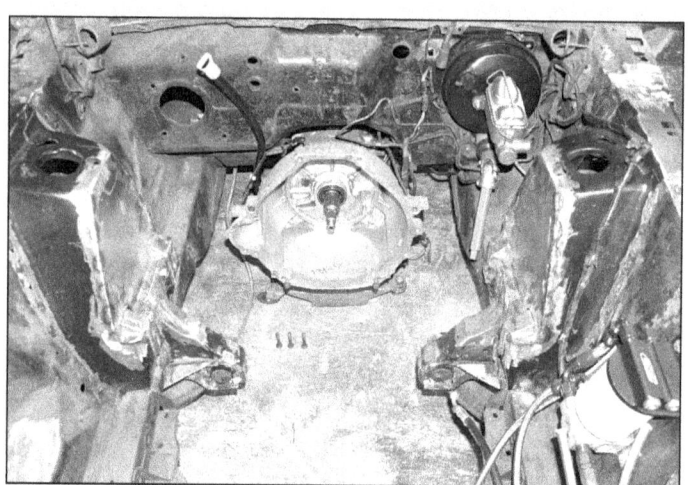

This car has had the towers cut back and new plates installed. Note that you will be cutting through several big, thick pieces of steel. A plasma cutter is excellent for doing this type of work.

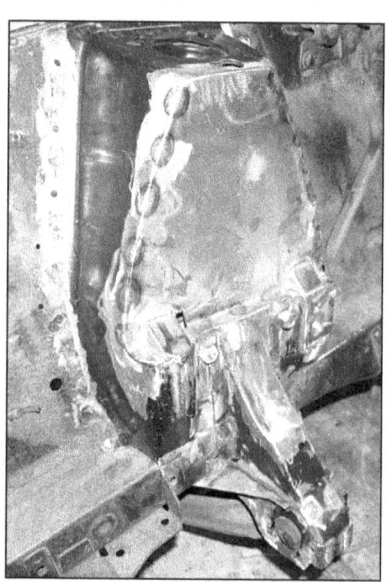

The center support was trimmed back for additional exhaust manifold clearance, and then it was capped off for strength. How much you need to trim depends on your engine and exhaust combination. This setup has a couple of reliefs for the upper arm installation. I have seen some that angle back for a smoother look.

INSTALLING THE MODULAR ENGINE IN A PROJECT CAR

Dave Stribling Restorations sells engine mounts that allow the engine to be mounted to the original 1967–1970 engine mount points in the chassis. They are designed to be used with the SN-95 Mustang engine insulators (see engine mounts section).

Canton Racing makes a front sump oil pan and pickup tube to fit both the 4.6 and 5.0 Coyote engines. They have pickup tubes for both 2V and 4V applications, and the pans are set up for a universal dipstick tube and a port for an oil level sensor if you wish.

With the spring installed, you can see there is still plenty of clearance behind the coil to install additional bracing to shore up the shock tower. Remember that Ford had to increase the bracing starting in 1968 ("wraparound" shock towers on big-blocks) because stresses on the towers were causing cracks. You need to make additional braces.

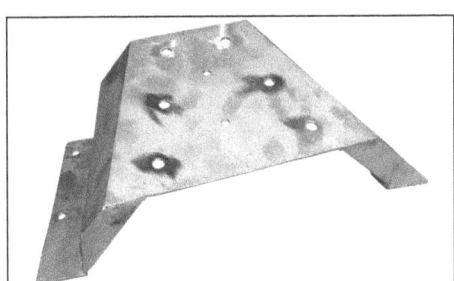

These heavy-gauge braces replace the wraparound shock tower pieces on the front and are gusseted to wrap around the spring. These will be welded into the backside of the tower.

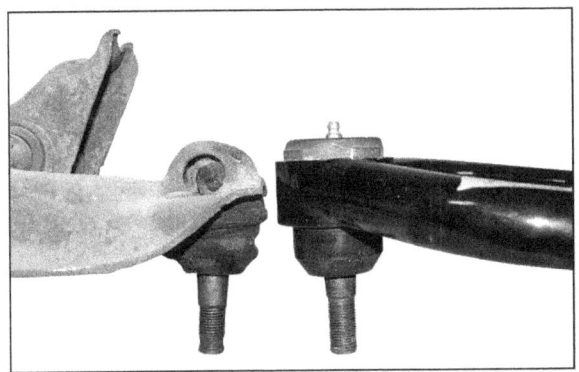

You should consider installing a set of aftermarket control arms with the stock-style suspension. The benefit is, several aftermarket builders have corrected the ball joint binding issues with the upper control arm drop, and mount the ball joint at a corrected angle. The stock arm is on the left, the Global West tubular arm is on the right. Global West has also redesigned its control arms to be dropped 1-3/8 inches, so the car has more negative camber while cornering.

CHAPTER 3

Swapping the Modular Engine into 1967–1970 Mustangs and Cougars CONTINUED

The engine sits between the shock towers. This car can now benefit from any of the aftermarket parts designed for the original Mustang suspension.

brake calipers for the rear are the same from 1994 to 2004, and in the United States they can be purchased at any Ford dealer or auto parts store. This may be a better choice than a custom-made caliper that has to be sent back to the manufacturer for rebuild. But it may not work as well.

4. What is your budget? Cost may be a big factor in what the final use is. For example, least expensive is to convert your original first-generation suspension to handle the modular conversion, next expensive is the Mustang II conversion, and on the high-end is the Griggs Racing conversion.

As with building a modular engine, my goal here is not to make you an expert on suspension and handling, but to help you get the engine into the chassis. Whether you are building a hot rod, pro touring car, dragster, or other type of car, a book is available about how to design and build a suspension for your needs. Choosing the right suspension depends on the eventual use for your car and is something you are going to need to research to get right for your project.

Early Mustang Suspension

The majority of modular engine swaps are into first-generation Mustangs, so I discuss them here. A lot of this information covers Cougars, Falcons, Fairlanes, Mavericks, and other Ford vehicles with layouts similar to the Mustang's.

The early 1965–1970 Mustangs used an uneven-length double arm suspension with a shock absorber mounted to the upper control arm. Most of the companies that sell "performance suspensions" tell you that this system is terrible. But the truth is, it isn't that bad. Over the years I have learned a lot about the original uneven-length double arm suspension on the Mustang. Companies such as Street or Track and its ST-6873TFEKIT take everything I have learned about the original Mustang suspension and make it much better than most systems on the market for the early cars. Although the original systems exhibited bump steer, the terrible original steering gear contributes to the condition. In addition, modern radial tires are often aligned to the original alignment specifications of the 1960s, which compounds the problem. To resolve this problem, you should consider upgrading to a rack-and-pinion steering system such as the Randall's Rack system or the Total Control Products rack-and-pinion designed to work with the original-style front suspension.

Shelby discovered that by dropping the upper control arm 1 inch it was able to eliminate some of the roll

INSTALLING THE MODULAR ENGINE IN A PROJECT CAR

The 1964–1966 Mustangs are only about 22 inches between the narrowest points in the engine compartment, and the 2V modular engines are about 25 inches wide. The upper control arms mount about 1½ inches farther in on the early cars, and that means that the upper control arm and the exhaust manifolds are going to occupy the same space. Major modifications likely need to be made to the exhaust and chassis to get the modular engine into this engine bay.

in the body during hard cornering. One of the drawbacks to this modification is that the upper ball joint can bind and wear out faster, so performance companies began building upper control arms with a revised ball joint angle to eliminate the bind when the control arm is dropped. You need to follow a few guidelines when installing the modular engine and using the original front suspension. Unfortunately, the modular engine is not compatible with the 1965–1966 Mustangs and Falcons; you need a different suspension setup because there simply is not enough room. Even with the control arm drop, the upper arms mount too far inboard to allow the engine to fit into the chassis. The modular engine exhaust and the upper control arm want to share the same space in the engine bay. You will be shopping for something else with these cars.

With the 1967–1970 Mustangs, you have enough room to install a modular engine. In 1967 Ford moved the upper control arm outward 1 inch to accommodate the wider FE 390 engines. The lower control arms were relocated to accommodate the change. All 1965–1970 Mustangs have the same frame rail width dimensions.

The FE installation was tight to say the least, and owners found it very difficult to change the spark plugs on these cars during routine maintenance. Drag racers found it unbearable but discovered a work-around. Turns out the angle of the shock and spring allows for the shock towers to be cut back to gain access to the center two spark plugs on a 390-428 engine. Ford did the same thing on the 1969–1970 Boss 429 to make room for the Boss heads.

Some 2V modular engines have been installed into Cougar and Mustang chassis by an "influence" from a tool (sledge hammer) on the shock tower. Rather than do that, you can cut the tower back to make room. With the towers cut back, the 4V engines will fall between the shock towers. There is plenty of room to reinforce the back side of the tower (which you just removed a bunch of) for strength. By lowering the upper control arm position 1 inch, you make clearance for the exhaust manifolds that want to lay right on top of the control arm bolts.

Mustang II Suspension

Originally designed for V-6 Pintos, the Mustang II suspension has blossomed into a product for the street rod industry because of its compact size and design, which adapts well to many other chassis. Hot rodders loved it for its compact size and its adaptability to frame cars, and it allowed for larger modern engines to be installed in older chassis.

Many muscle car owners adapted it as a replacement for the original suspension in some of the early Ford unibody cars because it eliminates the upper shock mount; the shock is mounted between the two control arms. The shock tower can be removed from unibody cars, which leaves plenty of room for a big, wide modular engine. These suspensions come with rack-and-pinion steering gears, which replace a not-so-good part of the old Ford chassis.

Several companies, including Detroit Speed, Heidt's, and Griggs, have taken the basic compact design of the MII and developed it into a road-hugging, race-winning system. Griggs Racing's designs are winning on the track and are an excellent choice for true performance vehicles.

The front clip needs to provide support and strength for the Mustang II suspension on a unibody car. As stated before, the unibody gets its strength from the sheet-metal panels welded together to create the chassis. The shock tower is a big, thick piece of steel welded to the front engine

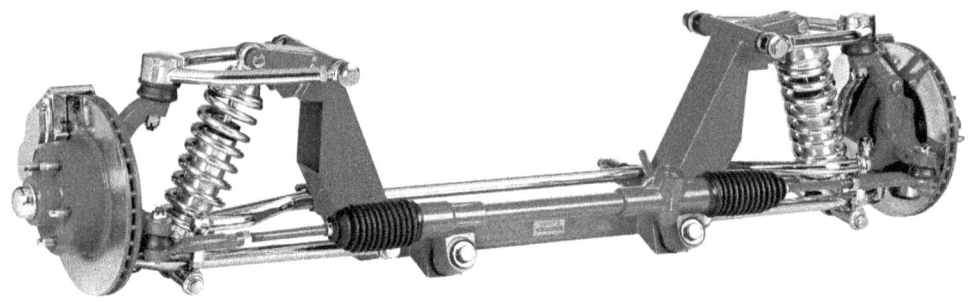

Heidt's has adapted the versatile MII suspension to numerous vehicles and trucks. The company developed a matching engine mount for all modular engines to work with its kits. This is the Superide II for a 1948–1952 Ford truck. (Photo Courtesy Heidt's, Inc.)

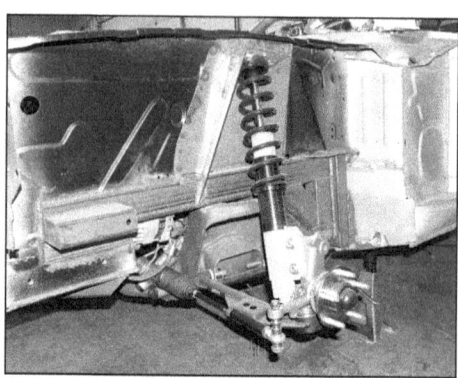

Dave Stribling Restorations has adapted the Mac strut system from the 99-04 SN-95 Mustangs to the first-generation Mustangs and Cougars. They retain all the original Ford geometry and mounting, which means that any aftermarket goodies developed for the later cars bolt on to the early cars. A new set of towers is used to make clearance for even the wide 5.4 engines. This is an in-house fabrication only and is major surgery.

Fatman Fabrications has adapted its MII system to more than 200 applications, including this 1956 Ford Victoria. Note the notch in the back of the crossmember to assist in clearing the modular engine oil pan. Its suspension can also be installed in any Fatman full frame to your specifications. (Photo Courtesy Fatman Fabrications)

Fatman Fabrications has developed a strut system that incorporates the original tower locations and uses spindles and steering from newer vehicles. It is designed to fit 1960–1971 Falcons, 1964½–1973 Mustangs, 1962–1971 Fairlanes, 1968–1971 Torinos, 1970–1977 Mavericks, and the Mercury variants. It uses a massive 5/16-inch K-member plate to shore-up the lower chassis and provide a strong mount for the rack steering. The system is available in rear steer with front steer available soon. (Photo Courtesy Fatman Fabrications)

compartment panels; it adds a lot of strength to the front end. The unibody system flexes a lot, and that is why the early Mustang is known in some racing circles as "the hinge." Taking out the towers doesn't help with that reputation. Successful MII installers take the extra step and reinforce the area on the back side and tie things together to gain back what is lost by removing the towers.

One other point I discovered about installing the modular engine with some MII kits is that the oil pan hits the crossmember on some of the early manufacturers products. Some MII kits now come notched for the stock pans.

Strut Suspensions

MacPherson strut suspensions eliminate the upper control arm and allow for a simplified geometry. Used widely in front-wheel-drive cars, this suspension system has been the staple in the Mustang camp since 1979; all the new engineering is designed around it. It doesn't interchange well into the original early chassis, though, so companies have worked around this problem to get the technology into the early cars. The Mac strut systems use rack-and-pinion steering, which also improves the handling of the earlier cars.

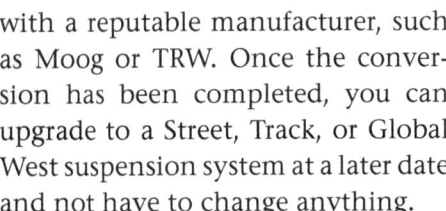

Gateway Classic Mustangs has a complete strut system available for Mustangs, Cougars, Falcons, Fairlanes, Meteors, Mavericks, Rancheros, Montegos, and Torinos. It has also adapted its technology to some vehicles already set up for Mac struts, such as SN-95 Mustangs. Its new spindles bolt right up to the original lower ball joint to simplify installation and are ride-height adjustable. (Photo Courtesy Gateway Classic Mustangs)

Fox-Body Mustangs and Thunderbirds

When installing a modular engine in your Fox-body car, you can adapt a later-model modular K-member to the early chassis. The struts are an inch shorter, allowing for extra underhood clearance. Some of the early T-birds from the Fox-body eras can also be fitted with the later modular engine K-members, making these swaps a breeze.

Other Designs

Several companies and their racing programs provide suspension systems that deliver excellent performance, as can compact designs such as the Corvette suspension systems. Many of these designs can be adapted to a variety of cars, but the best suspension choice depends on the car and its application.

When I am working with a customer on an early Mustang swap, I typically recommend three systems. If the budget isn't available for a big overhaul or the car is just to be used for mild street driving, I usually recommend retaining the original suspension.

To improve performance, I recommend replacing the stock steering gear with a rack-and-pinion system, but then you need to convert to a front sump oil system. In addition, you can select good quality Moog or TRW suspension parts. Keep in mind that some parts sold in "handling" packages are inferior quality, so stay

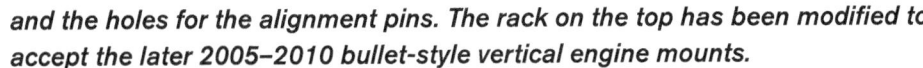

In 1979 Ford started using a K-member with the Mac struts in the Fox-body vehicles such as Mustangs, Thunderbirds, and Fairmonts. The later SN-95 modular engine K-member can be installed in the earlier cars and take advantage of the modular engine mount points. The rack on the bottom is a stock K-member showing the slots for the mounting bolt to slide in to and the holes for the alignment pins. The rack on the top has been modified to accept the later 2005–2010 bullet-style vertical engine mounts.

with a reputable manufacturer, such as Moog or TRW. Once the conversion has been completed, you can upgrade to a Street, Track, or Global West suspension system at a later date and not have to change anything.

A strut system is the next step up, and Dave Stribling Restorations offers a strut conversion that incorporates all the SN-95 K-members and struts without changing any of the geometry. This means that performance upgrades from Maximum Motorsports, Kenny Brown, or Steeda swap right in. The ride quality and handling are worth the additional costs if you can afford it. Strut kits are available from Gateway Classic Mustangs for many early cars, and they have tower cutback plates that allow for the structural integrity of the towers in the chassis and room for the modular engine.

If my customer wants to go racing, I look into the Griggs Racing GR350 suspension systems. Bruce Griggs has engineered his front suspension system to handle as well as any other system out there, and his cars win.

The modular engines swap into the early Fox-body Mustangs without any K-member or suspension modifications, so any suspension engineering improvements made for the Fox platform still work.

Engine Mounts

The engine mounts consist of two parts: the engine isolators that attach to the engine and the frame mounts that connect the frame to the isolators. Polyurethane isolators are available from Energy Suspension (PN 4.1127) for installing modular engines into early Mustangs and Cougars with original suspension and into a Fox-body chassis. UPR sells

CHAPTER 3

Detroit Speed has developed its Aluma-Frame front suspension system for 1964–1970 Mustangs and integrated it into its hydro-formed front subframes. This massive aluminum frame features forged spindles, tubular control arms, and a patent-pending alignment system. Engine mounts are available for all the modular engines and retain the stock frame rails with minimum fabrication. (Photo Courtesy Detroit Speed, Inc.)

Bruce Griggs Racing has been winning on the track for years and has developed its own double A-arm suspension system for many of the Ford platforms. The GR-40 suspension is track proven, and Griggs can custom tailor its K-members for most any application, even right-hand drive. Mustang Don's Garage is an expert on installing the Griggs suspension. Here they are installing the GR-350 system in a 1970 Boss 302 clone with a Boss 302 5.0 engine. (Photo Courtesy Mustang Don's Garage)

Total Control Products has been building subframes for years, and it has developed a front subframe clip to replace the flimsy factory versions in early Mustangs. This frame is vertically taller than the original 1964–1970 Mustang front rails, and one-piece design all but eliminates the flex and torque from the original setup. Total can install its G-Machine tubular suspension system or any number of different suspension systems to its subframe, and it has modular engine mounts to fit. This system along with its subframe connectors ties the frame together front to back. (Photo Courtesy Total Control Products)

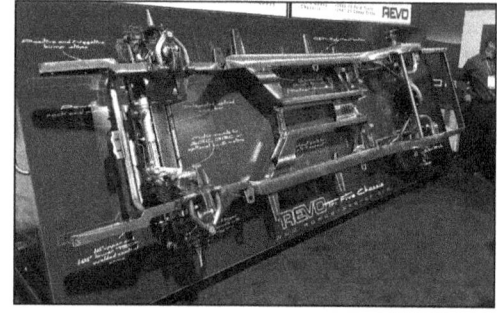

The Roadster Shop can install the Revo IFS suspension to any of its full frames or provide it as a bolt-in solution. The Revo suspension is a complete new design and incorporates a one-piece crossmember. It also uses a Wilwood forged pro spindle, steering arms, and tubular arms as standard. The Roadster Shop builds chassis for all popular muscle cars and street rods. (Photo Courtesy The Roadster Shop)

a K-member (PN 2005-79-MOD-50) that bolts in to the Fox chassis and mates with the above isolators. Maximum Motorsports also sells a conversion K-member (PN MMKM21). With the exception of the Fox body, some Mustang II conversions, and some early Mustang conversions, you may have to fabricate your own engine mount system.

The good news is, the isolator mount holes have not changed on the modular engine block, so half of the fabrication has been done and you should be able to adapt one of the existing isolators to your chassis. With few exceptions, you will probably be fabricating engine mounts for your project unless the suspension builder has already done that for you. You can use one of Ford's engine isolators, but you may be fabricating your isolator-to-chassis mounts yourself.

Motor mounts for early Mustang are available through Dave Stribling Restorations and use a 2003 GT isolator and mount in the stock 1967–1970 position. Late-model K-members for Fox-body cars are also available, as the mount is incorporated in the K-member.

Isolators

The isolators mount to the engine via a series of holes cast into the side of the block in a 100 x 80–mm rectangular pattern. Ford has used these holes for other things along the way, such as the GT500 oil cooler on the 5.4 engines.

The early-style isolator was a rubber bushing mounted fairly perpendicular to the block. With the start of the SN-197 Mustangs (2005), Ford went to a vertical isolator for the Mustang that was mounted on top of the factory K-member. Prothane makes polyurethane isolators for early applications (1996–2004) PN 6504BL and vertical (2005–2014) PN 6505BL.

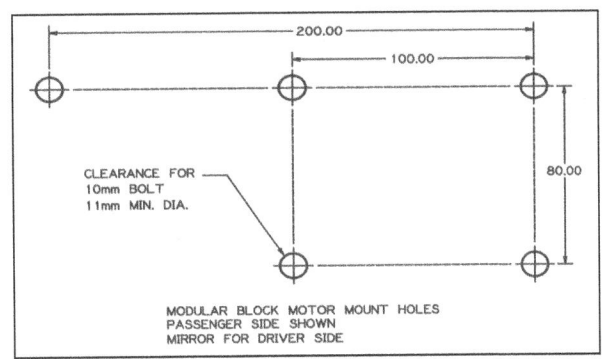

The Coyote block has a sixth mounting hole that completes the rectangle pattern.

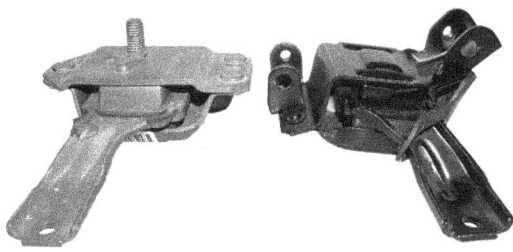

The engine mount on the left is from an SN-95 Mustang, the one on the right is from a mid-2000s Crown Victoria. The Mustang version sits slightly lower and uses bolt and alignment pins to mount to the factory K-member. There are aftermarket versions of the Mustang mount. For trucks the engine is usually mounted a little higher in the chassis.

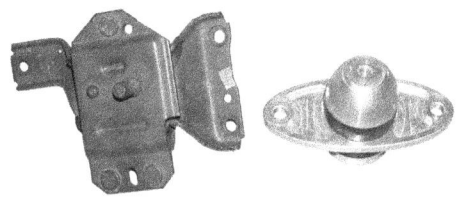

In 2005 Ford went to a vertical bullet-style mount with the introduction of the SN-197 Mustang. The engine bracket lies directly on top of this Prothane aftermarket mount, whereas the earlier mount on the left hugs the block.

Oiling System

The oil pan and oiling system is a big concern when installing the new engines in older cars, and it often interferes with other components. Most older cars have a steering system that is mounted behind the oil pan reservoir (front sump) whereas the modular engine installation uses a steering system mounted in

Fabricating Your Own Mounts

If your project calls for a set of engine mounts and no aftermarket solution is available, here is a set of quick and easy universal engine mounts that can be used to mount to side rails or to a K-member. If you are not skilled in proper welding (this is a chassis component, good welding is a must), take the attached drawing to your fabricator and have them make a set of mounts for you. This design is heavy-duty to handle the big iron-block supercharged engines, and the parts list comprises common parts normally found in stock at steel supply and performance parts outlets. You can modify this setup to suit your needs, but remember minimum thickness on steel components and note the recommended minimum thickness from the bushing manufacturer that you choose.

Parts List
- 3/16-inch or thicker plate steel; two pieces approximately 130 x 110 mm (5.12 x 4.33 inches) and four pieces 50.8 x 63.50 mm (2 x 2.50 inches)
- Energy Suspension bushings (or equivalent) PN 9-9111G
- DOM 1.5 inches (38.1 mm) tube with .187-inch wall (3.175 mm), 24-inch (60.96-mm) length
- 5/8 x 3–inch Grade 5 or greater bolts, washers and nuts, two sets

Tools
- Welder
- A means to cut out the plate steel and tubing (e.g., chop saw, cutoff wheel)
- Drill, 11-mm drill bit, and a 41/64-inch drill bit
- A tubing notcher or a means of putting a curve on the end of the pipe
- Proper safety equipment (face shield, gloves, hearing protection, welding safety equipment)

Fabricating Your Own Mounts CONTINUED

Using the supplied drawing, you can spend a couple of hours hand-cutting the plates from 3/16-inch steel and drilling them, or you can cheat and take advantage of new tools such as plasma, laser, or in this case, water jet cutting. It took an hour from the time I emailed him the DXF file to completion (you can create one with online free software if you don't have drawing software). For better results at a very reasonable price, I chose a common DOM 1½-inch tubing size. While having them cut the length I needed I also had the supplier cut two sections 1-9/6 inches long, then cut the remainder in half for the shafts. It only cost a couple dollars more and the cuts are nice and straight.

The hardest part of the fabrication is notching the ends of the long side shafts to fit the cross shafts. I am using an inexpensive tubing notcher purchased from a tool store with a 1½-inch hole saw. It is possible to do this with a barrel grinder or sander, but it is time consuming. The 1½-inch tubing is a popular size for roll bars and frames, so a local fabricator should be able to do the work for you. Weld the side shafts to the 1-9/16-inch cross shafts. Note: This is thick tubing and assembly. You can go with a thinner wall thickness and smaller outside diameter, depending on the bushings you choose.

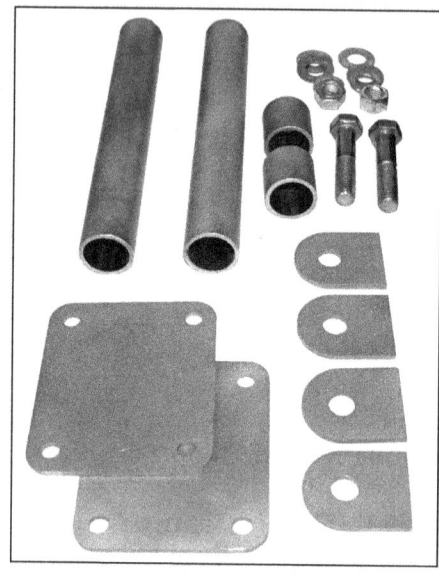

Here are all the raw materials ready for assembly. Use Grade 5 or better bolts and note your torque specs. This is heavy duty to handle big V-10s and supercharged iron-block V-8s.

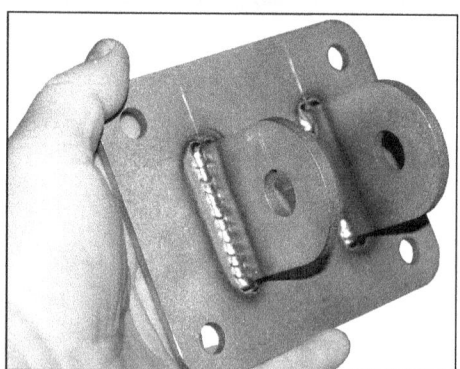

The tabs can be mounted anywhere on the plate; here I centered them for looks. You can mount the plates on the engine and temporarily set the engine in the chassis and check for clearances to see where the tabs best fit your application.

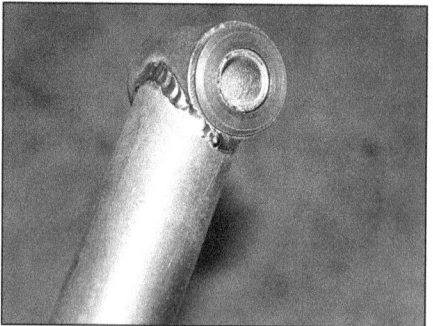

The Energy Suspension bushings are in its universal line (PN 9-9111G) and are very low cost. They press fit into the pipe we selected and use 5/8-inch hardware. If you use a different bushing and pipe, be sure to maintain the manufacturer's minimum wall thickness for the pipe.

Mount the shafts to the plates and then attach them to the engine. Use the four forward mounting holes in the block. This mount rotates 90 degrees for straight-down to horizontal if needed, so it is perfect for welding to a side frame or chassis with permanent crossmembers.

INSTALLING THE MODULAR ENGINE IN A PROJECT CAR

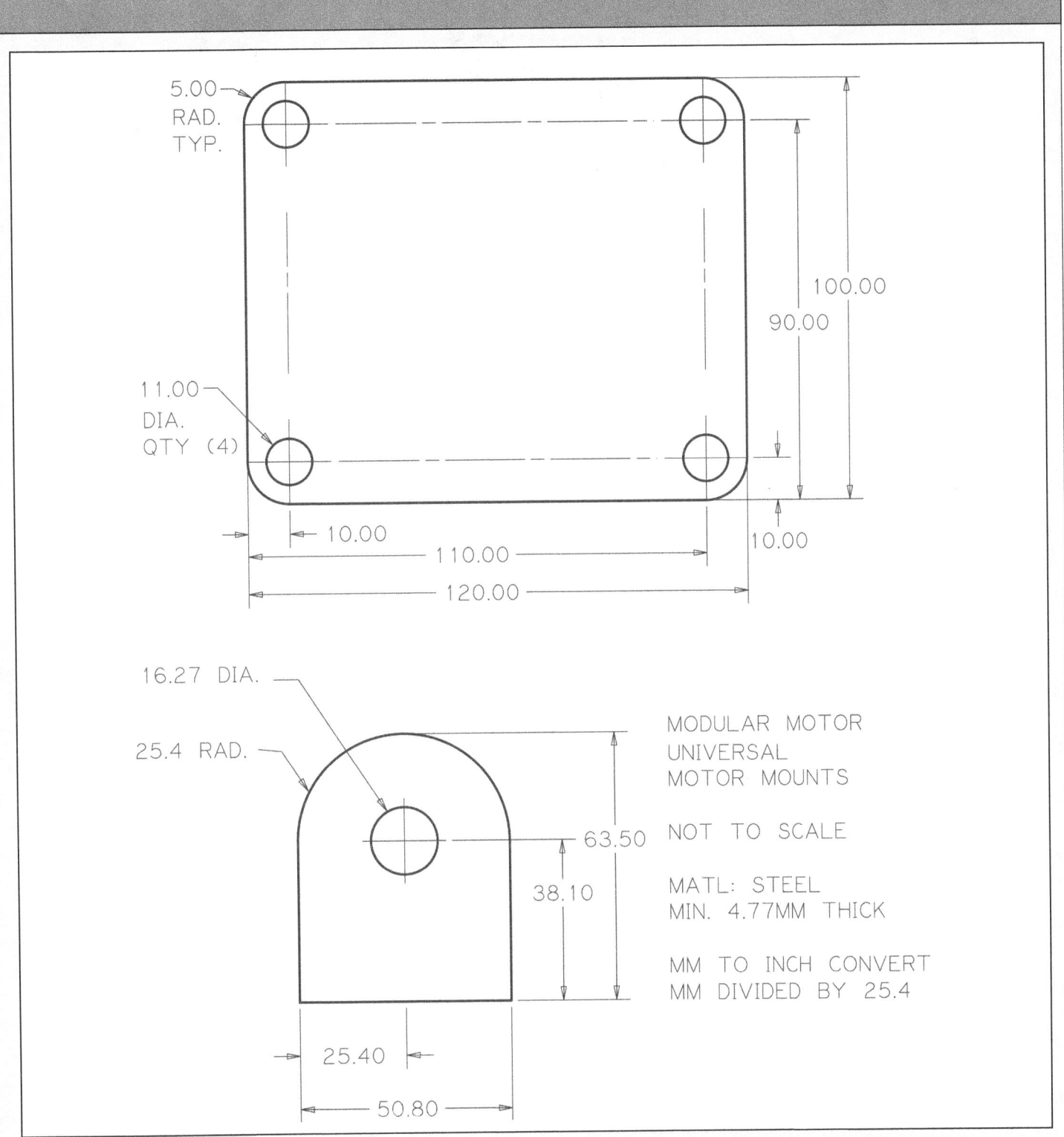

This drawing can be input into your drawing software to generate a .DXF file or file format your fabricator can use. Some shops may input it into their computer faster by hand (it is pretty simple). Measurements are in millimeters because of the block, but all the materials are in inches converted. You can always cut it out by hand, and the radiused edges are not required.

CHAPTER 3

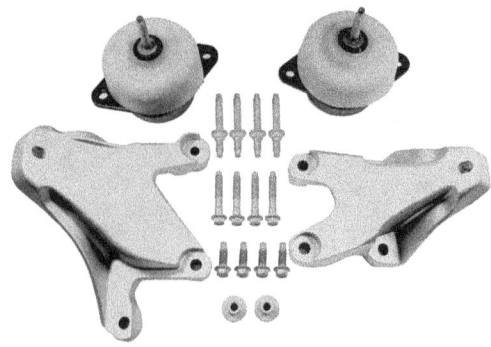

Ford Performance Parts markets new isolators for Coyote swaps (PN M-6038-M50). These stock 2011–2015 Mustangs come with the aluminum engine-to-isolator mount and hardware. (Photo Courtesy Ford Performance Parts)

Sean Hyland Motorsport also markets a set of conversion isolators for mounting the modular engines into 2005–2010 Mustangs or to adapt to your project. They feature steel engine-mount brackets and urethane isolators. (Photo Courtesy Sean Hyland Motorsport)

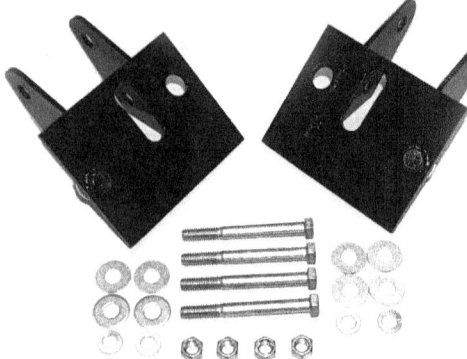

This set of frame mounts from Dave Stribling Restorations bolts in to the stock frame position on 1967–1970 Mustangs and Cougars and accepts the engine isolators from the SN-95 Mustangs. They can also be modified to use in earlier 1964–1966 Mustangs if using in conjunction with a strut-style suspension where the lower frame is retained.

Tin Man Fabrications has developed a set of engine mounts that employ the popular horizontal urethane isolator found in many street rod applications. These laser-cut, TIG-welded frame tabs adapt to many street rod frames and custom applications. (Photo Courtesy Tin Man Fabrication)

front of the reservoir (rear sump). In Ford modular-equipped cars, the lone exception to this is the front-wheel-drive 1995–2002 Lincoln Continentals. The rear sump pan's big advantage is that under hard acceleration the oil doesn't roll up and out of the reservoir, potentially starving the pump and bogging down the crankshaft. Even in cars already set up for rear sump oil pans, you may need a shallower pan and extra capacity, depending on the application. Moroso makes a low-profile road pan that works well in low cars such as Factory Five Racing roadsters, and Canton Racing makes a conversion oil pan and pickup to convert the rear sump systems to front sump to clear rear-steer steering systems, as well as drag and road racing pans for rear-sump installations.

Oil Filter and Clearance

On many installations, the oil filter hits the frame, particularly on unibody applications, because the oil and coolant passages exit in the same area on the earlier 4.6 and 5.4 engines. Ford changed this on the 5.0 Coyote engine and the inlet for the coolant is located at the front of the block on the driver's side. Ford pushrod engines have the oil filter mounting base cast into the block. However, modular engines use a bolt-on adapter, and this adapter can vary, depending on the application. Most of these designs place the oil filter out much farther than the older pushrod engines.

Several options are available if you run into this problem. Ford used a 90-degree oil filter adapter (PN F4UE-6884-BA) on some installations, such as the Police Intercep-

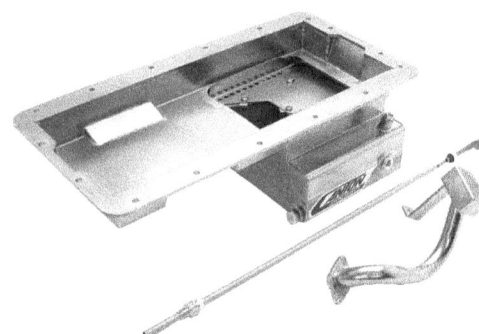

Canton Racing offers a full line of performance and conversion pans for modular engines. This front sump conversion pan (PN 15-738) and pickup tube (PN 15-739) are for a Coyote engine. The earlier modular pans won't interchange because of a change in the crankshaft trigger wheel and the front timing cover. Canton also has a front sump for the earlier blocks as well as a full line of pans and oil accessories. (Photo Courtesy Canton Racing Products)

tors and some vans. It is tapped and threaded for the metric modular oil filter. Ford Performance sells the same adapter (PN M-6880-M22), only the

INSTALLING THE MODULAR ENGINE IN A PROJECT CAR

Moroso's special low-profile rear sump pan (PN 20570) and the pickup tube (PN 24570) are used in many Cobra kit car applications. It works with the stock Coyote windage tray and has ports for low-level sensors, temperature senders, and supercharger drain back. Moroso has a full line of rear-sump modular engine pans. (Photo Courtesy Moroso Performance Products)

Installing a remote oil filter requires an adapter. On the left is a Canton Racing 90-degree adapter that attaches to the original oil filter pad and provides 1/2-inch NPT fittings to route to the filter. In the middle is a Canton adapter that replaces the original oil filter piece; the lower coolant hose is an AN fitting and the oil lines are 1/2 NPT. On the right is a modified Ford Performance Parts piece with a huge 2-inch outlet for the radiator and AN fittings for the oil lines; it is tapped for oil pressure and oil temp sensors.

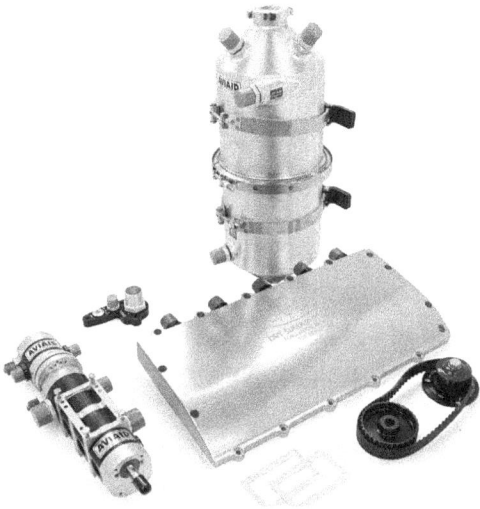

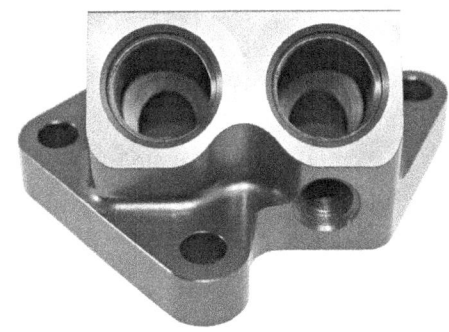

For the ultimate in ground clearance, Aviaid makes a dry sump oil system with a low-clearance pan for the modular engines. The system features a four-stage pump, a pickup oil pan, 3-gallon capacity tank, and a remote oil filter. (Photo Courtesy Aviaid)

Modular engines do not have an oil filter pad cast into the block as with earlier Ford engines, but rely on a filter mount adapter specific for the application. On the pre-Coyote engines, Ford had the coolant inlet mounted right above the two oil coolant passages for the oil filter (the big square hole), which complicated the oil and coolant layout for the early engines. The Coyote coolant inlet is on the front of the engine.

For Coyote applications, Ford Performance Parts has this remote oil filter adapter (PN M-6881-M50), which uses AN-10 O-ringed fittings. It is made of billet aluminum and is recommended for street applications. (Photo Courtesy Ford Performance Parts)

FPP unit accepts a standard FL1-A or 3/4-16 threaded filter.

Most manufacturers that made oil filter outlets for the more common FL1-A filters are now tapping them for the modular 22-mm threads because the mounting pad is the same. These can be used for a remote oil filter mount and external oil coolers using the original oil filter mounting pad.

Oil Coolers

Ford used radiator coolant to cool the engine oil. A circular intercooler was mounted between the filter and the inlet of the block. On some earlier engines, the intercooler worked in conjunction with the inlet design of the coolant passage next to the oil passages. On later 5.0 engines, the coolant lines tapped into the radiator lines. On the 2007–up 5.4 Shelby GT500, a van-style relocation adapter was made to mount the oil filter down the side of the block. This part was cast with 7R3V-6884-BB and may also carry PN 9R3v-6884-AA1.

HOW TO SWAP FORD MODULAR ENGINES INTO MUSTANGS, TORINOS AND MORE   43

CHAPTER 3

Modular Motorsports Racing also sells an angled adapter for the Coyote engine (PN 444832). It is angled for additional clearance, uses AN fittings to run the lines, and has a 1/4-inch NPT port for running a feed line for turbo/supercharger lubrication or an oil sensor. (Photo Courtesy Modular Motorsports Racing)

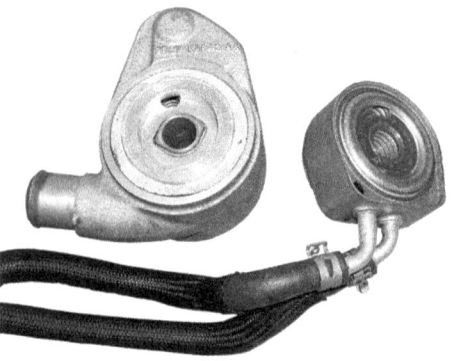

Ford uses engine coolant to cool the oil on modular engines. The oil cooler (left) for a 2003 Cobra engine plugs in to the outlet on the block adapter and then receives cooled coolant from the radiator. The unit (right) is from a Crown Victoria police car and has a separate line route to the lower radiator hose below the radiator. The Coyote cooler is similar to the Crown Victoria unit and is sold through Ford Performance Parts (PN M-6642-MB).

This picture shows the conflict between the driver-side exhaust outlet and the steering gear position on a rear-steer car. The original steering gear on this 1967 Mustang bolted up to the three holes to the left of the manifold. The stock exhaust manifold dumps right on the gear. If you want to run the original gear you need to change the outlet of the exhaust manifold. A better solution is to install a rack-and-pinion system as shown; the DD shaft clears nicely.

Steering System

The Mustang II conversion with rack-and-pinion steering system provides far more precise and controlled steering. The old worm and sector steering had a lot of issues with play and road feel.

The driver-side exhaust manifold or header frequently contacts the worm gear steering gearbox that's positioned on the side of the frame rail. The header often heats up the gear and causes premature failure or early wear. The rack-and-pinion conversion systems generally eliminate this conflict as there is usually a solid rod going from the steering rack to the steering column. Rack-and-pinion systems mounted behind the oil pan can cause interference with some traditional header designs (see Chapter 9), so take this into account when selecting a conversion rack for your car.

Several manufacturers now sell a conversion rack that replaces the original-style rear-steer system with a modern rack. Total Control Products makes a rack-and-pinion system for early Mustangs, Torinos, Falcons, and Fairlanes. In addition, Randall's Rack has designed a system to fit early Mustangs. Both of these companies took time to engineer out the bump steer issues, rather than just make a part that fits. These conversions usually use a modern pump, which is already pressure ready to run the rack-and-pinion system, so the conversion is convenient and you don't have to worry about the operating pressure. Some systems adapt the old-style pumps, but they are not designed to operate a rack steering gear.

In the late 2000s, electric steering was installed on some Ford vehicles and in 2012 it became standard on the Coyote Mustang. This eliminates

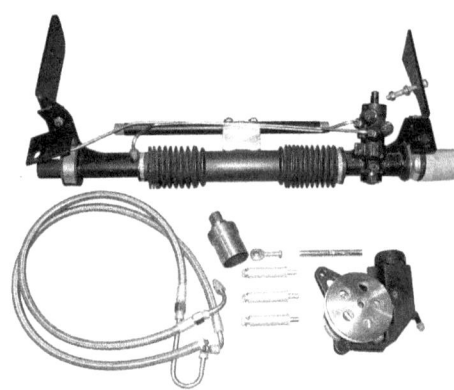

Randalls Rack was one of the first to adapt a modern rack-and-pinion system to the early Mustang rear-steering mount points and make a true bolt-in system. His system uses the steering box and idler arm mounting holes and uses the original engine crossmember holes for a second axis hold. His system uses original-style tie-rod ends, so there is no problem with custom parts.

the need for a pump and all those hydraulic lines, and also eliminates power loss due to having to spin a

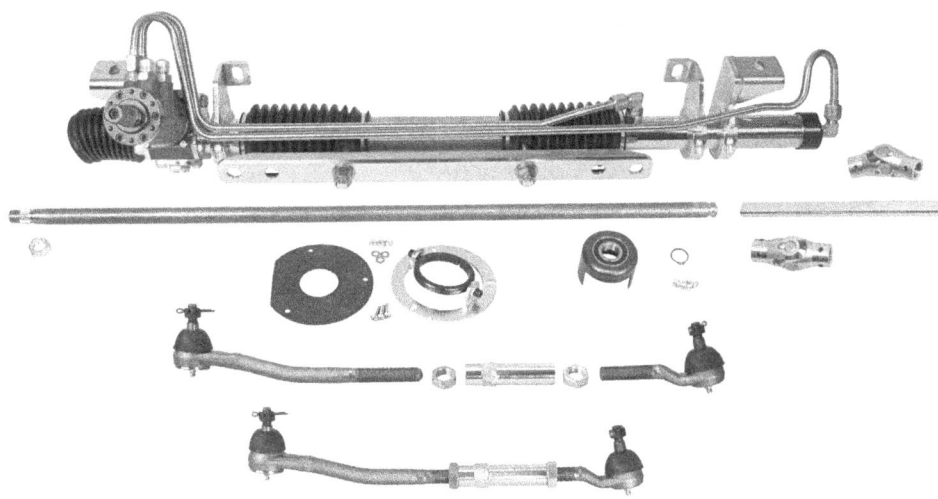

Total Control Products also makes a custom rack-and-pinion system for first-gen Mustangs and Cougars (1965–1973) and early Comets, Falcons, and Rancheros (1960–1965). The system is a bolt-in and there are options for additional clearances and for right-hand drive. (Photo Courtesy Total Control Products)

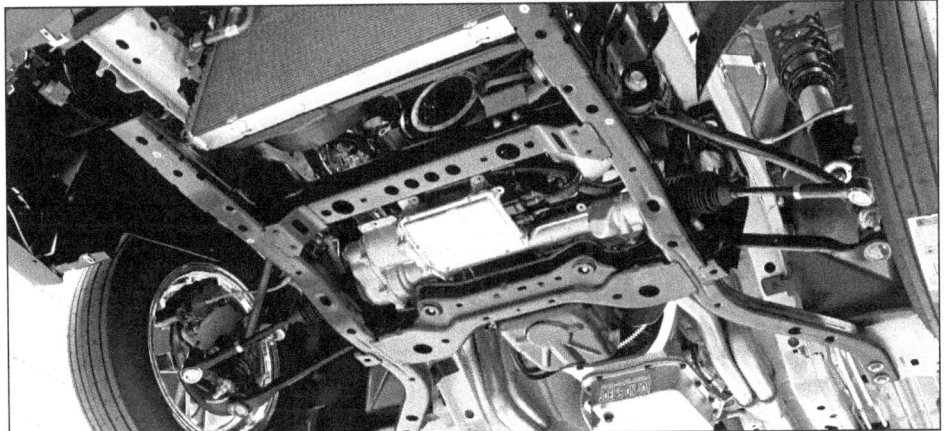

pump. Whether you are running a hydraulic or electric steering system, conversion pieces are available.

Power Brakes

The stock power brake booster on most cars contacts and occupies the same space as the driver-side cylinder head, and therefore you may need to find an aftermarket alternative that fits. The booster mounts behind the master cylinder on the firewall. These large, vacuum-actuated units extend into the engine bay on classic Ford and other muscle cars. When Kar Kraft was assembling the 1969–1970 Boss 429s, the company had to resolve the same brake booster/engine fitment problem. Ford developed a special brake booster and an angle plate to clear the big Hemi heads in the

In 2011 Ford began using electric steering on the Mustangs along with the new Coyote engine. Ford Performance Parts sells a rack system (PN M-3200-EPAS) set up for race applications and it is the same unit used in the Boss 302R program. (Photo Courtesy Ford Performance Parts)

Sean Hyland Motorsport has designed a power steering pump bracket that allows the use of the A/C compressor in the original positions. It mounts the pump on the passenger's side and comes complete with all the hardware needed for the conversion. (Photo Courtesy Sean Hyland Motorsport)

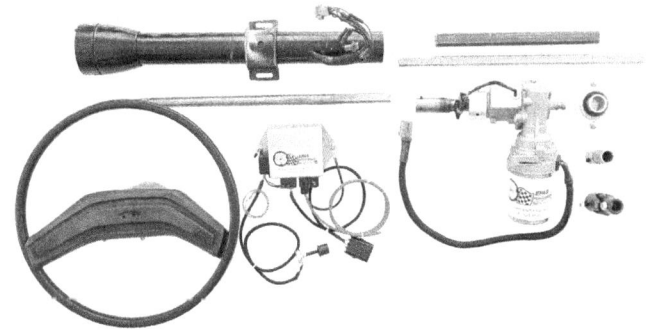

EPAS Performance makes a full line of electric conversion power steering systems to fit most vintage automobiles and allows you to operate the Coyote engine without converting to a hydraulic system. Its units require no welding and come pre-wired and ready to go. This unit is for a 1966–1975 Ford Bronco. (Photo Courtesy EPAS Performance)

CHAPTER 3

KRC makes a bracket to mount a power steering pump to the left side of the engine on a Coyote engine. The bracket works well with its famous KRC pumps. The system includes a water pump pulley adapter to run the pulley. (Photo Courtesy KRC)

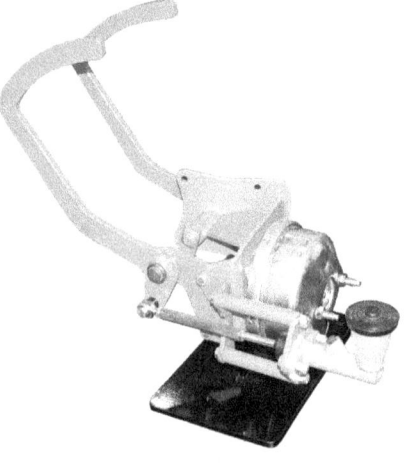

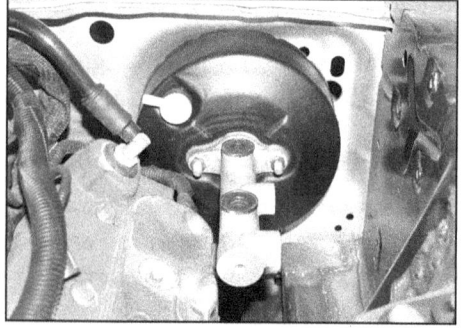

This 4.6 DOHC in a new Dynacorn 1967 Mustang fastback body is using a Mustang Steve's 9-inch booster conversion. Mustang Steve found a compact 9-inch booster that works with four-wheel discs and fits in tight spots. The master cylinder is a super narrow Ford unit from a 1993 Ford Thunderbird.

With the engine running down the center of the chassis, the original hydroboost from the SN-95 Mustangs and Cobras fits in the 1967–1970 Mustangs. The only requirement is a few additional holes in the firewall and it is a bolt-in using a non–power brake pedal.

For very tight street rods and vehicles with little room for the big DOHC heads, the vacuum brake booster can be mounted under the chassis to make more room in the engine compartment. This unit is made by Engineered Components to fit a 1935–1940 Ford chassis and includes both a power brake booster and a hydraulic master cylinder for a hydraulic clutch conversion (PN EC-404).

Hydroboost Power Brakes

During the SN-95 Mustang generation (1999–2004), Ford began installing a hydroboost power brake unit on Mustang GTs and Cobras. These units received hydraulic pressure from the power steering pump and worked well in the early Mustang chassis. In fact, it is almost a bolt-in using a non–power brake pedal in the 1967–1970 Mustangs. It is narrow and allows for the installation of the wider 4V heads in these early cars. In 2005 Ford went back to a vacuum booster (my guess is that the hydroboost was a more costly system).

Mustang chassis. It is the same with some of the big 4V heads, and very true with the wider 5.4 4V engines.

Street rod builders have known about this problem for years and have come up with clever ways to mount the power brake booster outside of the engine compartment, such as in the trunk or under the frame of the car.

You need to make sure power brake boosters are compatible with your setup. I have had to replace several 7- and 8-inch boosters because they just don't have enough push to operate four-wheel disc brakes, even though some of the manufacturers say they will. Some brands may work better than others, but I feel the better solution is a 9-inch booster.

Swap Spotlight: One Bad Kat

The Mercury Cougar entered the pony car field in 1967. The Cougar shares the same basic engine compartment dimensions as the 1967 Ford Mustang, so the techniques for installing the larger modular engine into the 1967–1970 Mustang chassis apply to the Mercury Cougar as well. (See "Installing the Modular Engine into the 1967–1970 Mustang and Cougar Chassis").

Rockstar Ridez in Chula Vista, California, decided that a first-generation Cougar needed a little rock star attitude to complement the clean Cougar lines. Owner Robert Emery and his crew are all about upscale attitude, and what better way to show this off than with the pony car that rises above the others in both areas? The result is this beautiful 1968 Cougar fitted with Ford Coyote power.

Rockstar began with a rust-free California (what else?) body and installed a complete roll cage front to back. The suspension features the Heidt's Pro-G Series I independent front and independent rear systems, a set of Ride Tech Shockwave airbag shocks rides on all four corners and uses a Ridepro coltrol unit. Wilwood's blocked-out series of brakes provides the stopping power using six-piston Forged Narrow Superlight brakes up front and the 11-inch inboard brakes on axle shafts in the rear. To clear the big four-cam heads the brakes are actuated by a 2003 Cobra hydroboost unit with a custom-modified angle plate similar to the one originally designed for use in the 1969–1970 Boss 429. The rear of the Cougar was mini-tubbed to accommodate the Work Wheels CR-2P 19 x 10–inch rims and BFG's 285/35/19 tires, while the fronts received 18 x 8–inch rims and BFG's 245/40/18 tires. The rims are Work Wheels CR-2P 18 x 8 up front and 19-10 in the back.

Up front is a Boss 302 engine pulled from a 2013 Boss Mustang putting out 444 reliable hp. The stock tubular headers were modified to clear the side rails and suspension pieces, and the stock air breather was removed in favor of a custom unit using a K&N filter mounted under the hood scoop to allow for ram air operations. The Ford Control Pack computer system was used to control the engine.

Backing up the Boss engine is the Gertrag 82 6-speed transmission from the 2013 Boss, using a McLeod lightweight-steel flywheel and 11-inch clutch. A Modern Driveline hydraulic clutch pedal conversion is used in conjunction with the stock hydraulic throwout bearing. With the lowered stance of the Cougar, the transmission tunnel was modified to accept the larger MT-82 6-speed.

A Tanks Inc. fuel tank with an in-tank pump feeds fuel through an Aeromotive fuel regulator (required for the Ford Control Pack). AN-6 fuel lines are custom bent and used throughout. Magnaflow multi-chamber mufflers and 2½ inch pipe were chosen for their quiet operation while cruising but performance and sound when the engine is cracked open.

I caught Rockstar Ridez during the final assembly of this 1968 Mercury Cougar. It received the full custom treatment on the outside, including badge and reflector removal, custom hood scoop, and spoilers. Under the hood, they added Ford Performance Coyote power. (Photo Courtesy Rockstar Ridez)

Rockstar Ridz installed the Heidts Pro-G front and rear suspension and custom fabricated the transmission mounts to fit the Getrag 6-speed into the chassis. Full 2½-inch exhaust and X-pipe flow into Magnaflow mufflers. Ridetech Shockwave air ride shocks and Ridepro control unit allow the Cougar to sit as low as you want. The Pro-G front crossmember is double braced to add extra strength when the towers are removed. (Photo Courtesy Rockstar Ridez)

This beautiful Cougar is finished in 2015 Harley Davidson Olive Gold Denim Green paint with 2015 Ford Tuxedo black for all the striping. The engine intake and engine covers were treated to the same highlighted color scheme, along with the custom transmission crossmember. The hood hinges are one-piece billet Ring Brother's hinges.

A 1967 Eliminator-style hood scoop was also given the rock star treatment by stretching the scoop and raising it 3 inches in front, for a little extra attitude. A custom rear deck spoiler was added, as well as the custom front spoiler. The Stars and Stripes are proudly worn on the side of this ride to honor the owner, who is a retired Navy SEAL.

Rockstar Ridez have truly succeeded in bringing upscale attitude to this 1968 Mercury: looks, performance, engineering, and overhead cams. Whether you're heading to the Sunset Strip to check out the live music or blasting down the Pacific Coast Highway, Rockstar can get you there in style. With attitude.

A 444-hp 5.0 Coyote from a 2013 Boss 302 sits in the engine bay of this car. Not much was needed other than a custom intake tube and a conversion to use the Ford Control Pack computer. (Photo Courtesy Rockstar Ridez)

Autometer Musclecar series gauges were selected for the interior and the engine computer was tucked under the middle of the dash on top of the transmission tunnel. (Photo Courtesy Rockstar Ridez)

The rear spoiler was custom made to match the lines of the Cougar, and the rear was tubbed to make room for the 19x10 Work wheels and BFGoodrich tires. (Photo Courtesy Rockstar Ridez)

The hydroboost from an SN-95 Mustang was installed to help clear the big hemi heads. A 2003 Cobra power steering pump conversion mounted with custom-made brackets powers the booster. The hood hinges are billet Ring Brothers units. (Photo Courtesy Rockstar Ridez)

CHAPTER 4

POWERTRAIN CONTROL MODULES AND WIRING

Once you have chosen an engine, it is time to select a computer and wiring harness to control the engine. While many industry names have been used to describe the computer that controls the engine, Ford refers to its system as the Powertrain Control Module or PCM. Wiring the system is the most difficult part of any swap, and with all the changes Ford has made over the years and the upgrades to computers, it is a source of apprehension to most builders. Unlike other makes where the basic scheme doesn't change much, the Ford system has changed considerably over the years and has had at least four base configurations as of this writing.

You can choose between an aftermarket or the factory system that originally came with your engine. Both types have benefits and drawbacks. Follow the recommendations in this chapter to select the best computer and wiring system for your engine. The newer the engine, the more difficult it is to use a factory system. If you have a Coyote engine, therefore, you should strongly consider an aftermarket or Ford Control Pack system, which will allow you to tune your engine according to your application. If you use a factory Ford computer and harness, make sure you acquire or have all the necessary parts, including sensors, boxes that bolt to the firewall, etc. You know that the car runs with all the components plugged in; you can determine later if a component isn't needed.

Determine what, if any, other components from the donor vehicle you would like to use (e.g., transmissions, ABS, electric windows). Some of these systems are best controlled using a factory computer. If you want to use only the engine, an aftermarket computer may be your best option. Make sure that the system you choose is legal. Some of these systems cannot be used in pollution-controlled vehicles.

Factory Systems Overview

The factory system allows you to use and control components such as automatic transmissions, ABS units, and fuel systems without extra controllers. Retaining the original

Two of the biggest advantages to the modular engine are the amount of data you can retrieve from the computer system, and the ability to tune the engine through re-programming. Error codes and data logging help determine what components may need attention, and most systems now work over Wi-Fi. This is an SCT X3 programmer being used to download a new performance profile into a modular-engine 1968 Mustang.

computer and harness for your engine type is simpler and easier than using an aftermarket computer because you can use the factory plugs and the original wiring and sensors. In addition, you don't have to verify the sensors that are installed on the engine, as some aftermarket systems require a change to generic sensors.

Ford has used at least four different computer systems to control the modular engines. These computers are all mass airflow design, so they must use an airflow meter to measure the amount of air going into the engine. Ford made constant improvements to the engines and controls throughout the years, and along with the base computer, the control systems also changed.

The location of components can be a disadvantage and often an obstacle with the factory system. For example, the PCM mounting on the donor vehicle may be in a place that doesn't work on your swap, and changing the placement may be difficult. And the same goes for the wiring; you may have to extend, trim, or tuck away wiring that doesn't quite fit. Ford also has used some creative routing for some of the wires, requiring you to get all the wiring harnesses from your donor car.

Ford is generally very good at keeping wire colors consistent, but is notorious for changing the location of signals in a connector and changing the sex of the connector, even within model years. Ford made it increasingly difficult to mix and match the wiring harnesses because of various options on the vehicle. Ford may have multiple harnesses within a year and model that cannot be interchanged.

If you are going to use a Ford harness and computer in your swap,

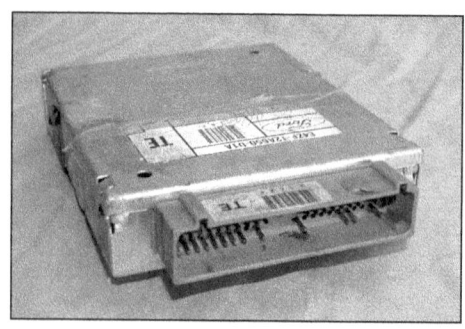

The first modular engines installed in full-size Fords used the reliable but now aging EEC-IV computer from the 1980s. The wiring for the early Crown Vics and Grand Marquis does not convert well to other chassis. Its larger pins and unique plug keying identify the EEC-IV computer.

This EEC-V is from a 2003 Mustang Cobra, and it features an additional row of pins and the different keying from the EEC-IV unit. These computers can be programmed through the DLC connector or through a chip mounted on the back side.

make sure you get all the wiring and electronic parts from the donor car. Buying every sensor or component from Ford can be very expensive.

The following are brief synopses of the Ford computer systems:

EEC-IV (1991–1993)

The EEC-IV computer was installed on the earliest modular engines in full-size Ford cars. Ford used this computer system throughout the 1980s and EEC-V replaced it in 1994. All of these systems were the mass airflow type and used coil packs (modular engines do not use a distributor). The EEC-IV computer module is easily identified by its three rows of pins on the main plug. These systems were unusual in layout because they had some extra relay boxes, and this makes the conversion a bit cumbersome compared to later wiring harnesses.

EEC-V (1994–2004)

Ford implemented the EEC-V computer to comply with the mandated On Board Diagnostic II (OBDII) industry standard. Several versions of the EEC-V system were developed and installed on Ford vehicles. During the EEC-V era, Ford transitioned away from coil pack ignition to a coil-on-plug (COP) system. Ford also introduced a returnless fuel system for which the PCM regulated fuel pressure. As a result, the old mechanical fuel pressure regulator and fuel tank return line were eliminated. About 1999, the Passive Anti-Theft System (PATS) was improved, and installing aftermarket components such as instrumentation became difficult. The EEC-V computer can be identified by the four rows of control pins in its main connector.

EEC-VI (2005–2013)

As more gadgets continued to consume computer resources, the computer needed to evolve. The jump to EEC-VI and improvements such as drive-by-wire technology and Variable Cam Timing (VCT) came in 2005.

EEC-VII (2014–)

The EEC-VII system uses a computer housing similar to the EEC-VI's, but it uses the three connectors on the end or top. As regulations and

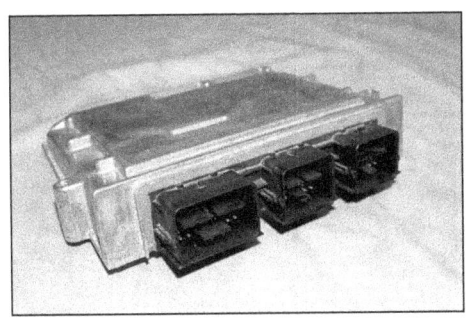

The three connector plugs easily identify the 2005 and up computers. Many of these computers were mounted in the engine compartment rather than inside the interior as with earlier computers. This can make the mounting using original hardware difficult in tight engine compartments.

features are added to new vehicles, its computers will be replaced with greater frequency. In 2015 the control box shape changed slightly, going back to a two-connector design.

Ford Wiring and Connectors

Using Ford factory wiring harnesses is an option for most engines and projects. However, the newer the engine and vehicle, the more difficult it is to use the factory components. When using factory computers and wiring, pay close attention to the connectors. Ford frequently changed them, even within model years. For example, a 2003 Mustang Cobra uses a male plug on the engine harness, and on the 2003 Mustang GT it is a female. Ford also changes the wire locations in the connectors. A Crown Victoria engine and a Mustang engine may have the same connector, but Ford changes the pinouts of the wires in the connector. Ford is very good at keeping the wiring colors consistent, but it doesn't really want you interchanging harnesses.

Here are some of the bigger hurdles to consider if using a Ford wiring harness and computer.

PATS

The Passive Anti-Theft System (PATS) has evolved over the years and the newest system is now the biggest hurdle to overcome in an engine swap. Starting in 1996, the Ford Securilock system was integrated into Ford cars and trucks, and in 1999, Ford upgraded to the PATS II system. The PATS II looked at the serial numbers of certain components such as the gauge cluster and wouldn't start if they had been changed. However, a simple software jump in the PCM programming could defeat these systems.

About the time the VI-VCT engines came out, Ford improved the PATS system to the point that aftermarket performance tuners found it difficult to bypass the system. Programmers were first told that PATS was hard-wired into the computer, but this turned out to be not true or they were able to get around it. The problem has been resolved, and now programming the new computers is no problem. But it may prove more challenging as Ford continues to improve its security systems.

Throttle-by-Wire

In 2005 Ford introduced the throttle-by-wire system that actuated the throttle plate using an electric motor rather than a traditional cable. The gas pedal is an electronic device that sends signals to the throttle motor via wiring. This means provisions need to be made in your swap to accommodate the throttle-by-wire gas pedal.

The throttle-by-wire systems include this servo motor that's attached to the throttle body to move the throttle plate. The throttle-by-wire system helps the engine run smoother under acceleration and deceleration and changing torque conditions.

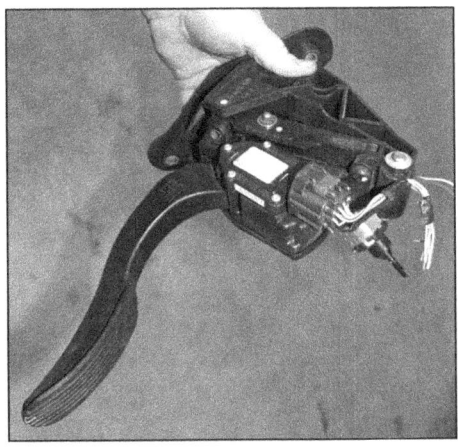

An accelerator pedal that uses a potentiometer to identify the position of the pedal is matched to the throttle control. This police car unit is very big and difficult to use in a swap due to the speedometer calibration system.

Returnless Fuel System

In the late 1990s Ford introduced the returnless fuel system that eliminated the mechanical fuel pressure regulator and fuel return line used since the 1980s. The PCM controls the voltage applied to the pump and reads the pressure via a pressure transducer mounted on the fuel rail.

Unless you will be using the stock pump and controller in your

CHAPTER 4

In a returnless fuel system, the PCM uses this pressure transducer mounted on the fuel rail to measure the fuel pressure at the engine. The PCM can then adjust the voltage to the fuel pump and reduce or increase the pressure without the need for a mechanical regulator and return line back to the tank.

The round port with the plug just above the oil fill is the servo for the Variable Camshaft Timing (VCT). This servo can advance or retard the intake camshaft to increase the performance of the engine. VI-VCT used on the Coyote engines does the same for the exhaust cam and eliminates the need for an EGR system and improves emissions.

existing tank, you need to reprogram the computer to tell the fuel pump circuit to maximize output all the time and run an old-style regulator and return line to the tank.

Variable Camshaft Timing (VCT and TI-VCT)

Ford introduced variable camshaft timing starting in 2005. VCT allows the computer to advance or retard the camshaft timing via a control solenoid. Many aftermarket computers cannot control the variable timing, and the camshafts have to be locked down. VCT and the improved PATS system make using the factory wiring more difficult in most cases.

Ford PCM Communication

As I outlined in the introduction, one of the advantages to a modular engine swap is the ability to get information from the computer for both maintenance and performance tuning. This information is useful not only for drag racers with laptops; familiarity with the capabilities of your engine's computer system and ways to optimize your engine swap will help you meet the goals for your project.

Even the earliest EEC-IV computers could communicate running information and errors incurred. They did this through a series of binary pulses that generated engine error codes with the Key On Engine Off (KOEO) test. The computer could also run checks on the sensors in Key On Engine Running (KOER) mode. An old swing-arm voltmeter could be used to read the pulses put out by the computer.

With the introduction of the EEC-V system in 1994 came the OBDII (On-Board Diagnostic II) set of standardized error codes, which are still in use as of this writing. Along with the standard industry error codes, each manufacturer has some proprietary codes that are available to cover specific features of its vehicles. The latest systems cannot only give you the basic error codes, but can log information on the engine and systems when an error occurs, provide

You plug a scanner into this industry-standard DLC port to communicate with modern cars. It is usually found on the driver's side of the interior under the dash. This port allows you to read error codes, look at logged and live data, and change computer programs. This one is tucked up under the dash of a 1952 truck.

real-time running information on the performance of the engine, and be programmed over the Internet for engine and drivetrain improvements for both performance and efficiency.

All communications with the computer are done through the DLC (Data Link Connector), which is a standardized plug that is usually mounted under the driver's side of the dashboard. This plug connects to the Ford communications network and to the PCM.

Reading Error Codes

There are three levels of communication with the PCM, and these three levels require three different tools. The first is a basic low-cost code reader, the second is scan tools and data loggers, and the third is programmers. The basic code reader can read error codes stored in the computer. Error codes are primarily used

POWERTRAIN CONTROL MODULES AND WIRING

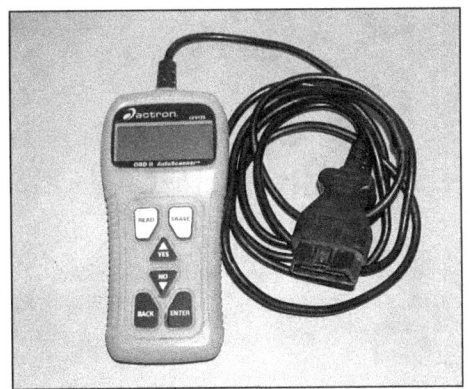

A simple error code reader can be had for little cost at most auto parts stores. These read the codes from the computer, and then you can check your manual or online for a solution. Most error codes are for emissions systems, but there are codes assigned to manufacturer specific problems. In 2003 Ford went to a faster data channel, so older code readers won't read newer computers.

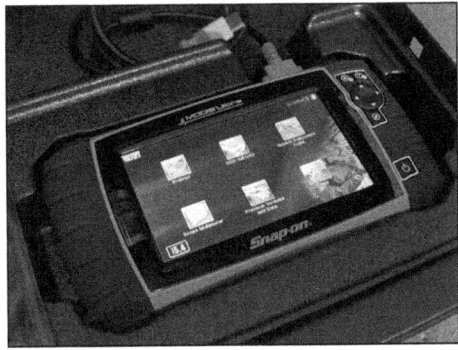

Gone are the days of using the old oscilloscope to analyze your engine's performance. Most professional mechanics have a scan tool that not only reads the error codes, but it can track data live while the car is running and look at data stored by the computer. This Snap-on Modis Ultima can graph performance data, run tests on individual components, watch data live and can even provide tips and recommendations based off of the data received. Most diagnostic tools now have ports to talk to computers and the Internet for even more capabilities.

for emissions issues, and when your PCM senses a problem, it stores a DTC (Diagnostic Trouble Code) and turns on the check engine light on the dash. The DTC follows the industry standard OBDII numbering system. Low-cost code readers, available at most auto parts stores, read these codes, and can erase them, as well. With the exception of being able to erase codes, this is pretty much one-way communication, but it is still beneficial.

Scan Tools and Data Loggers

The next step up is the ability to read the data stored in the computer and the ability to perform specific tests on certain items controlled by the PCM. For this, you need a scan tool, which costs more than the error code readers, depending on what level of features your scan tool possesses. This is more of a two-way communication with your computer, and the computer can respond to your inquiries and perform tests for you.

Over the years, improvements in the PCM and the software running the PCM have increased the level of communication and the amount of data acquisition. With this level of communication, you are going to hear your tuner or mechanic talk about specific terms. Here are just a few that you need to be aware of:

Parameter Identification (PID)

This allows a scanner to access the analog and digital sensors that are controlled by the PCM. OBDII rules dictate a standard set of PIDs that all scan tools can read; Ford has some proprietary ones that may or may not be readable by non-Ford scan tools. This function can test whether a sensor or switch is turning on or off, can measure the percentage of sensor in use, or the voltage reading of the sensor.

Output Test Mode (OTM)

With this mode, you or your technician using a scanner can turn on and off specific items in the car. An example would be a two-stage fan relay module. Through the scanner you can turn on the low and high fan outputs on the Ford system before you fire up your engine and know you will have the cooling fans on first start.

Freeze-Frame Data

With more and more information being stored by the computer systems, one thing that comes in handy is the freeze frame data. When your computer sets an error code, it records exactly what was happening when the error occurred. The newer the computer and the greater the number of sensors, the more information there is available. Freeze-frame data records the engine performance, as well as speed, emissions, what gear you were in, everything. (A friend test drove a newer Mustang GT and while he was cruising at 95 mph and backup system threw a minor code.

The computer recorded all the data of the vehicle at the time of the error, including his "test drive" speed. He had some explaining to do.)

Gone are the days of the old oscilloscope, and now every mechanic has a scan tool to talk to the computer. The computer can tell you more about what is happening with the engine than any external device. New diagnostic equipment scans live and stored data, graphs operating conditions, and even recommends a plan to correct the problem.

CHAPTER 4

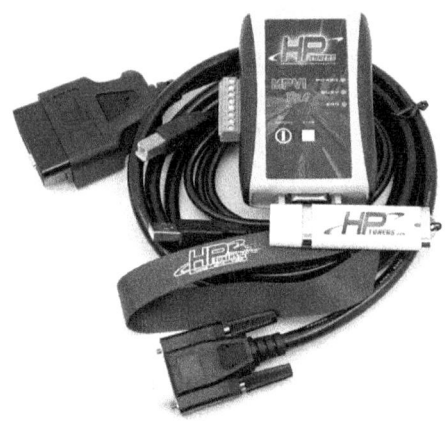

HPT's VCM Scanner is a computer-based diagnostic tool that allows you to download and analyze real-time data, allows you to chart information to look for intermittent problems, and also allows tests to be run on individual components and systems. It plugs right into the DLC just the like pros use and can be used across multiple models and brands with licensing. (Photo Courtesy HPT)

The EEC-V computers have a port that allows a programming chip. SCT's Eliminator Switch Chip is a plug-in device that can store up to five custom programs on one chip. With an optional selector switch, you can change programs instantly for track or road use. (Photo Courtesy SCT)

Diablosports InTune i2 compact tuner can hold as many as five custom tunes, log data real time, and talk to your favorite tuner via the USB port, allowing it to be programmed from a remote site from anywhere. The small compact size makes it handy when traveling (e.g., if you want to carry different tunes for different grades of gas), and it can be licensed to tune more than one vehicle, so no need for a separate tuner for each of your rides.

Programmers

The third level of communication allows you to reprogram your computer system, and this is what you need to get around systems such as PATS. Most aftermarket programmers have data logging and error code reading capabilities built in, so they are all-in-one solutions.

Some earlier EEC-V computers have a port where you can plug in an external computer chip and override the original program. These chips, depending on their complexity, can store multiple tunes for different uses (e.g., driving to the dragstrip and changing the tune for your passes; changing the tune on your truck when you are pulling for max torque).

Some system's computers can be reprogrammed via the Internet through built in Wi-Fi or through a laptop. Tuning an engine is a science, and most companies who sell the programmers work with trained tuners to maximize the performance and efficiency of the engine. Some sell pre-programmed tunes based on experience, but specific tunes are generally left to the experts. You can certainly purchase a programmer and work with tuning your vehicle, but there is a learning curve to becoming adept with tuners. If you plan to develop your ride for racing or top performance, a programmer may be right for you.

Unless you are a wizard with fuel curves and shift points, you will be working closely with a tuner, and they will probably use the tuner they are most comfortable using (see Chapter 10). A programmer manufacturer can give you a list of tuners in your area, or you can work with one over the Internet.

Programming Factory Computers

With the factory PCM, any time you change something on the engine, you need to reprogram the PCM to accommodate the change. You need to program around the PATS system,

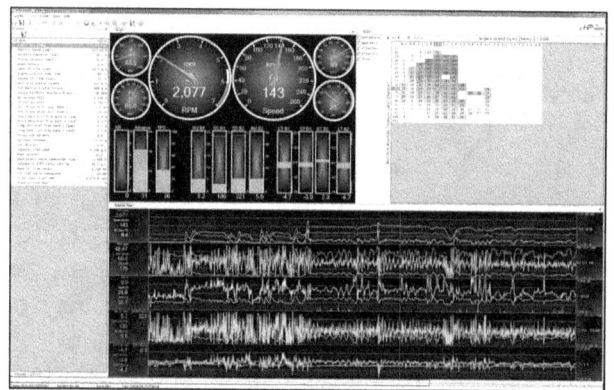

The HPT Tuner Suite puts the power of a professional tuning shop on your home PC. You can download and reflash the original code, run data logging and charting, lock in changes, and can be licensed for multiple vehicles and lines. (Photo Courtesy HP Tuners)

something most aftermarket companies say they can do (but check with your tuner). Anything that can affect what the computer thinks it is seeing needs to be addressed. You need to notify the tuner of any changes to items such as the intake, injectors, oxygen sensors, or any hardware that affects the performance of the car.

If you bypass items such as the EVAP or EGR for off-road use, or you are converting a mechanical fuel pressure regulator, you need to let the PCM know what you are changing. Some tuner dealers don't like to deal with swaps because the owners generally don't tell the tuner everything they have done, or the swap builder makes a mistake with the wiring and blames the failure on the programmer. Find a good tuner dealer and work closely to get your conversion right.

Factory Wiring Notes

If you plan on using the factory computer and wiring, here are the requirements: It is best to have a complete donor car; it gets very expensive running back to your dealer every time you are missing a sensor. Ford tends to route wires through multiple harnesses, so you need them all, and depending on the year, you'll need items such as fuel pumps and controllers, perhaps even components you won't be using. If you can't get the entire donor car, try to get as much as you can: computer, all the wiring harnesses, throttle pedal (if using throttle-by-wire), fuel pumps, and controllers.

You will be shortening, lengthening, and removing circuits from your harnesses in almost every case. Make sure you have a good, professional multimeter, quality crimp tools for general connections, and the proper pin insertion/removal tool for your job.

You need to buy a wiring diagram! Whether you prefer a physical book, CD, or direct online schematics, it is up to you. Wiring diagrams for Ford can be purchased online at helminc.com. Other services are available for online wiring and diagnostics.

Purchase the tools you need to successfully lengthen and shorten wires, or remove and install pins. Typical installations do not use all the wiring from a factory harness, and to save space and weight you will be pulling some wires out of the harness. You may also have to move pins within connectors if you have mismatched harnesses, or if you are trying to combine harness connectors.

Factory Computers with Aftermarket Wiring Harnesses

It is possible to run your factory computer using an aftermarket wiring harness. Through the years, numerous companies have attempted to build harnesses, and I have tried many of them, with varying degrees of success. Some harness manufacturers require you to send in your old harness so they can reuse

A typical vintage muscle car had 5 to 10 fused circuits. Modern cars have more like 50, and they are split into the fuse block and power distribution box, depending on how much current they carry. If you eliminate some unneeded circuits, you may be able to patch your original wiring harness systems, such as the lighting circuits, into unused fuses on your new system and consolidate.

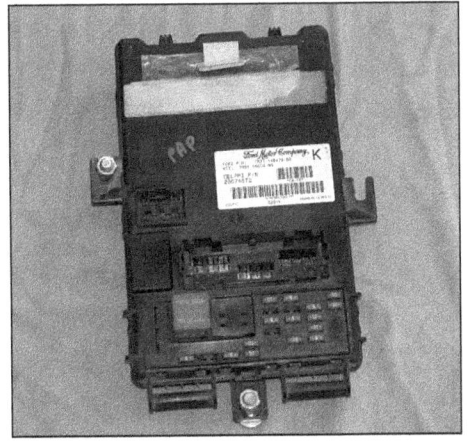

As the cars became more complex, Ford needed new ways to bring circuits together. This is a Smart Junction Box (SJB) from a 2007 Shelby GT500. Circuits from the engine area and interior terminate here, and if you plan on using the original harness, you need to get all of the special items like this. Ford changes the circuit pathways through the harnesses frequently.

Ford wiring diagrams are available to the public through Helm Inc. (helminc.com). They are available in book or digital format for your computer. It is a must for anyone using the original Ford harnesses in a project, and it's a good idea to have one even if you are planning on using an aftermarket harness.

CHAPTER 4

Installing an Aftermarket Wiring Harness

I have tested several different harnesses over the years, and I recommend the one from Hot Wire Auto. The Hot Wire Auto harness has some advantages over other harnesses on the market:

- The more connections you have in a circuit, the greater the possibility of a bad connection. Harnesses that use old-technology junction boxes require twice the number of connections as a one-piece harness. An enthusiastic owner usually makes these connections and doesn't have fancy pneumatic crimpers to ensure a good connection. Spade terminals are 1950s technology. The Hot Wire Auto part is a one-piece solution requiring a minimum amount of external connections, and that reduces problems after install.
- No bulky termination system to mount.

- Some of the harnesses currently on the market have exhibited quality issues. While it is true that you may need to send your old harness in to have some of the connectors reused, this may be preferred to using aftermarket housings, which may differ from the Ford units.
- Custom-length harnesses are not a problem. While other harnesses give you plenty of wire to mount components where you wish, Hot Wire Auto works with you on making a custom-length harness to mount your PCM where you wish.
- Simplified installation. A one-piece harness is closer to plug-and-play than one that is only partially fabricated. Depending on your application, you may need to send them your old harness to provide some of the hard-to-source connectors. The test mule for this install is the 1970 Mach I with a 4.6 SOHC.

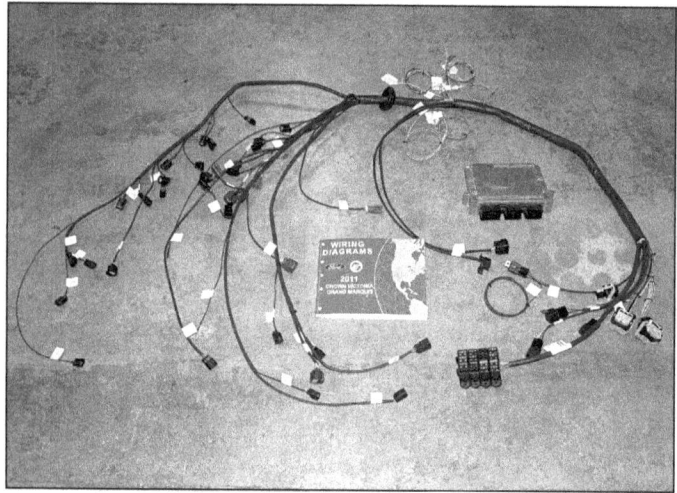

After sending Hotwire Auto the old harness, the company sent back this ready-to-go, fully labeled harness for this project. Hotwire Auto makes a wiring harness that uses the factory plugs for the computer and sensors to eliminate bulky breakout boxes, and it adds wiring for aftermarket gauges and accessories if needed. For this install I chose its standard length cable, but Hotwire Auto will work with you on custom lengths if you wish. You can also have four or two oxygen sensor systems, and the harness came with the automatic transmission connections. I also highly recommend getting a copy of the wiring diagrams for your engine. Also shown is the EEC-VI computer, which you must have re-flashed to operate properly.

Here is why I recommend the wiring diagram for your project: a lot of these connectors look the same, but may be keyed differently. I needed to locate the cylinder head extension cable, and by using the cross-reference in this book I was able to identify the correct extension.

Hotwire Auto will work with you on custom setups. I turned this intake elbow around to make more room on the driver's side, and that moved the TPS and ETC circuits to the passenger's side. Hotwire Auto moved them for me at my request. I started the layout by temporarily laying in a few of the connectors to aid in routing the harness to the firewall.

POWERTRAIN CONTROL MODULES AND WIRING

This owner is using the stock 1970 gauges, so I needed to add a coolant temperature sender to the engine. This nice crossover port is located at the front of the intake, and it has this big undrilled boss that worked perfectly. All-composite intakes may be more difficult to modify.

I installed a 1970-style coolant sender and Hotwire Auto ran a line in the harness to attach to the original gauge point.

With the dash partially removed, I looked for a good location for the wires to come through the firewall, and the lengths on the standard harness work well using the original factory engine exit hole. At this point, if you need a custom length on your harness, take the measurements from your computer mount location and fuse block mounting point to the location where your harness exit the firewall and send them to Hotwire Auto. When measuring for clearance add an inch or two to allow for sharp bends or obstacles in the way of the harness.

The firewall outlet requires a 2 3/8 inch hole for the harness to pass. The original wires coming out of the firewall at this point were the engine controls and the wiper circuits. Because I don't need the cable from the accelerator pedal, I moved the wiper circuits to the hole vacated by the accelerator pedal and opened up the original hole with a holesaw.

Pull the harness off the engine and feed it through to the engine bay from the inside of the interior. Note the larger hole where the accelerator cable was; this is for a standard-size grommet for the new location for the wipers. Attach your connections to the engine.

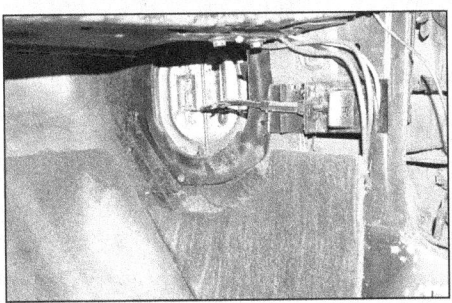

Our favorite place to mount the computer is not available on a 1969–1970 Mustang, as the cabin vent takes up the inside of the kick panel area. On your build, if you want to mount the computer here, you may need to have the harness lengthened to reach.

The dash on a 1969–1970 Mustang is very scalloped and does not allow for much to be mounted under the dash, especially a bulky computer and three big connectors. I went over to a friend's house to use his 1970 Mustang to make measurements and found the perfect spot, right between the bottom of the dash and the lower console. The standard length harness did not need any changes for this to fit here.

HOW TO SWAP FORD MODULAR ENGINES INTO MUSTANGS, TORINOS AND MORE

CHAPTER 4

Installing an Aftermarket Wiring Harness CONTINUED

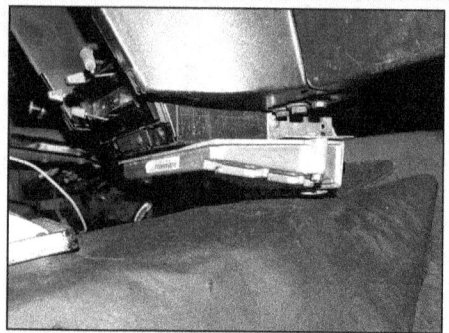

A simple set of adjustable brackets hold the computer to the bottom of the dash, and can be adjusted once the carpet and console are in place. A simple cover painted black hides the computer and blends it to the interior. Allow some space for cooling.

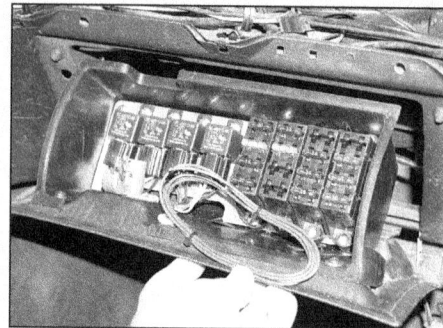

The Mustang console has a small storage compartment, which made the glove box available for us to mount the fuse block and power relays. I made a small shelf to fit inside the glove box, then attached the components to the shelf. No more crawling under the dash to change these fuses.

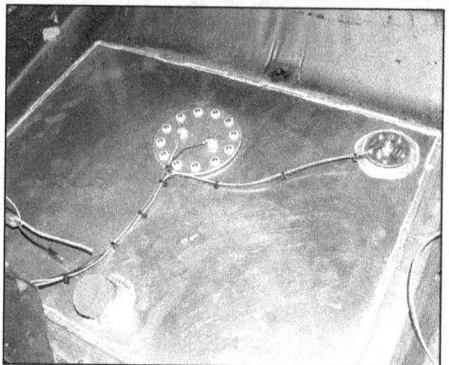

This customer opted for a custom fuel tank with a built in fuel pump from Mustangs to Fear. The sender unit in the corner has a standard 1970 Mustang output, and the fuel pump output is run to the relay mounted in the glove box.

The stock Ford fuel pump cutout switch was mounted to the rear taillight panel support for easy access. Route the fuel line power from the fuel pump relay to the switch, and then run it down to the fuel pump.

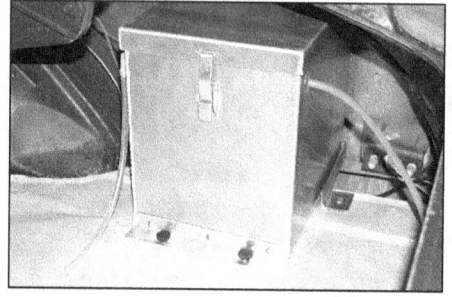

The battery box is tucked deep into the passenger-side quarter panel. A custom shelf was built to hold the battery to raise the floor up to protect the fuel pump and wiring. Ford always runs ground and power lines directly to the battery, and I did too. The Hotwire Auto harness has a single ground wire that attaches to the engine, and I went from there to a direct connection to the ground cable at the battery.

With the battery tucked away and difficult to access quickly, its a good idea to add a power cutout switch inside the trunk in case of emergencies. This makes a nice connection point to run direct battery power for the computer and battery power to the keyswitch. It also allows easy access for the battery charger connection.

The DLC connector was attached under the driver-side dash with a small custom-made bracket. Note the throttle-by-wire accelerator pedal in the background.

One of the better advantages to using the Hot Wire Auto harness is that the automatic transmission connections are the exact length needed and mimic the Ford routing. No fuss, no muss. This car is ready for the computer to be re-flashed and ready to fire.

some of the original Ford connectors, which may be obsolete and not readily available (some that are available are not good quality). Others can get the connectors, and some use a central junction point that permits remote mounting, but it is big and bulky. Some other harness suppliers require you to convert to GM-style generic sensors, which may make it difficult in the future to remember what is installed in the car.

You need to have some experience in wiring and making proper connections, and these aftermarket harnesses only control the engine and, if equipped, the transmission, and may not be capable of running any other components from your donor car.

Ford Performance Power Parts Control Pack

For the later throttle-by-wire engines, Ford has developed a control pack that uses a stock-style Ford computer and a plug-and-play wiring harness that controls just the engine. For the later VCT engines, the Ford Control Pack will also control the variable cam timing. The early 2005–2006 engines require a modification to the wiring harness to work with the control pack.

Using the control pack requires you to convert your system back to a mechanical fuel regulator and return system. It also requires the use of the 2011–2013 Mustang GT airbox and inlet hose, which can be cumbersome when installing in a non-Mustang application. Your tuner may be able to help you program around this.

Aftermarket Computer Systems

You have several aftermarket systems to choose from, but the choice boils down to three different types: Mass Air Flow, Speed Density, and Alpha-N. Which you choose depends on the type of driving you plan for your project. Here is a brief overview of the different types of computers

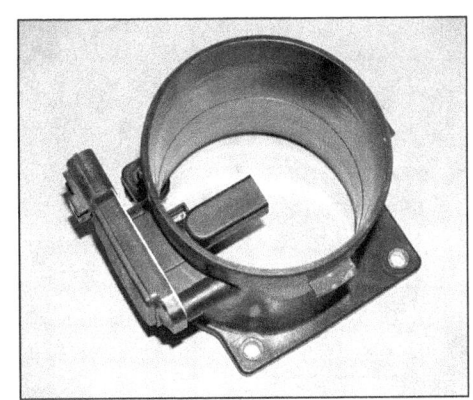

All Ford modular engines come with mass air fuel injection systems from the factory. The mass air meter heats up a small wire and then measures the resistance in the wire. As the air moves past the wire, it cools the wire and changes the resistance, and the computer can read the change. Mass air systems do not require many fuel curve tables and can calculate the most efficient ratio on the fly. Major changes to the engine may require a change to the size of the mass air meter.

and how they work. With the introduction of the Ford Control Pack, it has taken over as the best and easiest-to-use computer control system. Holley and FAST both sell speed density systems that will work with the modular engine and have specific Coyote harness converters to run these engines.

Mass Airflow

All Ford modular engines came with Mass Airflow (MAF) computer systems for control. A mass airflow system features a meter mounted ahead of the throttle plate that measures the amount of air going into the engine. The computer calculates the amount of fuel to be delivered to the engine based on air volume, air temperature, manifold pressure, and exhaust gas mix. Most MAF systems

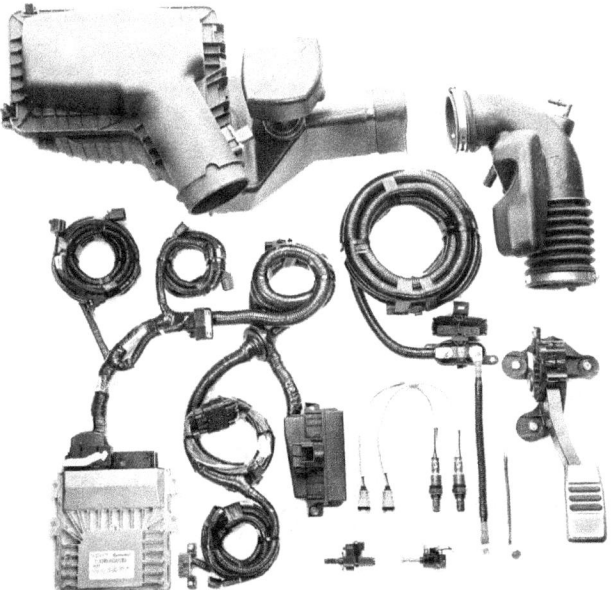

Currently, the best choice for operating the Coyote engine and later engines with VCT is the Ford Performance Control Pack. Designed for installation in street rods and engine swaps, it is a complete plug-and-play system that comes with the drive-by-wire accelerator pedal and a harness designed to run only the engine. The computer is already programmed to fire without the PATS system and it can be tuned just like any other Ford computer. (Photo Courtesy Ford Performance Parts)

Selecting an Aftermarket Computer

Selecting an aftermarket PCM is dependent on your engine choice and performance needs. Keep in mind that some aftermarket PCMs are not legal for street use, so be careful when choosing a PCM for your project. Choosing between mass air, speed density, or Alpha N depend on the application of the car. The ability of the PCM to control items, such as automatic transmissions, VCT, distributorless ignition (coil packs and COP), and other items also needs to be considered. Because Alpha N is fairly simple, most PCMs can operate in Alpha N mode. ∎

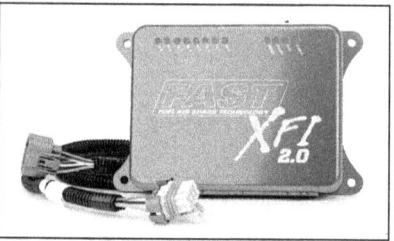

The FAST XFI 2.0 is available to control the 2011-and-up Coyote engines in both speed density and Alpha N modes. This self-tuning racing system comes with power adder control, fuel and cooling controls, and even individual cylinder RPM reference. It can be set for sequential or bank-to-bank fuel injection. Harnesses for Coyote crate engine applications are available, and you need to lock the cam phasing down and run a cable-style throttle body. (Photo Courtesy Fuel Air Spark)

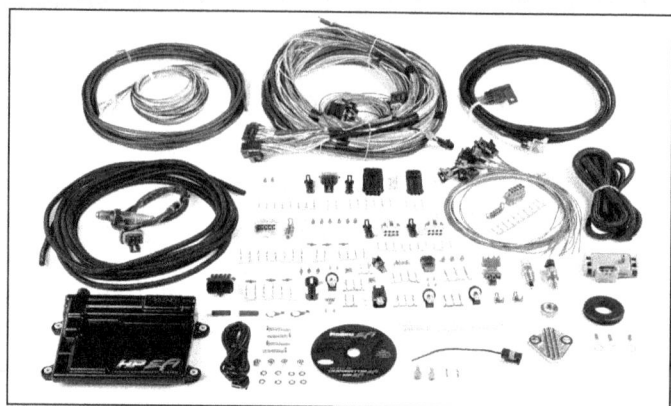

The speed density Holley Pro EFI operates the Coyote engines. It comes with a plug-and-play harness and options for drive-by-wire applications. It has inputs for boost control, water or methanol injection, and fuel pump control. VCT needs to be locked down to use this system. (Photo Courtesy Holley Performance)

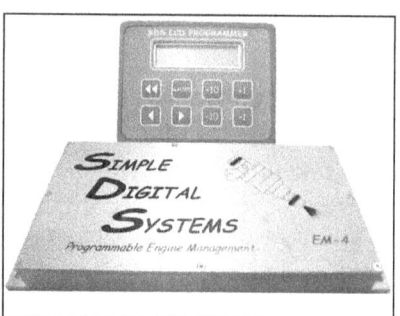

Simple Digital Systems has a speed density racing PCM that is just as advertised, very simple to install and use. However, it is fully capable of handling engines with more than 1,000 hp. It features quick plug-and-play setup and can operate with or without a laptop (it comes with a handheld programmer). The computer works in conjunction with an aftermarket ignition control module. (Photo Courtesy Western Motorsports)

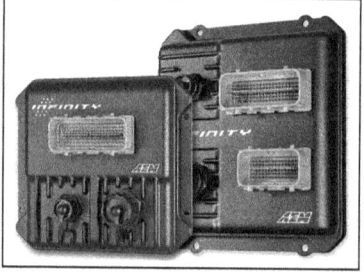

AEM's Infinity computer is a racing speed density system that is fully compatible with drive-by-wire and VI-VCT camshaft timing. AEM has a harness that works with the Ford Performance Coyote crate engines, and it also has solutions for installing MAF and AIT sensors, as well as adapting to the Ford Performance Boss 302 alternator kit. AEM has a solution for 2V, 3V, and other 4V applications as well. (Photo Courtesy AEM)

This Haltech Elite ECU is running a Supercharged Coyote engine on an engine stand. Haltech's Elite ECU system handles it all: mass air or speed density, variable cam timing, drive-by-wire, supercharging, whatever you need. Haltech also offers several different wiring harnesses for different applications as well as a universal harness that can be adapted to your application. (Photo Courtesy Haltech Engine Management Systems)

use sequential fuel injection, which means the fuel injectors are only firing once per cycle, making them more efficient than some speed density systems that fire every revolution (also called waste spark).

Mass air systems are typically less tolerant of big tuning changes than speed density systems due to the sizing of the mass air meter. A big change in fuel injection or camshafts may mean that a larger MAF meter is required, and the system can't be tuned without changing several items at once.

Speed Density

Some aftermarket companies use speed density systems to make big horsepower because they are easier to tune and do not have some of the restrictions of mass air. The speed density system calculations are based on engine speed, manifold pressure, exhaust output, and a Manifold Absolute Pressure (MAP) sensor to measure the pressure in the

Some manufacturers still sell speed density systems, and they use a Manifold Absolute Pressure (MAP) sensor to measure the pressure inside the intake manifold. The sensor on the left is from a mid-1980s 5.0 Mustang, but the one on the right is from a GM application and is used on most aftermarket speed density systems. Speed density systems use on-board fuel curves and data to calculate the best operating conditions. Speed density is still used by some aftermarket systems due to its ability to be tuned without having to change the mass air meter.

intake manifold and then calculate the fuel required. It doesn't measure the volume of air coming into the engine; it uses a big internal table of fuel curves and uses these calculations to determine the amount of fuel to deliver to the engine. Ford used speed density on engines from 1986 to mid-1989, when they converted to mass air systems. Some manufacturers still use speed density. Most aftermarket systems still use speed density to run the engine because it allows for flexibility in tuning without having to change major components.

Alpha N

Alpha N computer controls are a simple form of fuel injection. Fuel is delivered based on throttle plate position and engine RPM, and the computer reads the manifold vacuum and controls fuel accordingly. While this is a simple system used in some race cars, it is not recommended for most street and street/strip applications, as it doesn't take into consideration any exhaust gas information or emission information. Because of this, it can sometimes be very inefficient on fuel mileage.

Spotlight Build: 1967 Pro/Street Cobra Mustang Coupe

The 2003–2004 Cobra Terminator engines continue to be a popular swap engine because they are easy to modify and produce a lot of power. In addition, they don't have some of the issues with throttle by wire and VCT. Programming the computer is very easy and the wiring from the donor Cobra can be used.

This build-in-progress is a 1967 Mustang coupe and it is receiving the

This pro street 1967 coupe is being fitted with the still popular 2003–2004 Cobra Terminator engine. It doesn't require drive-by-wire or control of variable cam timing, and there are plenty of aftermarket power adders to make the Terminator a good choice for a swap. This car will be fitted with the T-56 6-speed and Cobra independent rear suspension. The car has received a mini tub in the back and all four fenders have been flared 1½ inches.

full pro/street build out with a complete running driveline from a 2003 Ford Mustang Cobra donor car. Like with the Mustang in Black (see Chapter 2), this owner wanted to take full advantage of all the capabilities of the newer Cobra such as ABS, modern cruise control, and returnless fuel injection.

To start the conversion, Rod and Custom Motorsports performed extensive fabrication work and installed a Mustang II front suspension. The shock towers were removed to make room for the wide DOHC heads. The engine and transmission were set back about 4 inches to help with the clearance of the stock Eaton-style supercharger snout, as this build will use a stock 1967 turn-signal hood. This required a set of custom fabricated mounts to place the engine back far enough. The crossmember was notched slightly to clear the curve of the factory oil pan. This also allowed the T-56 shifter to protrude into the original shifter hole without any modifications. The factory air-intake tubing was used and mounted to the old battery area. The only other fitment issue was the IAC solenoid, which was mounted on top of the supercharger intake. It was contacting the factory underframe, so it was turned 180 degrees and rewired and no longer touches the hood. A custom-made transmission crossmember was fabricated to hold the transmission to the firewall extensions.

The rear suspension is also out of a 2003 Cobra, but it's slightly modified to work with the mini tubs provided by Autoworks International. The IRS cradle was narrowed to make room for the 11-inch-wide rear wheels. A set of custom-made subframe connectors was also installed. The rear IRS is already equipped with the ABS wheels, and the front spindles are retrofitted. To get the pro/street look the factory fender flares have been widened 1½ inches in the back and 1 inch in the front.

The fuel system was custom designed to use the components from the 2003 Cobra. New stock 1967 fuel tanks are being fabricated out of stainless steel, and this was the choice for modifications for the 2003 dual fuel pump. The fuel ring from a donor tank was grafted to the top of the tank and a custom baffle was installed for the in-tank pump. The stock fuel pump controller was mounted down in the driver-side quarter panel. The battery was also relocated to the trunk.

The hydroboost from the Cobra was mounted to the original 1967 brake pedal, and a hydraulic clutch conversion from Modern Driveline works with a McLeod throwout bearing. A Lokar throttle cable is used along with an accelerator pedal from a 1970 Mustang to run the throttle body. Up front, the Cobra radiator and cooling fan fit nicely between the frame rails and the intercooler is mounted between the radiator support and the hood latch bracket. The original Bosch intercooler pump is mounted on the underside of the original battery tray. A remote oil filter mount and oil-to-air cooler are also used. Electronic speed control is tucked under the driver-side splash shield.

The exhaust features a custom 2½-inch pipe system with off-road X pipe running from the stock Cobra manifolds. Electronics are also borrowed from the Cobra donor car and the stock EEC-V computer is re-flashed. The air conditioning is adapted to the original

The 2003 Cobra engine puts out 390 hp in stock form. The biggest challenges to installing the engine are the width and height. The SN-95 Mustang engine compartment is wider and longer than the first-generation engine compartment. The engine bay needs to be modified to make room for the bigger engine.

This customer opted for a Mustang II front-end conversion from Rod and Custom Motorsports. It eliminates the shock towers and optional modular-engine mounts are available. A set of custom engine mounts was added to this MII crossover bar to move the engine back 4 inches to make room for the Eaton Supercharger.

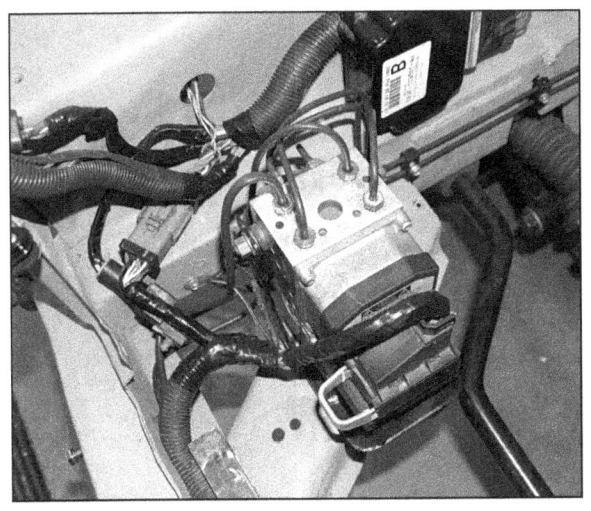

Using the original harness allows you to run options such as the original ABS unit from the 2003 Cobra. The Bosch base unit fits nicely on the 1967 strut rod mount, and sensor rings will be added to the front Mustang II spindles. The independent rear suspension is already equipped to run the ABS.

1967 A/C box. A custom set of Speedhut gauges including a GPS speedometer is used.

With 390 hp, the 2003–2004 Terminator engines continue to be a popular option when making a modular engine conversion. They have horsepower, can make more horsepower very easily, are not as complicated as a newer throttle-by-wire engine, and look fantastic under the hood.

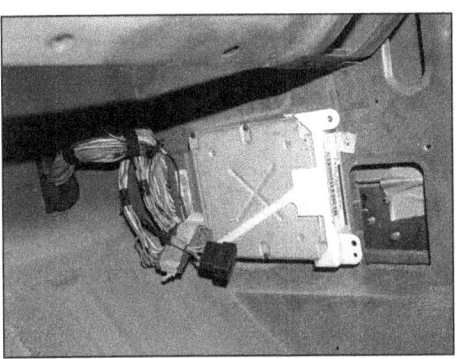

The PCM mounts to the passenger-side kick panel area, similar to the way it is mounted in the 2003 Cobra. The wires wrap around the heater box and the secondary connectors are part of the under-dash wiring. The stock 2003 computer mounting bracket is used to mount the computer and provides proper grounding.

West Coast wiring guru David Toth has found that the Ford Controls Pack computer lays in perfect on older Mustangs and Cougars by mounting the PCM in the old battery tray area. (Photo Courtesy Classic Resto Garage)

The PCM harness comes out through the side panel and into the passenger's side through the corner firewall. A second oval grommet from a salvage yard harness seals the harness as it passes through the firewall. This wire can be run behind the splash shield on a Mustang to protect it.

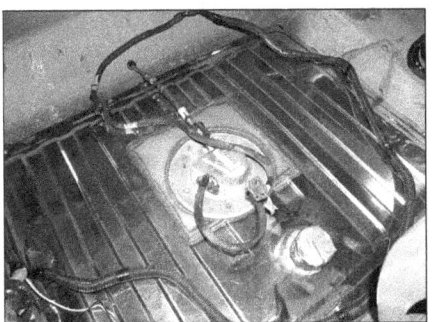

The factory supercharged 2003 Cobra engine uses a special dual fuel pump to handle the extra fuel needs. This owner wanted to retain stock control of the fuel pump and the returnless fuel system. An aftermarket stainless-steel stock tank was modified to accept the 2003 fuel pump assembly and locate the fuel pump at the correct height. A custom baffle was built into the insert to keep the pump from starving under heavy acceleration and turning.

Note how far back the engine is placed. Non-supercharged engines can mount over the front axle if desired. With the radiator and intercooler plumbing, the empty space in front of the engine goes away very fast. Using the 2003 Cobra hydroboost also aids in moving the engine back to the firewall.

CHAPTER 5

INTAKES AND INDUCTION

Even though modular engines were delivered with mass air intake systems, you don't have to stick with Ford's design. The aftermarket intake manufacturers have offered a wide selection of units for modular engines over the years, so you should find an air delivery system that fits the look and feel of your conversion project.

As mentioned in Chapter 2, "modular" doesn't mean that lots of things cross over among engines, and intake manifolds are no exception. Just like the small-block Ford 351W and 302 manifolds, the 4.6 and 5.4 won't interchange because of the difference in block deck height. The shape and size of the ports have changed over the years, even if they look the same. And, of course, the manifolds are designed to flow enough air to feed one or two intake valves per cylinder.

All Ford factory intake manifolds are made of composite plastic, aluminum, or a combination of both. Most of the early performance engines and 4V setups came with aluminum manifolds. The early 4.6 manifolds developed a problem with the coolant crossover, requiring a fix from Ford in the early 2000s (see Chapter 2). Starting with the 3V engines, Ford went back with an all-composite intake and continued with that material up through the 5.0 Coyote; factory supercharged engines required an aluminum manifold to handle the extra pressures.

The early 4.6 SOHC cylinder heads (pre-1999) were fine for street cars but started to run out of steam around 5,000 rpm. In 1999, Ford introduced the PI (Performance Improved) heads that work much better, and the intake port and intake manifold changed. Both intake ports have the injector mounted in the upper "corner," but the port shape on the PI head was changed considerably. A head change requires a matching change to the intake manifold. Most aftermarket intake manifolds are designed for the later PI intake port. This design became the standard in the 2V engine through its production run.

The first 4V heads used a dual-port intake manifold that consisted of a square port primary intake runner and a round secondary port for use above 3,000 rpm. These heads work

Intakes need not be industrial, plastic, and boring. This 2012 Cobra Jet Dragster features a supercharged Ford Performance 5.4 Cobra Jet Engine and a fully custom intake fabricated by Mr2 Performance in Lebanon, Indiana. Handcrafted from aluminum, it is adorned with a custom raised-cobra-scale pattern. And it works well, too; just like all cold-air intakes it eliminates curves and bends and draws air away from the heat flow of the engine.

INTAKES AND INDUCTION

adequately, but have some issues with low rpm torque. In 1999, Ford redesigned the intake port into a Tumble Port design, which means that the air "tumbles" into the cylinder rather than swirls in. These oval ports have the injectors mounted in the middle of the port, and though they look the same, the size of the port varied through the engine's revisions. A reminder about swapping heads and intakes: with a few exceptions (as when using adapter plates mentioned later in this chapter), when changing heads the intake manifold needs to be changed to match.

With the 4V heads still needing an increase in performance in the

A shot of the underside of an early 4.6 SOHC intake. Note the teardrop-shaped intake and the injector in the corner. Also note the placement of the intake runner below the ports taking up the room under the manifold.

Here is the PI intake that most aftermarket companies duplicate. The port shape was changed to improve high-RPM performance.

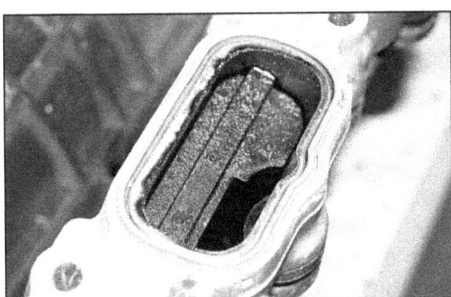

The IMRC plate inside the intake manifold is shown. At low RPM, this plate closes off the port and increases the velocity of the incoming air charge, which improves low-end torque. As the engine increases in RPM the plate opens and allows full airflow. Many high-performance engine builders delete this system for high-horsepower engines because it's a restriction at high RPM. Special thanks to Brenspeed.

The underside of the 3V intake shows the wider "tumble port" design and injector mounted centrally to feed both valves. The aluminum plate holds the IMRC system to help with low-end torque. It is also interesting to note that the runners are higher placed in this manifold than in the SOHC variety, and it also sports a dual-port throttle body. Special thanks to Brenspeed.

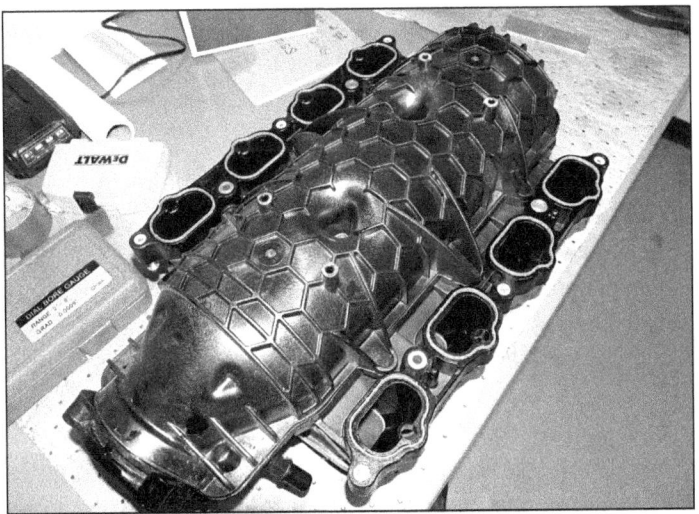

The 5.0 Coyote intake features larger ports and the runners running lower in the center of the intake. The IMRC has been removed from this intake, and the port size changed from the earlier 3V intake manifold. Note also that Ford went back to a single-blade throttle body design for the Coyote. Special thanks to Brenspeed.

CHAPTER 5

Engine Air Intake Systems

When it comes to intake systems, bigger is not always better, regardless of what the performance manufacturers claim. It's a system that needs to work together. Since the beginning of hot rodding engines, we have been guilty of overdoing the intake system. Even Ford is guilty. The 429 CJ engines were great at 8,000 rpm, but drag racers soon found out the smaller ports of the 429 police interceptor heads worked better than the sewer pipe 429 CJ head for low-end torque, which meant they worked better on the street, too.

When selecting induction pieces, it is more important to match the components of the intake system to the proper use of the engine than to buy the biggest parts possible. Bloggers say to install this part or that component, not even understanding how they work. It is important to understand how each component works in the intake system and why the builder is recommending certain pieces for the project.

A V-8 engine is a big air pump. It draws air in, burns it, and pushes it out. The pistons are drawing in air, and if they had no restriction they would be drawing air in at atmospheric pressure, which at sea level is about 14.7 psi (101 kPa or 29.9 HG). The intake ports, valves, intake manifolds, and all the tubing can and usually do act as a restriction to flowing complete atmospheric air (which is why for maximum output most engine builders make these things as big as possible).

There are three basic physics considerations used when designing engine intakes: air volume, air velocity, and air inertia. And they all interact.

Volume

The more air drawn into the cylinder, the more fuel that can be added, and the more power that can be made. Volume is directly affected by the restrictions up to the cylinder; the bigger the openings, the more volume. However, the larger the opening, the lower the velocity. The larger the volume of air, the more effort it takes to move it around.

Velocity

The faster the air is drawn into the cylinder, the greater the volume at a chosen RPM. Think in terms of your thumb over the end of a garden hose; the water comes out faster, but the volume is less. To increase the velocity at low RPM, you want a smaller, longer port. This becomes a restriction in high-RPM engines because the engine can't get the volume of air needed to run. Engines that make big power at high RPM do not make much low-end torque due to the low velocity created by the bigger openings at low RPM (which is why dragsters launch at high engine RPM).

Inertia

Newton's first law of motion states that "Every object in a state of uniform motion tends to remain in that state of motion unless an external force is applied to it." What this means in an engine is that when air is running through the intake manifold and the valve closes, the air builds up behind the valve as it tries to continue forward and builds pressure. It has to go somewhere, so it reverses direction in the form of a shockwave heading back into the manifold. Since the early days of race engines, designers have varied port runner lengths specifically to take advantage of the shockwaves bouncing back and forth in the intake manifold, and timing them to bounce back in time to hit the valve just as it is opening again (like a mini supercharger!).

An engine creates a vacuum (called manifold or runner vacuum) when the availability of air is restricted to the cylinders by either a butterfly valve in a carburetor or the throttle plate in the throttle body. The engine is pulling more air out of the manifold than can be replaced when the throttle plate is closed. At wide open throttle, few or minimum restrictions are present, and the atmosphere can replace the air drawn from the manifold quickly, resulting in very low or no vacuum pull. When the throttle plate opens, more air may be drawn into the cylinders at atmospheric pressure. The in-rushing air replaces the vacuum in the intake manifold. When the throttle plate is closed, the air in the intake is drawn in quickly and the engine builds manifold vacuum again, which slows the engine down.

The inlet tubing feeding the engine can be compared to a big straw. At a given vacuum, a small straw flows less air at a higher velocity, and a bigger straw flows more air, but at a lower velocity. Changing items such as heads and camshafts to get more air in and out of an engine requires changing the size of the intake system (straw) to match both the speed and volume of air required by the engine, and the sensors need to match the new straw size. However, by increasing the size of the tubing, the speed at which the air enters the intake is slowed, and this can cause stumbling at low RPM as the slower speed of the air cannot fill the vacuum quickly enough.

Modern fuel-injected engine controllers need to know how much air is being delivered to the engine, how dense it is, and its temperature. Denser air puts more oxygen into the

INTAKES AND INDUCTION

cylinder, and the computer has to increase the amount of fuel to compensate. Colder air is denser air, and air in the mountains is not as dense as air at sea level. The speed of the air entering the engine changes the density of the air contained in the intake manifold, so the size of the intake tubing is critical for maximum efficiency.

All the components from the air filter to the valves need to be matched to the purpose and capability of the engine, not the advertising claims of the component manufacturers. Installing a big throttle body and mass air meter on a stock engine does nothing to improve the efficiency of the engine, likewise big cams and valves trying to draw through an undersized throttle body doesn't work either. The components need to be engineered together, as a system. ■

---

low-RPM range, Ford developed the Intake Manifold Runner Control (IMRC, sometimes called the CMRC) for the 4V engines. This is a plate that is opened and closed to partially block the ports to the heads, increasing low-end torque. Some builders of high-performance engines pull these plates out because they hamper high-RPM flow. (See later in this chapter for information on the IMRC delete plate system.)

Factory Intake Manifold Considerations

As noted in Chapter 2, truck intake manifolds tend to be taller than those used in Mustangs or LTDs. If the build requires an intake manifold to fit in tight quarters, swapping can be done within the engine family (3V truck to 3V Mustang, for example).

The length of the runners is designed to enhance the velocity of the air charge going into the cylinder. When the valve closes, a pressure wave bounces back from the valve and travels through the runner port and back. The goal is to time this pressure pulse such that the shock wave arrives at the valve just as the valve is opening, to increase the amount of air going into the cylinder. Engines that are supercharged or turbocharged maintain positive pressure in the manifold that forces air into the cylinders, so the port runner design has less of an effect on pressurized engines. The higher the rpm, the shorter the runner length required.

The valley between the cylinder heads on a modular engine is dry; there are no lifters or camshaft mounted here to keep lubricated. Ford took advantage of this area to tuck in the port runners. In the case of factory superchargers, a liquid-to-air intercooler is installed here that lowers the intake charge temperature.

The 4.6 SOHC uses an elbow to angle the intake tubing to one side or the other just like with the older fuel-injected pushrod small-blocks. The intake opening is symmetrical, so the elbow can be reversed. Reversing the elbow may require moving wiring and cables, and the EGR may need to be re-routed. On an LTD engine, the elbow goes to the driver's side, on a Mustang, it goes to the passenger's side. The 2001 Ford Mustang Bullitt

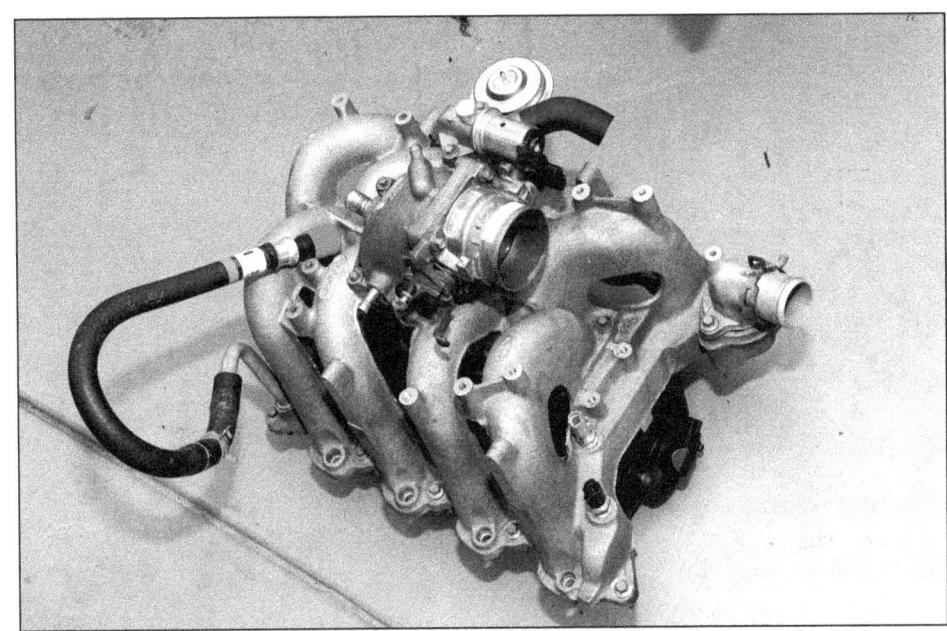

Truck engines require low-end torque for pulling, so they are equipped with long, narrow runners to make low-end torque. Because trucks generally have taller engine bays, Ford can make manifolds that help with low-end torque. This 4.6 SOHC truck manifold shows how Ford can take advantage of the extra space and make the port runners longer. (Photo Courtesy James Smart)

CHAPTER 5

uses a manifold similar to the one sold by Ford Performance, and the entry to the manifold is on the back.

Engines that are supercharged or turbocharged have a constant pressure in the manifold that forces air into the cylinders, so the port runner design has less effect on air delivery. All the factory supercharger manifolds are aluminum.

Intake Manifold

A wide range of intake manifolds is available for the modular engine family, and you can find one to accommodate everything from carburetors to stack injection to compact supercharger applications. Ford Performance still carries a line of intakes for most of the modular engine applications. Through the years Ford Performance has also supplied many of the factory performance intakes through the parts catalog, so used manifolds are in good supply at the swap meets and online. Here are some of the manifolds currently available:

Original Style

The term "original-style manifold" refers to a multi-port injection intake manifold similar to, or a duplicate of, the original style of intake manifolds found on the modular engines. These may or may not allow the use of factory components such as injectors and throttle bodies.

Ford Performance Parts 3V manifold (PN M-9424-463V) is a composite design that works well with forced induction. It has a port for mounting a MAP sensor (used with some forced induction and speed density computers). It works with stock or Ford Performance and aftermarket throttle bodies. (Photo Courtesy Ford Performance Parts)

Ford still makes available the PI version of its manifold for 4.6 SOHC (PN M-9424-P46). It has the upgrades to eliminate the early intake issues and with a matching set of PI heads works very well on the earlier 4.6 engines. (Photo Courtesy Ford Performance Parts)

The Boss 302 manifold (Ford Performance PN M-9424-M50BR) used on the Boss 302 production and race cars features composite construction and short port runner length for high-RPM power. It is designed for manual transmissions as it does not have an output for an aspirator tube. (Photo Courtesy Ford Performance Parts)

The Cobra Jet intake manifold was designed along with Ford Performance's Cobra Jet racing engine program and is available for Coyote applications (PN M-9424-M50CJ). A composite manifold, it still works well with forced induction. Stock Coyote fuel rails fit this manifold, and the short runners make it good to 7,725 rpm. It is made for manual transmissions only as it does not have a provision for an aspirator tube. (Photo Courtesy Ford Performance Parts)

INTAKES AND INDUCTION

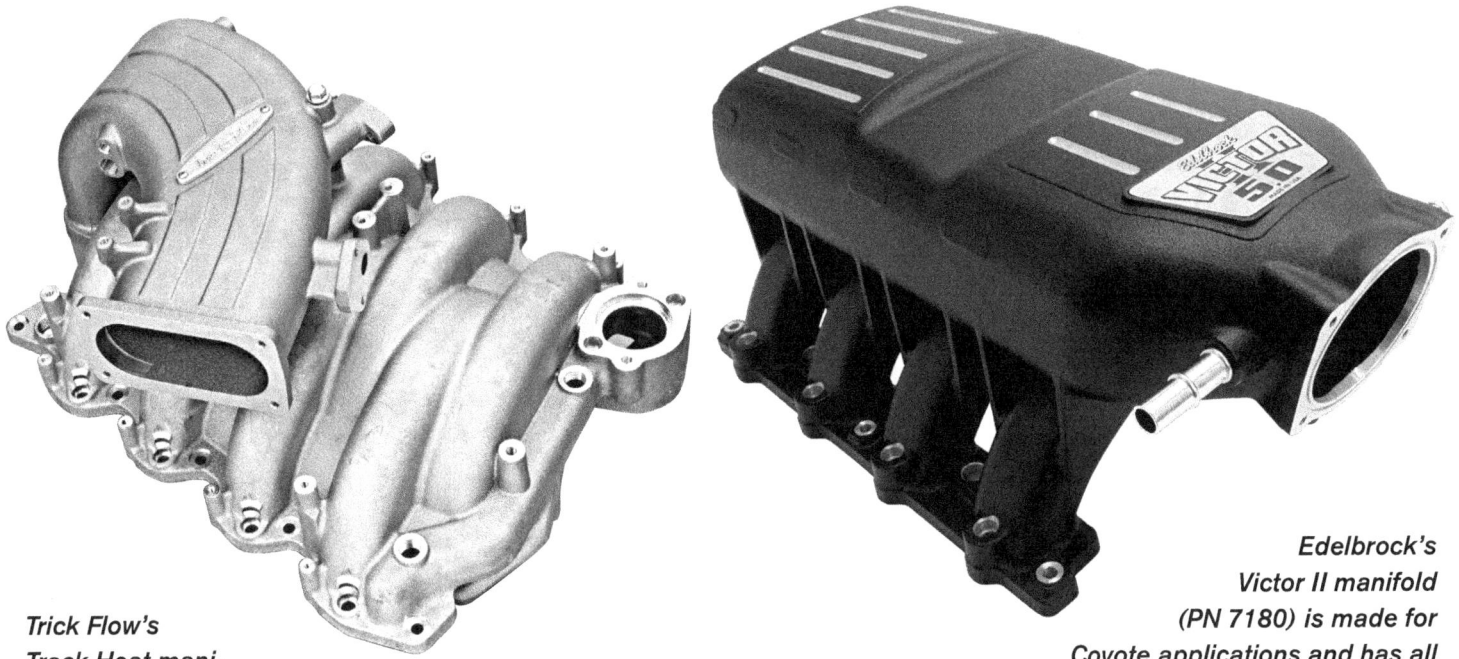

Trick Flow's Track Heat manifold (PN TFS-51800002) is an all-aluminum manifold that's designed for power ranges of 2,500 to 7,000 rpm for the Streetburner series or 3,500 to 8,000 rpm for the Track Heat configuration. The elbow can be adapted for a 75-mm round or oval dual-bore 57-mm throttle body. (Photo Courtesy Trick Flow Specialties)

Edelbrock's Victor II manifold (PN 7180) is made for Coyote applications and has all the emissions ports and works with stock components. It has a crossover port design that gives it a lower height, which may help in some tight installations. (Photo Courtesy Edelbrock Corp.)

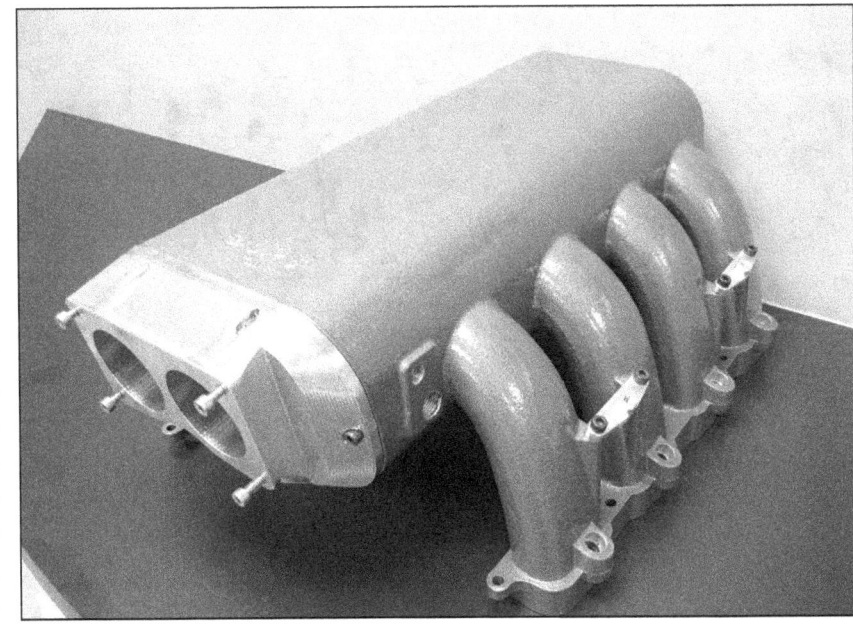

JPC Racing has an aluminum 4.6 3V manifold that has multiple front mounting plates for a variety of throttle bodies. This low-profile manifold eliminates the CMRC system and fits under low-profile hoods. It is also plumbed for most Ford factory equipment including EVAP and a vacuum port for power brakes. (Photo Courtesy JPC Racing)

Trick Flow makes three intake manifold versions for the 4.6 2V engines. Similar to the manifold used on the 2001 Bullitt engines, the elbow comes off the rear of the manifold rather than the center. JPC Racing has an aluminum 4.6 3V manifold that incorporates a billet aluminum front throttle body mount that can be changed for different TB applications. Edelbrock's Victor II manifold for the 5.0 is an aluminum construction, which allows it to be used with forced induction and nitrous.

Carburetors and Central Fuel Injection

It is possible to run a carburetor on a modular engine; there are both low-profile and tall-ram manifolds. These manifolds can also be adapted to run central fuel injection metering and even multi-port fuel injection.

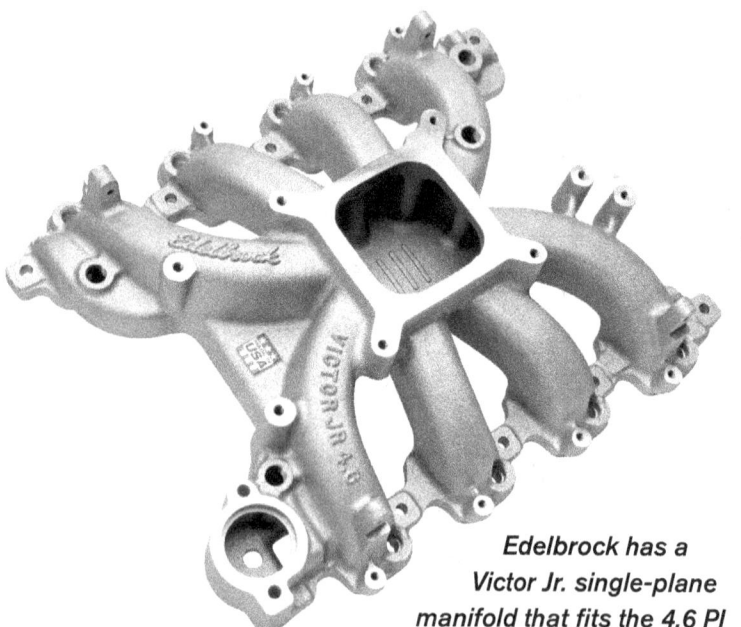

Edelbrock has a Victor Jr. single-plane manifold that fits the 4.6 PI heads and allows for carburetion, central fuel injection, or port injection. PN 2838 is not machined for individual injectors and 28385 is machined for fuel rails. Aluminum construction makes it ideal for forced induction and nitrous. (Photo Courtesy Edelbrock Corp.)

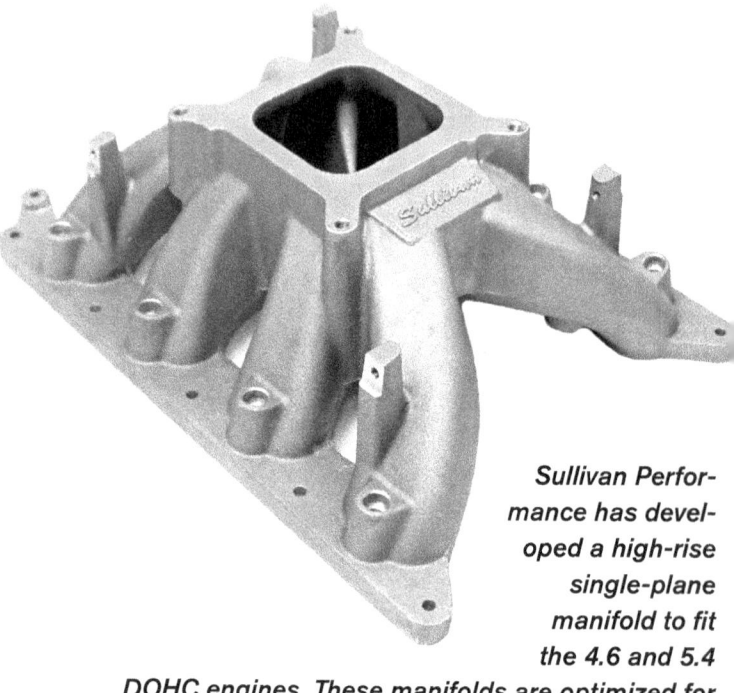

Sullivan Performance has developed a high-rise single-plane manifold to fit the 4.6 and 5.4 DOHC engines. These manifolds are optimized for use between 2,500 and 7,500, and come with a standard Holley bolt pattern. They also come with plenty of material for mounting vacuum parts and nitrous ports, and come with or without fuel injector ports already machined. Bosses for fuel rails are cast in and they also work with aftermarket central fuel injection systems. (Photo Courtesy Sullivan Performance)

Dr. DOHC has done extensive work with the early 4.6 dual port and 2V engines, and it custom builds carburetor intake manifolds to work as a dual-port and a single-port system. These manifolds can be configured in low or high profile, single or dual carburetor, and all kinds of custom touches. This early 4.6 4V coil pack engine is decked out like an old gasser engine with custom finned pieces, low-profile Holley carb and intake manifold, and a custom set of coil-on plugs arranged to look like a distributor. (Photo Courtesy Dr. DOHC)

It is possible to run Weber downdraft carburetors on the modular engines, and Dr. DOHC can custom fit a set for 2V and 4V. This engine is fitted with chrome stacks; all the standard Weber configurations (air filters, ram tubes) are available. Check out the custom valvecovers on the 4.6 4V. (Photo Courtesy Dr. DOHC)

INTAKES AND INDUCTION

Stack Injection

Probably the biggest advantage to the individual injection stacks is the fact that each port has its own throttle plate, and this can reduce the airflow losses associated with the bigger single or dual bore throttle bodies. Plus they just look fantastic. The downside to some of the systems is fitting the throttle-linkage-specific engine compartment configurations.

Sheet Metal and Custom

For the full-bore racing set, numerous manufacturers have developed a sheet-metal intake that can be

Kinsler now offers its race-proven fuel injection setups for 4.6 and 5.4 4V engines and the 4.6 3V. It is a three-piece design so the center can be changed for different deck heights and widths. It can be fitted for EFI electronic injectors or old school mechanical constant-flow fuel injectors. The fuel rails can be mounted inboard or out, and the manifolds can also be custom-machined to fit other modular engine port specifications. They can be made of magnesium on special order. (Photo Courtesy Kinsler Fuel Injection)

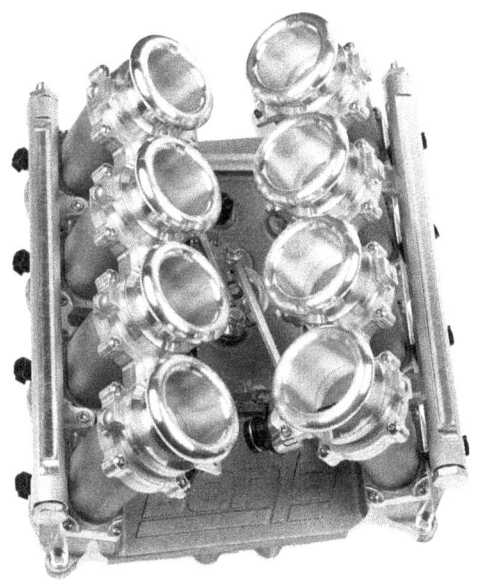

The Borla Induction stack injection system for the 5.0 Coyote (PN 200125 and 200126) comes in either straight or semi-cross ram configuration. The semi-cross ram allows for extra hood clearance, and the big 55-mm throttle plates allow for huge airflow capabilities. The air horns, throttle bodies, and even the linkage is all CNC-machined from billet aluminum and has mounting points for high-capacity injectors and fuel rails. The aluminum intake is fully flow-matched to the Coyote intake ports. (Photo Courtesy Borla Induction)

EFI Hardware in Australia has developed its own stack injection system for the 4.6 and 5.4 DOHC engines and is developing one for the 5.0. It comes fully or partially assembled with either street or full race throttle bodies, ram tubes in blue or black, and fuel rails. It is also machined for a special MAP sensor collector for speed density applications. The plenum chamber underneath is designed for vacuum creation to run a brake booster and is connected to all eight throats to allow for electronic idle speed. (Photo Courtesy EFI Hardware)

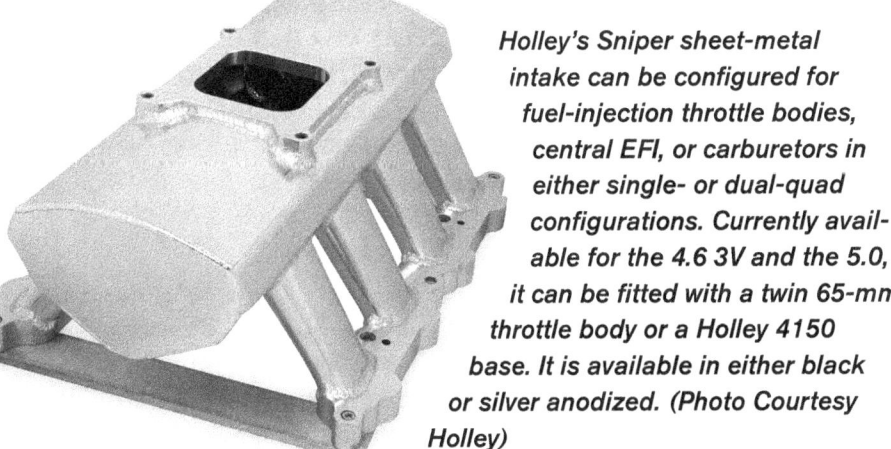

Holley's Sniper sheet-metal intake can be configured for fuel-injection throttle bodies, central EFI, or carburetors in either single- or dual-quad configurations. Currently available for the 4.6 3V and the 5.0, it can be fitted with a twin 65-mm throttle body or a Holley 4150 base. It is available in either black or silver anodized. (Photo Courtesy Holley)

CHAPTER 5

On its way to creating the world's fasted modular-engine dragster, Modular Motorsports Racing has developed a line of sheet-metal manifolds for many of the modular platforms. This Coyote manifold is full race with custom injector rails, front throttle body mount, and removable top for additional tuning. (Photo Courtesy Modular Motorsports Racing)

Hogan's Racing Manifolds can fabricate just about anything you can think up, including carburetion, EFI, Webers, stack injection, supercharged; just tell them what you need. Any of the modular head and block combinations are possible. This manifold is designed for a 4.6 4V EFI with a 90-mm throttle body. (Photo Courtesy Hogan's Racing Manifolds)

BBK makes a one-piece high-flow elbow and throttle body for the 1996–2004 4.6 2V. The throttle body is available in 73- or 78-mm versions and comes in black or polished finish. Ford factory IAC and TPS work with this elbow, with 10- to 15-hp gains with this bolt-on alone. (Photo Courtesy BBK Performance)

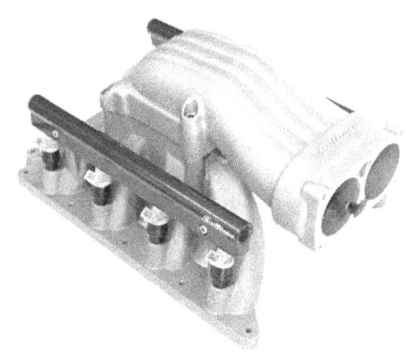

Sullivan Performance sells an adapter that not only fits its manifolds, but it fits a Holley 4150 base pattern to convert to a Cobra dual-throttle body or a single Accufab throttle body. It is also machined for use with a factory Ford IAC and EGR. (Photo Courtesy Sullivan Performance)

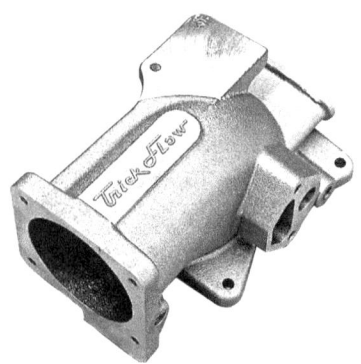

High-flow upper plenums are available for 2V applications that use stock components such as this Trick Flow upper Plenum (PN TFS-51800001). It flows 100 cfm more than stock and is compatible with throttle bodies up to 75 mm. (Photo Courtesy Trick Flow Specialties)

designed for everything from old-fashioned GMC Roots blowers to modern fuel injection to tunnel rams with carburetors.

Intake Elbows

Most 2V manifolds used an intake elbow to direct the airflow to the manifold from one side of the engine compartment. The aftermarket designs have improved on the factory pieces and allow more combinations with the SOHC engines. Factory elbow design allows for cost and manufacturing concerns, noise reduction, and space restrictions, whereas aftermarket designs can concentrate on performance.

INTAKES AND INDUCTION

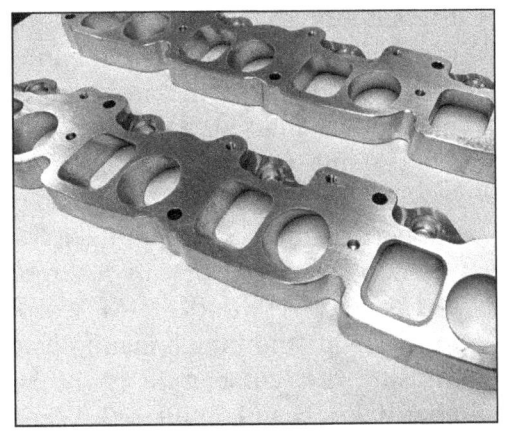

Modular Motorsports Racing has several IMRC delete plates available to eliminate the restriction caused by the plate system in the vehicle. This version (PN 900876) is made of billet aluminum and is designed to replace the 1996–1998 dual-port IMRC plates. They can be ported for maximum flow and are a direct replacement for the factory components. (Photo Courtesy Modular Motorsports Racing)

Intake Adapters

As with the pushrod small-block, more intake manifolds are available for the lower deck height engines than the taller engines. Modular Motorsports Racing and Professional Products make adapter plates to retrofit a 5.4 engine with 4.6 intakes. They are application specific and have to keep within the "family" of cylinder heads (e.g., 5.4 DOHC to 4.6 DOHC of the same year).

IMRC Eliminator Plates

While the IMRC (Manifold Runner Control) is good on a stock engine for helping with low-RPM torque, it creates a restriction for high-revving engines. Steeda and Modular Motorsports Racing make eliminator plates that remove these restrictions on high-horsepower engines and maintain factory intake manifold height and geometry.

Intake Tubing and Components

Factory Ford intake systems use a throttle body, an IAT sensor (intake air temperature), an MAF (mass airflow meter), a length of tubing to draw the air from a remote location, and an air filter/filter box. Speed density systems use a similar setup without the MAF; instead, they use a manifold absolute pressure sensor or MAP. Some supercharged or turbocharged setups may use both. The engine build determines the choice of components.

Throttle Body

The throttle body meters the amount of airflow into the engine by using a blade or blades to meter airflow. The throttle body needs to match the airflow requirements of the engine. If the throttle body is too small, the engine can't get enough air and loses performance. If the throttle body is too big, the speed of the air coming into the engine is too slow and the engine loses horsepower and throttle response.

Cable versus Drive-by-Wire

Prior to 2005 Ford used a mechanical throttle cable to open the throttle body. In 2005 Ford began using drive-by-wire on modular engines. This consisted of a sensor mounted on the accelerator pedal and an electric motor mounted on the throttle body. If you're buying an engine and harness from a donor car, you need to get the pedal and the underdash harness, so you have the equipment to properly run the engine. Aftermarket pedals are available, but some pedals don't work well in some vehicles, such as the Crown Victoria pedal. Ford has kept the connector fairly consistent, so swapping a pedal from different vehicles is not a big problem. (See Chapter 6 for more information.) Some aftermarket PCM systems do not work with drive-by-wire and require a conversion back to a cable-style throttle body.

Single- versus Dual-Bore

Ford has used both single- and dual-bore throttle bodies on its factory engines. Why a particular style was chosen goes along with the

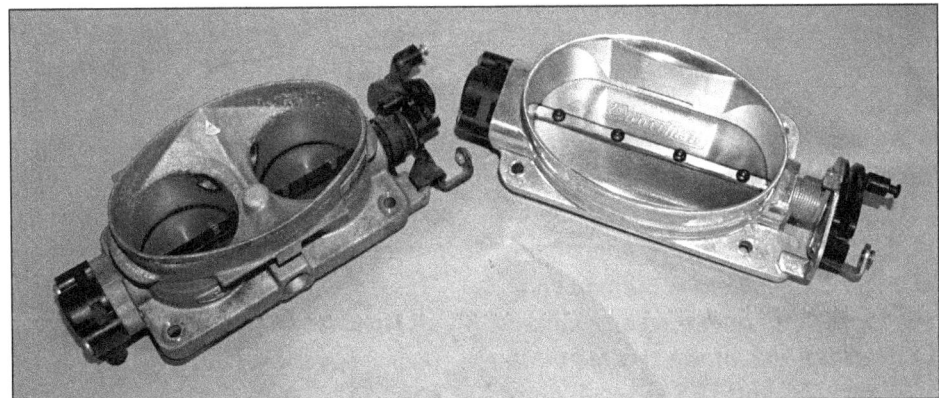

A comparison of two Terminator throttle bodies, the stock 57-mm dual on the left and an Accufab single blade on the right. The dual bore allows for more air velocity at low RPM, but is restrictive at high RPM due to the splitter between the bores. The single blade flows a considerable amount more as it opens, flowing 1696 cfm compared to the stock 1,089 cfm at WOT.

CHAPTER 5

Ford Performance sells throttle bodies for both drive-by-wire and cable operations. This is the drive-by-wire 90-mm throttle body for the Coyote (PN M-9926-M5090). Ford has adapters available to mount the throttle body to stock Coyote and Boss intakes, and reducers can be used to adapt it to stock 3.5-inch intake tubing. (Photo Courtesy Ford Performance Parts)

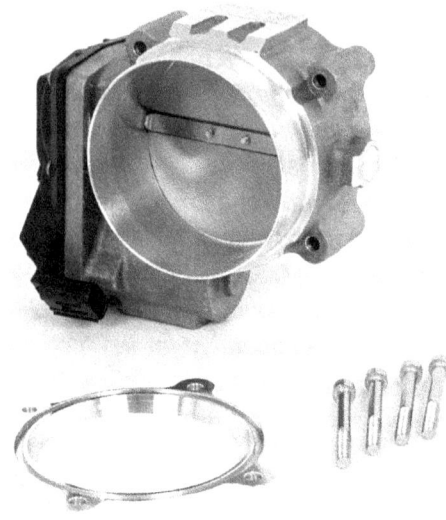

BBK also has a full line of cable and drive-by-wire throttle bodies. Its Coyote TB comes in at 90 mm and comes with an adapter to mount to the factory intake manifolds. They accept all factory parts and work with the factory tune (depending on other modifications). (Photo Courtesy BBK)

FAST makes a throttle body for the Coyote engine when converting to a drive-by-cable configuration or when working with some aftermarket computer systems that do not support drive-by-wire. The 87-mm bore is larger than the stock 80-mm, and works well with both the stock intake or the Boss 302 intake. It is fitted with GM-style IAC and TPS sensors. (Photo Courtesy Fuel Air Spark Technology)

overall engineering of the engine. A 4.6 3V has a dual-bore throttle body and a 5.0 Coyote has a single bore. Most of the supercharged engines have an oval dual-bore setup.

While a large single-blade throttle body allows greater amounts of airflow, the engine can be sluggish at low RPM. One way to improve engine response is to have the same air volume run through two bores to increase the air velocity. However, the dual-bore throttle bodies have a "splitter" in the middle, which restricts airflow at higher RPM. At high RPM, the single-blade throttle body may move more air without the restriction between the bores.

Intake Air Temperature Sensor

The Intake Air Temperature (IAT) sensor works similar to the coolant temperature sensor: as the air heats up, it changes the resistance in the IAT and the computer can change the amount of fuel delivered to the engine. Later mass air systems integrated the IAT into the mass airflow meter. Both mass air and speed density systems use an IAT.

The location of the IAT is usually close to the inlet of the air intake system. Supercharged or turbocharged engines use a secondary IAT sensor mounted in the intake manifold to measure the temperature of the air after it has been compressed. When a supercharger or turbocharger compresses air, the air temperature is increased.

An IAT sensor must have the correct resistance range for the PCM being used and should be mounted away from heat sources, such as the engine or radiator.

Mass Airflow Meter

Engines equipped with a mass airflow system use a small wire in the MAF, which is electrically heated, and as air flows past the wire the air cools the wire and changes the resistance of the wire. The resulting change of resistance is sent to the PCM to determine the amount of air that is flowing into the engine. This information, along with the IAT, tells the engine the volume and density of the air entering the engine.

Remembering the analogy that the size of the "straw" used determines the volume and speed of the air passing through the MAF, it is important to match the size of the mass air meter to the required volume of air entering the engine. This is one of the advantages of the speed density system; no MAF to change out when changes to the engine are made. Matching the MAF, the throttle body, and the tubing are all important when designing the intake system.

INTAKES AND INDUCTION

Supercharging and Turbocharging

The modular engine responds very well to supercharging or turbocharging. The preferable type of forced induction and how it fits is dependent on the project and how much room is available. A few notes on forced induction:

1. Ford used an aluminum intake manifold on its factory supercharged systems. Some aftermarket suppliers have successfully used composite intake manifolds for 7- to 8-psi boost range, and Ford Performance has tested its composite racing manifolds to pressures up to 20 psi. Although the composite manifolds are better for heat transfer, aluminum versions can handle more pressure.

2. Ford used dual fuel pumps in many of its factory supercharged applications (see Chapter 6 for more details).

3. Ford also used a liquid-to-air intercooler system to lower the temperature of the intake charge. As noted earlier in this chapter, the dry valley between the cylinder heads is a great place to mount an intercooler, and most aftermarket systems take advantage of this space. Accommodations for mounting the pump and heat exchanger somewhere in the airflow must be considered in the system design. Turbocharged systems usually use an air-to-air heat exchanger, which typically requires larger tubing and a larger heat exchanger than liquid-to-air systems.

Turbocharging has been as popular with the late-model crowd as supercharging, and the top drag racers are using twin turbocharger setups such as this Hellion system. Headers for Fox-Body conversions already exist (see Chapter 9), so building a system for a Fox conversion is easy. Hellion custom designs systems for many vehicles. (Photo Courtesy Hellion Power Systems)

Centrifugal superchargers still remain popular on conversions, such as this Procharger setup on a 1967 Eleanor with Coyote power. Procharger SC-series superchargers do not require external oil lines for lubrication, which simplifies installation and the design allows them to run cooler than other centrifugal chargers.

Kenne Bell's twin-screw superchargers come in a range of displacements from 2.3 to 4.7 liters. The Mammoth series (shown) is liquid cooled to greatly reduce the air charge temperature in comparison to the competition. Kenne Bell has developed one-piece intakes for all popular modular engine platforms that work with factory and aftermarket throttle bodies. (Photo Courtesy Kenne Bell)

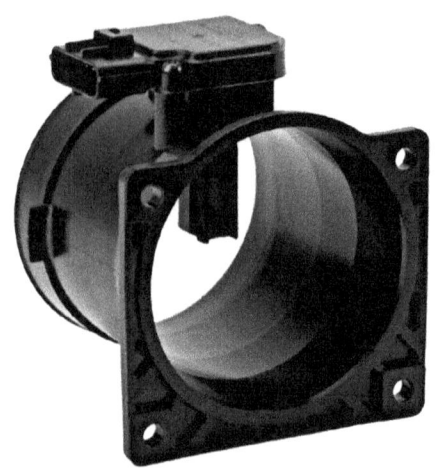

Ford Performance still offers the Lightning mass air meter (PN M-12579-L54). It is a 90-mm air meter for big intake-tube designs and has provision to mount the stock air filter box. (Photo Courtesy Ford Performance Parts)

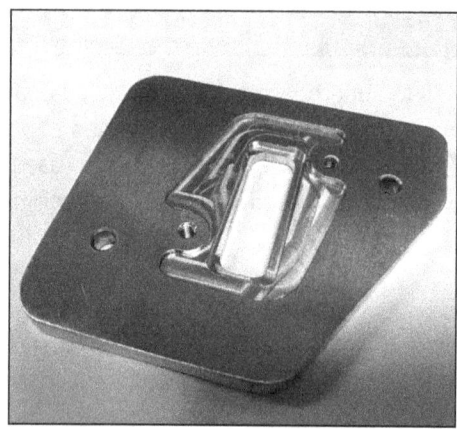

When fabricating custom intake tubing, VMP Performance offers a weld-in MAF mount. This mount is made of stainless steel and mounts a 2005-up MAF. It is good for tubing between 3½ and 5 inches in diameter. (Photo Courtesy VMP Performance)

BBK sells an 86-mm mass air meter for 1996–2002 SOHC applications. It comes fully calibrated for stock or cold air kits, is made of CNC aluminum, and can mount factory air boxes. Cobra calibrations are also available. (Photo Courtesy BBK)

There are two basic types of MAF meters: blow-through and draw-through. Normally aspirated engines use a draw-through meter and some supercharged and turbo applications use a blow-through MAF. These are exactly as named: a naturally aspirated (non-super or -turbocharged) engine uses a draw-through system. Forced air systems can be equipped with either, but the routing of the blow off valve and tubing is different for each application.

Manifold Absolute Pressure Sensor

Most speed density systems and some mass air systems use a Manifold Absolute Pressure (MAP) sensor. The computer needs to have three pieces of information to command the proper amount of fuel: the pressure of the air inside the intake manifold, the density of the air, and the load that the engine is working under. The MAP sensor measures the pressure in the manifold relative to a perfect vacuum; that is, no pressure from the outside air. Barometric pressure (the air pressure around you right now) is greater at sea level than up in the mountains, and barometric pressure can change with the weather. The MAP measures pressure from absolute vacuum (no pressure; outer space) up to 1 bar (around 14.7 psi, 29.9 inches of mercury or 101 kPa). Aftermarket MAP sensors can measure up to 5 bars, or approximately four times atmospheric pressure.

The speed density system uses the speed of the engine (RPM) and the density of the air going into the engine to determine how much fuel to supply at any given time. The speed density system uses a series of internal fuel curve maps to calculate this fuel/air ratio.

Intake Tubing and Filters

Matching the intake tubing to the rest of the components in the intake system is also critical when designing the system and tuning the computer. As noted in Chapter 4, the Ford Control Packs come with a preselected intake system and the PCM is programmed for this specific tubing set.

Cold-Air Kits

One of the cheaper horsepower add-ons is a cold air kit. Well-designed cold air tubing systems do two things: they draw air from an area away from the engine and radiator flow to equalize the intake air temperature to the outside air, and by reducing unneeded bends and silencers, they can reduce restrictions, increasing airflow to the engine to make more power. They also typically use a low restriction air filter to further increase airflow.

INTAKES AND INDUCTION

Along with the Cobra Jet throttle body, Ford Performance has a cold air intake to match with a 102-mm inlet. Compact and adaptable to other applications, it comes with a low-restriction filter and plastic filter bucket. (Photo Courtesy Ford Performance Parts)

Western Motorsports developed a cold air kit for the 2005–2009 engines that takes air in a straight shot over the radiator, eliminating all the bends and turns in most kits. The kit comes with a new mass air meter and low-profile air filter, and might be adaptable to other chassis. (Photo Courtesy Western Motorsports)

K&N makes a full line of cold air kits, and I found that the 1999–2004 Cobra cold air kit (PN 57-2523-2) works perfect with 4.6 4V installations such as the Mustang in Black. Once the battery is relocated to the trunk, it requires only a bracket to mount the filter shield to the bottom of the battery tray area.

JLT Performance specializes in cold air intakes and it has systems for both stock and custom installs, naturally aspirated and supercharged packages, and a host of options. Its intakes are available in standard black, color matched, or a carbon fiber look. Tuning is available with all its kits. (Photo Courtesy JLT Performance)

JLT Performance, Ford Performance, Western Motorsports, K&N, and others offer cold air intake for the modular engine. Because there is a wide range of modular engines, there is also a wide range of cold air intakes to fit them, and each engine type has its unique flow requirements. While most cold air kits are designed for a specific late-model application, some might work in a different engine compartment. Some aftermarket tubes do not have a provision for an aspirator tube, which allows for power brake operations in automatic-equipped vehicles.

Swap Spotlight: Double Trouble

Before he gave the world the *Equadroline*, master fabricator Gordon Tronson built *Double Trouble*, a built-from-scratch 1927 T that proved that a modular engine masterpiece can blend new technology with old school chassis, and do so seamlessly.

Double Trouble was built with no plans, from scratch. The plan was to build something that nobody else had. Gordon had seen dragsters and custom cars with engines inline, but Gordon wanted to build a car with engines side by side. Some serious engineering would need to be worked out to make everything work.

You would think that a side-by-side engine build would have you searching for a pair of narrow engines, but Gordon established the bar by starting with a pair of wide-bodied, all-aluminum 4.6 DOHC engines and a fiberglass 1927 T body, then he went to work. Almost everything on the car is hand fabricated by Gordon. The chassis was built out of 1.5-inch tubing custom bent by Gordon to accommodate the modular engines. The entire frame was then powder-coated for durability because his creations are driven. Gordon then custom-fabricated the front suspension using an unequal-length double A-arm design using coil-over shocks. The rear axle is a Jaguar independent unit with inboard brakes. Rear brakes are matched with a pair of Corvette spindles and brakes on the front. The rack-and-pinion steering unit is similar to ones used on sandrails. The brake booster is mounted under the floor.

This is Gordon Tronson and one of his creations, Double Trouble. *This 1927 T-bucket roadster has 1,200 hp emanating from two all-aluminum 4.6L DOHC engines. (Photo Courtesy Gordon Tronson)*

After acquiring the body and engines, Gordon hand fabricated the frame to accept the side-by-side configuration of the engines. Temporary spacers hold the engines in place while fabricating. (Photo Courtesy Gordon Tronson)

A custom fuel tank was fabricated and works in conjunction with a Procomp high-flow electric fuel pump. Griffin Thermal Products made the custom radiator for cooling the dual engines. The headers and side exhaust were made from a street rod kit then custom bent to fit the engines.

Even though the engines are new with overhead-cam technology, Gordon went old school for the look on this ride. Its engines are not only carbureted with

Holley 4150s, but they run through several (yeah, I said several) Weiand Roots superchargers. The original combination used two superchargers and was good for around 1,000 hp. But with Gordon, more is better, so he fabricated new intake manifolds to allow *twin* superchargers and carburetors per engine. Now *Double Trouble* puts out around 1,200 streetable horsepower.

Other improvements to the engines include a conversion back to distributors run off the back end of the camshafts. The Procomp CDI systems are reminiscent of the flathead designs of the late-1930s Fords. Twin starters work in tandem to start both engines at once.

The transmission is an unassuming Ford C5 automatic worked over to handle the horsepower. A custom transfer case was engineered and built, and it transfers power to the transmission via a pair of steel sprockets and a jackshaft that drives a Gates 90-mm poly chain belt. Micar Fab did the heavy machine work.

With the drivetrain in place, Gordon then fabricated everything else in the car (windshield screen, seat pans, dash, wiring, plumbing). The body was painted a beautiful Candy Apple Blue. Billet Specialties 15 x 14–inch wheels went on the rear with 15 x 7–inch wheels on the front with Mickey Thompson tires.

You would think that a car with that much horsepower would be a beast to drive, but in fact it has very accommodating road manners. Seeing around all those superchargers can be a challenge, and hold on if you decide to light up the Mickey Thompson tires.

Gordon Tronson comes to the United States via his home in Napier, New Zealand, where he developed his hot rod building skills. With *Double Trouble* and *Equadroline* under his belt, I can't wait to see the next project to come from the master builder.

The transmission is a mid-1980s Ford C5 3-speed, which is mated to a custom transfer case to drive both engines. The custom fabricated bellhousing was used to match the transmission to the transfer case. (Photo Courtesy Gordon Tronson)

A single-drive belt spins all four Weiand superchargers. The intake manifolds were hand-fabricated, and four Holley 4150 double pumpers feed them. The special wide radiator was custom built by Griffin Thermal Products and serves both engines with two inputs and outputs. (Photo Courtesy Gordon Tronson)

Gordon Tronson adapted old-school technology when it came to the ignition systems. The distributors have a magnetic pickup used for old flathead Ford engines, and these are mated to a Procomp CDI ignition. The distributors are mounted on custom brackets and are driven from the back of the camshaft. (Photo Courtesy Gordon Tronson)

The headers come from a kit, but were modified by the owner. With the exception of a few items, the owner did all the fabrication and engineering. (Photo Courtesy Gordon Tronson)

CHAPTER 6

FUEL SYSTEMS

As I stated in the introduction, the goal of this book is not to make you an expert on building a monster modular engine. The goal is to help you get the engine in your chassis and make you aware of the options available for the project. The fuel system is a prime example because it can be set up many different ways. I could fill an entire book explaining it all. The engine builder and dyno data determine the ultimate choice on fuel systems (see Chapter 10). For more in-depth information on fuel systems and what works best for you, I recommend the book *Designing and Tuning High-Performance Fuel Injection Systems* by Greg Banish.

While you can install and use carburetors on a modular engine, fuel injection is the preferred fuel system for most owners and swappers, and therefore, this chapter deals primarily with fuel injection. Always keep in mind, fuel injection works at higher pressures, and improper design can lead to leaning out the engine, which can lead to burning a piston or other damage.

Returnless versus Mechanical Return Line Fuel Systems

In a carburetor, the fuel bowl fills up with fuel, the needle is pushed into its seat, and it closes. The flow of fuel stops until the float lowers enough to re-open the seat. Carburetors run at about 5 to 7 psi, just enough to maintain fuel flow into the bowl. If there is a loss of fuel pressure, it isn't noticeable until the bowl is empty.

Fuel injection works at pressures of 32 psi or higher, depending on the application, but you need to consider both the fuel rail pressure and differential pressure. Fuel rail pressure is the actual pressure inside the fuel lines, and differential pressure is the pressure working on the fuel injector at any time. Recognize that differential pressure can be different from rail pressure. When a naturally aspirated engine is at idle, intake manifold vacuum is present in the engine. The vacuum draws more fuel through the injector when it opens, increasing the differential pressure on the

What did I just see? Yes folks, after years of Chevy 350 and LS swaps, it has finally happened. This 1978 Pontiac Trans-Am has a 4.6 3V Mustang GT engine. Why? Because the owner wants to go fast.

FUEL SYSTEMS

Prior to electronic reading of the fuel pressure in the fuel log, a mechanical fuel pressure regulator was used to divert excess fuel back to the fuel tank. The vacuum port on top was attached to the intake manifold. When the engine is idling there is a vacuum (or less than atmospheric pressure) in the manifold, and this can have an effect on the actual pressure in the fuel log. The regulator uses the manifold vacuum to adjust for pressure readings.

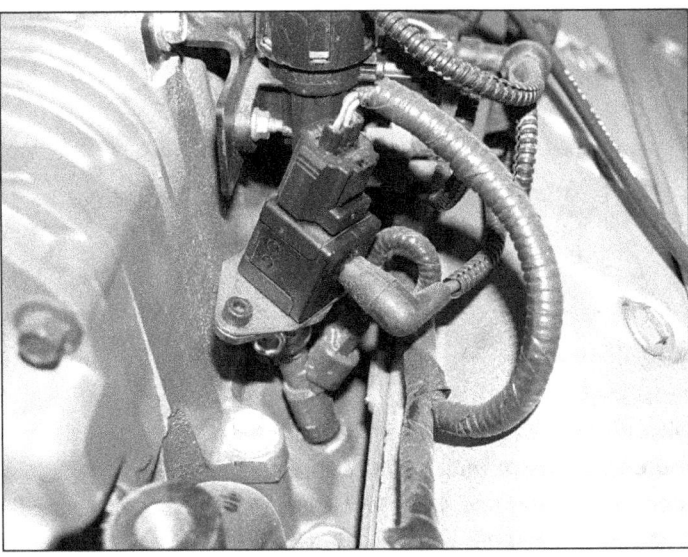

The Fuel Rail Pressure Sensor (FRPS) replaces the mechanical regulator on returnless fuel systems and sends a signal to the computer, which adjusts the voltage to the fuel pump to maintain proper fuel rail pressure. There is still a vacuum port on the side of the regulator that can be used for vacuum or boost readings on this supercharged 4.6.

injector. With a forced induction system, pressure increases in the intake manifold as RPM increases. This pressure acts against the pressure driving the fuel through the injector and reduces the differential pressure on the fuel injector.

Ford used a fuel rail pressure regulator mounted at the end of the fuel rail up through 1998. The fuel pressure regulator system maintains fuel rail pressure with a spring and valve. These allow the regulator to open at a specific pressure and divert the excess fuel flow back to the fuel tank. By sensing the intake vacuum or pressure, it can adjust the rail pressure up or down to maintain the correct differential pressure across the fuel injectors.

A mechanical fuel regulator has one drawback. When fuel is pumped from the tank, it can be heated while passing through the engine compartment, and it can return to the tank at higher temperatures. The boiling point of gasoline can be as low as 90 degrees Fahrenheit (35 degrees Celsius). So it is easy for the fuel to turn into vapor, which can create more hydrocarbons and increase vehicle emissions levels.

In 1999 Ford elected to use a returnless system, in which an FRPS (Fuel Rail Pressure Sensor) regulates the fuel pressure. Mounted on the fuel rail, this sensor tells the PCM the fuel pressure at the engine. The PCM adjusts the voltage to the fuel pump to keep the fuel pressure in the required range. The FRPS also measures manifold vacuum/pressure to adjust the differential pressure. One of the big advantages is the elimination of some of the evaporative emissions issues listed above. One drawback to this system is that the fuel can sit longer in the engine bay and absorb heat, but the FRPS can sense this condition and compensate.

Aftermarket Fuel-Bypass Regulators

Externally mounted bypass regulators work similar to the Ford-mounted units, with a little more accuracy. They typically are designed to use AN-style or O-ring fittings. They should be mounted at the end of the fuel rail if possible, which means that you have one or two lines feeding the regulator after they have passed over the fuel injectors.

Which regulator you choose largely depends on how much fuel is required. In general, you should use pumps, regulators, and filters as a system from the same manufacturer because they are designed to work together.

Several builders opt for the Aeromotive 13129 series regulators as a good universal regulator. It features O-ring ports and a vacuum port that can be used for boost or intake

CHAPTER 6

When using a Ford Control Pack computer system, or many aftermarket computers, the use of a mechanical regulator is usually required. This Aeromotive unit is fully adjustable and includes a port for intake vacuum or boost adjustment.

vacuum. Fuelab's 535 series regulators are compact to fit in tight spaces, and the Fuelab 529 series of electronic pressure regulators work with its Prodigy fuel pumps and reduce and maintain the return-line flow, which can reduce overheating of the fuel caused by constant pressure of the pump.

Single versus Dual Fuel Pumps

Ford typically installs dual fuel pumps on factory supercharged modular engines. Running two smaller pumps is better than running a big pump all the time because you can shut one down if needed. In most cases, a large single pump that runs at a constant voltage with a mechanical regulator and return line pumps more fuel to the engine than it requires. The excess fuel is returned to the tank, resulting in more vapors and heat, and in some cases, the pump may be louder.

Mounting the fuel pump in the tank reduces the chances of pump

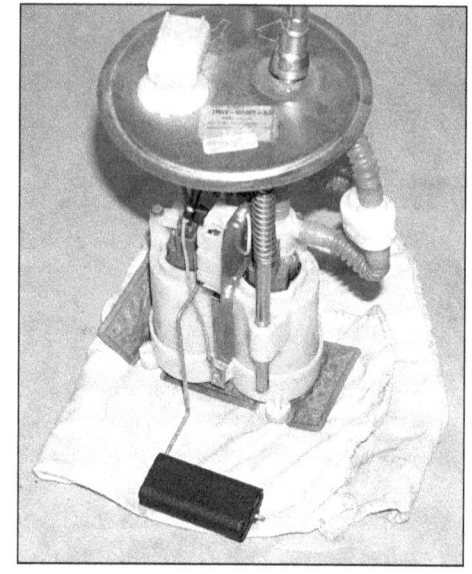

Factory supercharged applications got a dual fuel pump to feed the engine under boost. Using a dual fuel pump is quieter than using a bigger single pump, and you can turn one off if you wish when it is not needed. This unit is out of a 2007 Shelby GT500.

cavitation and starving the fuel system. The fuel also keeps the pump cool. When the pump is mounted externally, restrictions in the inlet tube can cause a drop in inlet pressure and allow bubbles to form and cause cavitation. The advantage to the external pump is that you don't have to drop the tank should you need to access the pump, and the pumps are not limited to tank size or design.

An important thing to consider when choosing a fuel pump is that superchargers and turbochargers increase the amount of air going into an engine, requiring more fuel. Make sure to follow the manufacturer's recommendation for fuel delivery.

Aftermarket Fuel Pumps

An aftermarket pump doesn't care about the brand of engine it is supplying, so you have virtually an unlimited number of pump options. Some work with the Ford returnless design. The PA series of in-tank pumps from Tanks Inc. can be adapted to most fuel tanks and come with its own baffling, so no internal baffles are needed. The Aeromotive Phantom fuel pump is made to adapt to most non-EFI, non-baffled tanks and comes complete with a foam ring that acts as a baffle. The Phantom system can also be used with the 1999 returnless fuel system, as it can be adapted to the pulse-modulated output from the factory computer and fuel pump modulator. The Walbro GS series of pumps have been the standard upgrade for inline fuel pumps since the 5.0 pushrod engines, and work fine with the modular engine conversions.

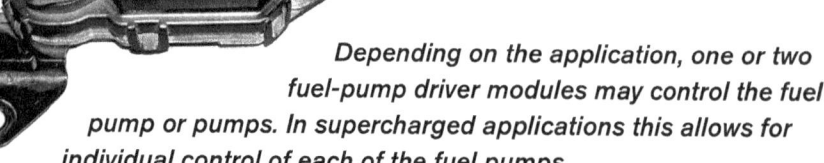

Depending on the application, one or two fuel-pump driver modules may control the fuel pump or pumps. In supercharged applications this allows for individual control of each of the fuel pumps.

HOW TO SWAP FORD MODULAR ENGINES INTO MUSTANGS, TORINOS AND MORE

FUEL SYSTEMS

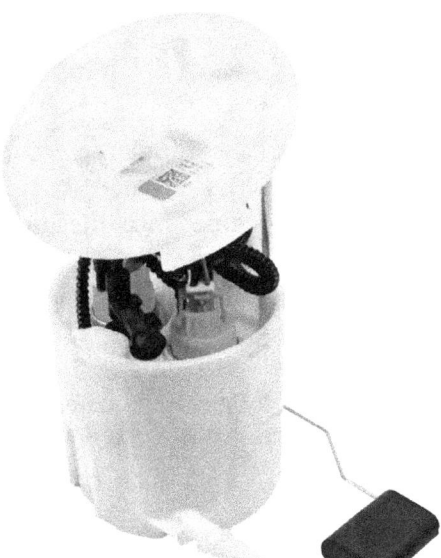

Ford Performance Parts sells this Aeromotive dual fuel pump setup originally found in the 2011–2014 Shelby GT500s (PN M-9407MSVT). It supports more than 850 hp. The unit works with factory wiring and can be adapted to other applications. (Photo Courtesy Ford Performance Parts)

Fuel Pump Voltage Boosters

As the fuel pump reaches 100-percent capacity when the engine is at wide-open throttle (WOT) and operating high RPM, it may not produce adequate fuel volume and/or pressure, which could cause the engine to lean out, resulting in damage. This is especially true with forced induction and nitrous, where additional fuel needs to be added as the engine RPM increases.

One alternative to using a larger fuel pump is to increase the voltage to the existing pump. Pumps are designed to work at 12 volts, but some manufacturers have designed their pumps to tolerate and operate at voltages of 20 volts or more. Increasing the voltage increases the output of a pump. By delivering this voltage when needed at WOT, a smaller pump runs cooler, and it can be used to power an engine that requires more flow when needed.

Caution: increasing the voltage to a fuel pump not designed for higher voltage will likely result in damage to the fuel pump.

Because supercharging requires additional fuel, Kenne Bell has been on the front edge of voltage boosters for fuel pumps with its Boost-a-Pump line. Its systems open when needed at WOT and maintain accurate pressure flow. JMS FuelMAX V2 voltage boosters can increase fuel volume up to 85 percent and allow for user control of the ramp-up rates to correct and eliminate voltage spiking when the voltage is increasing.

Fuel Injectors and Rails

A fuel injector is nothing more than an electronic fuel control valve. The computer grounds the circuit to the injector and opens the nozzle, or pintle, for a selected amount of time to allow fuel to flow into the cylinder. A few terms you may hear about when selecting injectors:

Flow Rate

In the United States, the fuel flow rate is measured in pounds per hour. A standard Coyote injector flows 24 pounds of fuel per hour at 43.5 psi (about 300 kPa) at 100-percent duty cycle; that means it's open all the time. You need

Aeromotive has the Phantom series of pumps that can be operated in a return mode or returnless mode using the Ford fuel-pump modulator. The top mount can be adapted to most fuel tanks, and the foam baffle prevents fuel starvation under acceleration and cornering. The phantom system is available in either single- or dual-pump configuration. (Photo Courtesy Aeromotive Inc.)

Kenne Bell's Boost-A-Pump system (shown for both single- and dual-pump applications) is designed to provide additional voltage at WOT and increase pump output 75 to 100 percent only when needed. The Boost-A-Pump can also maintain pump voltage to 1 percent, which can drastically reduce fuel flow fluctuations. Street version can boost voltage to 17.5 volts, while competition versions can boost to 20 volts. (Photo Courtesy Kenne Bell)

to determine the correct size of fuel injector for the engine's fuel requirements (see formula below). Changing the size of the injectors may or may not have any effect on the performance of an engine. In fact, you could harm performance if you install the wrong size of injector. If the engine is not designed for the fuel delivery by the bigger injectors, hesitation or stumbling may result, or the computer monitoring the air/fuel ratio may turn the fuel injectors on or off at a different rate, resulting in the same fuel delivery as a smaller injector.

The formula for calculating what size injectors you need is:

Flow Rate = Engine HP (at the flywheel) x BSFC (brake specific fuel consumption) ÷ 8 (the number of injectors) x .85 (maximum desirable duty cycle for the injectors)

Duty Cycle

This specification measures how long the injectors are open and closed. An injector running at 50-percent duty cycle is open and closed in equal parts. A street engine should not be operated at a duty cycle above 80 percent. If an injector operates at 100-percent duty cycle (open all the time), it is operating in a static mode, which can cause damage to the injector, and higher than 85 percent may mean it is trying to close while trying to reopen again in the cycle, which can cause erratic fuel delivery. Although injectors are tested at wide open (100-percent duty cycle) to test the flow rate, they should never be operated in this condition. Operating at a duty cycle greater than 80 percent indicates the injectors are too small for the application.

Impedance

Impedance is the electrical resistance in the injector. This resistance is a result of the design of the electrical coil and materials used. Most factory injectors are high impedance for cost reasons. Most racing platforms use low-impedance injectors due to their ability to open and close faster.

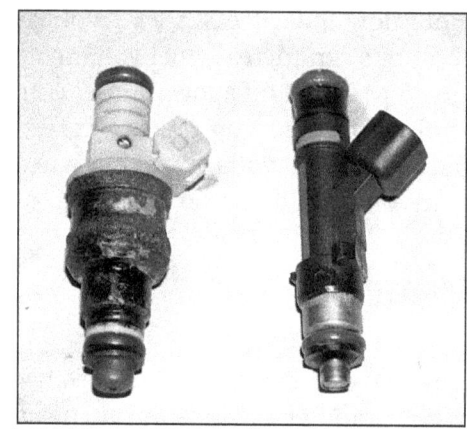

Most aftermarket computers can control either, so it is not necessary to convert to low-impedance injectors if there is no requirement for their use.

Boosted versus Naturally Aspirated Engines

As previously stated, when you boost the engine and add pressure to

The evolution of the 4.6 SOHC fuel injector demonstrates that care needs to be taken when selecting fuel injectors for a modular engine. The late 1990s version (left) and the 2011 version (right) are shown. The injector nozzle, the solenoid driver, the inlet, and the connection are completely different on these two injectors. Depending on the application, the fuel rail, intake, and computer all play a role in determining the ideal injectors.

Here are the two primary styles of injector connectors: the Jetronic/Minitimer style on the left and the USCAR-style connector on the right. The connections function the same, and adapters are available to convert your injectors to your wiring harness connections.

Ford Performance Parts sells converters to go from either style of fuel injector connector to the other. Shown is the M-14464-A8, which converts a USCAR-style fuel injector to a Jetronic/Minitimer harness. The adapters to go the other way (PN M-14464-U2J) are also available. (Photo Courtesy Ford Performance Parts)

FUEL SYSTEMS

Injector Dynamics has partnered with Bosch enginesports to bring out a full line of performance injectors. The 1300 series (shown here for a Shelby GT500, PN 1300.48.14.14.8) and flows 127 pounds per hour. With all stainless internals it stands up to fuels such as alcohol and other corrosive types. (Photo Courtesy Injector Dynamics)

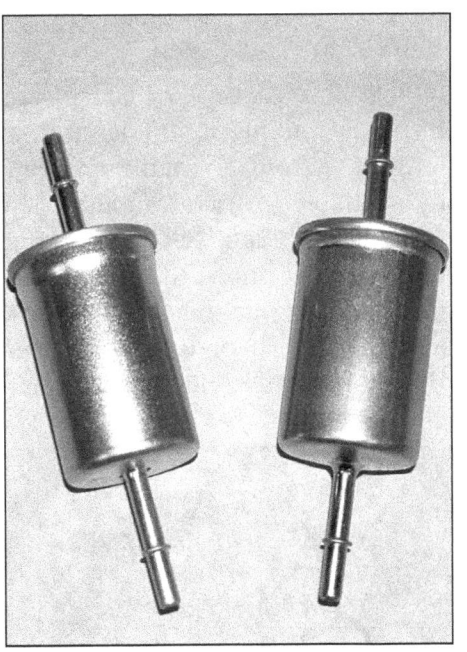

The Ford fuel filter used in most 4.6 and 5.0 applications is a good unit with plenty of surface area. However, you need to know what you are using. The filter on the left is for standard gasoline, and the one on the right is for flex fuel applications. Running the incorrect fuel in any style filter can destroy the filter.

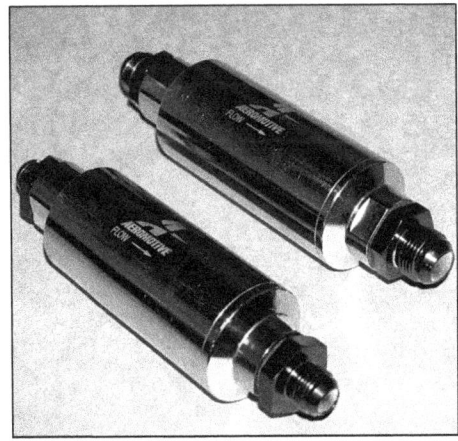

These Aeromotive fuel filters are good for applications up to 1,300 hp. When planning for high-end applications, you need two filters. The filter on the top is a 10M Pro 10-micron filter for use before the inline pump. The bottom filter is a 40M Pro with 40-micron filtration after the pump.

the intake manifold, the increased intake pressure counteracts the fuel rail pressure in the injector and resists the fuel flow from the injector. As boost increases, you need to add an equal amount of fuel pressure to compensate for the boost resistance.

Injectors come in numerous flow rates and body shapes. Some intake manifolds have specific hard mounts for fuel rails, so fuel rail mounts may dictate the actual usable length of the fuel injector body. Take care to note that there are two types of connectors used in the different injectors on Ford engines: the JetRonic/Minitimer connector and the USCAR connector.

Fuel Filters

An in-tank pump either has a fuel filter mounted on the pump or a screen on the inlet. Inline pumps generally recommend an inlet filter to prevent damage to the pump, but using the wrong filter can also cause damage. A filter that is too fine can cause excessive restriction and cavitation if it's mounted before the filter. To make sure the filter isn't a bottleneck in the fuel path, use a filter with the same size openings as the fuel line, and the greater the surface area of the filter, the better the fuel flow. A small, screen filter is not recommended because it clogs faster, resulting in damage. Some Ford applications have a non-serviceable fuel filter mounted on or in the pump. Although the factory Ford filters are inexpensive and work in some street applications, as performance increases you should look toward micron specific filters for better filtration. Aeromotive sells a complete line of inline filters that filter between 100 down to 10 microns and come in AN or O-ring, fitting from -6 to -10 sizes.

CHAPTER 6

Fuel Tanks

EFI conversions for classic cars have become more popular and, as a result, retrofit fuel tanks are readily available for many models. The key factor when selecting a fuel tank is to get one with internal baffling. Baffling in the tank prevents a sudden slosh of fuel away from the pickup, as under hard acceleration or cornering. This can cause the fuel pump to draw in air, or cause cavitation, which results in pressure problems with the fuel system. When using an in-tank pump and return line, avoid the return port dumping directly on or near the pump, as this can dump heated gas into the pump suction screen, potentially resulting in premature pump failure.

Aeromotive sells a line of fuel tanks for a wide range of vehicles with its stealth fuel system already installed. An A1000 or Eliminator pump is installed in the 18685 tank that features full baffling and a 100-micron filter already installed. This unit fits Fox-body Mustangs from 1986 and up. (Photo Courtesy Aeromotive, Inc.)

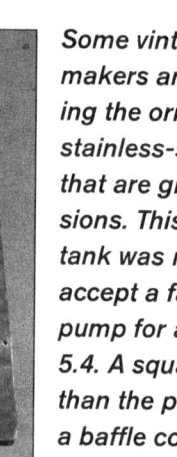

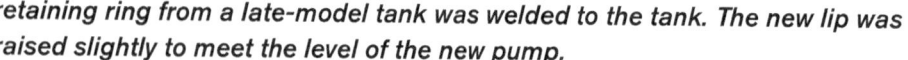

Some vintage fuel tank makers are now making the original-style stainless-steel fuel tanks that are great for conversions. This 1967 Mustang tank was modified to accept a factory dual fuel pump for a supercharged 5.4. A square hole bigger than the pump was cut so a baffle could be installed in the base, then the retaining ring from a late-model tank was welded to the tank. The new lip was raised slightly to meet the level of the new pump.

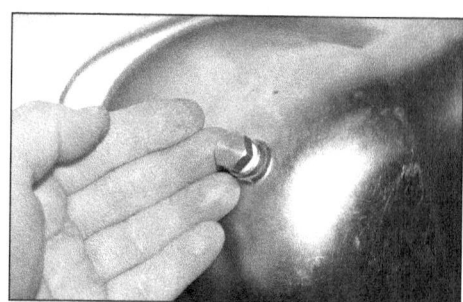

An old trick used back in the 5.0 pushrod days was to run the fuel return line back to the factory drain plug if you didn't have a port for the return line. Make sure you shield any loops in the line if they run low on the body.

Mustangs to Fear makes an aluminum tank for its modular engine conversion Mustangs and Eleanors; it features an Aeromotive stealth pump and choice of sending unit resistance ranges. It can be made for stock filler location or for the Eleanor side fill.

The ultimate in safety and performance is a fuel racing cell. They are fully baffled and the bladder prevents fuel spraying in a wreck. This one is for a 1970 Mustang (Fuel Safe PN EM-ED), uses an external fuel pump, and is plumbed for EFI return and venting.

FUEL SYSTEMS

If you are going to use the stock fuel rails, you need an adapter to mate to the Ford-style pressure connector. This Russell 640880 adapter mates the original Ford spring-loaded pressure connector to a male AN-8 fitting.

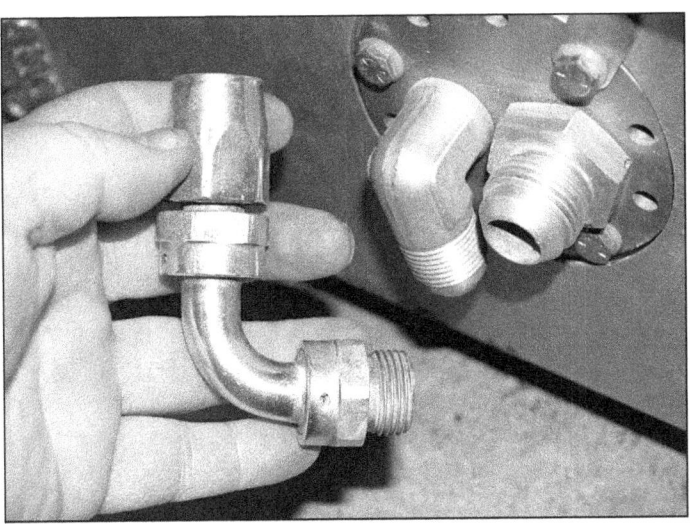

A quick note about fittings: when laying out your fuel system, avoid hard 90-degree turns such as the one plugged into this tank. The tube-style 90-degree fitting reduces the pressure loss from the hard turn and reduces heating up of the fuel.

Hoses and Fittings

Hoses and fittings need to be matched in size to the outlet of the pump so they do not create a restriction in the fuel line. Fittings and hoses should have radiused bends and no sharp angles.

Rubber hoses for carbureted and fuel-injected systems have different specifications, so make sure all the flexible hose is fuel-injection spec. Fuel lines can be steel, aluminum, or plastic, braided or woven hose.

EVAP System

The EVAP system takes vapors from the gas tank and flows them into a charcoal canister, where they are stored until they are pulled into the intake manifold and burned. This not only helps the efficiency of the engine by burning fuel vapors that would typically be lost, but it lowers hydrocarbon emissions.

The pressure in the fuel tank increases or decreases as fuel heats and expands or cools and contracts. Before emission control systems were put in place, these gases were vented into the air and replaced with the atmosphere through a vented gas cap. An emissions system draws the vapors from the tank but also replaces the vapors with air through a valve. The EVAP maintains a specific pressure level in the tank, and when the gas cap is left off the filler tube, the computer generates an error code.

When the valve or gas cap fails, vacuum or pressure can build up in the tank. Pressure can cause the gas cap to vent fuel when opening, and vacuum can counteract the fuel pump's ability to draw fuel from the tank. Both conditions can cause the gas cap to become difficult to remove.

In some racing and some regional situations, the EVAP system can be eliminated, and along with it the lines and hardware needed for it to operate. Most aftermarket fuel tank manufacturers do not have provisions for the EVAP system. To run the EVAP, it may be necessary to retrofit a tank that already has this provision, or modify an aftermarket tank. If the EVAP system is not used the PCM needs to be programmed to compensate.

Drive-by-Wire Gas Pedal

In 1969 Ford started using cable-operated throttle controls on some models, continuing to use cable systems until the throttle-by-wire systems went into production in 2005. For

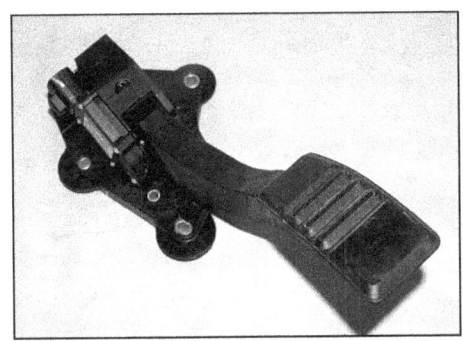

This drive-by-wire gas pedal from the 2005–2009 Ford Mustang is a nice, compact unit for converting from drive-by-cable. With its vertical mounting surface it adapts easily to most firewalls. It is included with the Ford Control Pack and the Ford part number on it is FR3Z-9F836-BD.

HOW TO SWAP FORD MODULAR ENGINES INTO MUSTANGS, TORINOS AND MORE

CHAPTER 6

Fuel System Mistakes to Avoid

To save time, money, and hassle, you need to properly plan out the fuel system requirements and order all the parts as an integrated system. Therefore, injectors, fuel rails, fuel lines, fuel pump, and other numerous related parts complement one another so your engine provides superior performance and reliability. On the other hand, if you do not take your time and properly plan the entire fuel system, you may make some key mistakes. Take some tips from the pros, who still, unfortunately, make some of these mistakes on a regular basis. Mistakes in the fuel system design can be costly.

Undersized/Oversized Components

Think of the horsepower in the engine as actual horses, and think in terms of watering those horses. You don't want 700 horses drinking from a trough designed for 300. You also don't water 300 horses with a pump designed for 700. Although more is better than leaning out, oversized components can lead to stalling, hesitation, louder noise, and component failure. Sending way too much fuel to the engine only to have it pick up heat and return it to the tank can cause vaporizing of the fuel.

Running Components Where They Don't Belong

The big mistake is running fuel lines near exhaust components, but also be careful of running them unprotected or where they can be damaged, such as under frame rails or near frame mounts. Driving over something and having the fuel line torn out or scraped is dangerous.

Never run fuel lines inside the passenger compartment. Don't run mechanical fuel pressure gauges inside the passenger compartment and expose the interior to fuel. Try to mount fuel pressure regulators as close to the intake manifold as possible.

Venting or Non-Venting Gas Caps

The number one reason for throwing an engine error code is forgetting to tighten the gas cap. In a conversion, you can't run an EVAP system and run a vented gas cap. Likewise, you can't run a non-vented cap on a conversion with a blocked off emission system.

Improper Plumbing

Take time to use the proper plumbing components in your system. Installing the fuel sender on the end of a 4-inch pipe nipple into a tee is a recipe for vibration stress cracking. Using a sharp-bend or 90-degree fitting is like adding distance (and more work) to the pump, so avoid sharp bends if possible. Use tube-style rounded fittings or, better yet, two 45-degree fittings if possible.

Cavitation

Fuel pumps are designed to flow liquids, not gases. Introduction of gases (air) into the fuel line causes the pump to cavitate and lose its ability to push fluid. Heat can cause this, and in the old days, it would like to vapor lock. Restrictions in the inlet tube to the pump, or fuel moving away from the inlet of the pump during acceleration or cornering would contribute to it as well. Modular engines don't have a provision for mounting a mechanical fuel pump (which is a source of heat), but plenty of other places along the fuel path pick up heat. Pushing fuel through lines itself causes heat from friction. A good fuel system design limits restrictions to delivering fuel to the engine in all conditions.

Component and Fuel Mismatch

Make sure the parts selected are compatible with the fuel being used. Many fuel blends contain alcohol, and alcohol can attack components such as plastic pump gears and rubber lines and seals. Some alcohol blends can be corrosive to metals in the fuel pump, carburetors, and regulators.

Octane Rating

The octane rating on gasoline does not define power level, rather it tells how much a fuel can be compressed before pre-detonation starts. Higher performance engines with higher compression ratios and forced induction require higher octane fuels to avoid pre-detonation, but some modular engines are designed to run on lower octane fuels. Sometimes premium fuel isn't necessary.

Volume versus Pressure versus Flow

It is important to understand that different components in the fuel system are measured by different means. Injectors are rated by how many pounds of fuel they flow in an hour (weight); fuel pumps are rated by how many gallons or liters per hour they flow at a certain pressure (flow and pressure). As with the 700-horse trough illustration, it takes a certain amount of water to water 700 horses. How you deliver that fuel is important. In Chapter 5, I noted that when pressure increases, the flow decreases. It is important to understand how the manufacturers rate their products.

FUEL SYSTEMS

Incorrect Gauges

Analog or digital, it is easy to get them mixed up and nothing reads right. It happens even to the pros. The computer and data channel control some of the gauges, and a second pickup may be necessary for an aftermarket gauge. ∎

Mustangs and Cougars prior to 1969, the 1969 gas pedal can be adapted to run a cable throttle. Depending on the computer control system selected, it may be necessary to convert back to a cable-operated throttle pedal.

Lokar makes a billet aluminum throttle-by-wire pedal that fits the Ford wiring harness (PN BDBW-FORD01). They can also be programmed for more than 1,400 OEM and aftermarket harness applications. Lokar offers the pedal in bright or black anodized finishes. (Photo Courtesy Lokar Inc.)

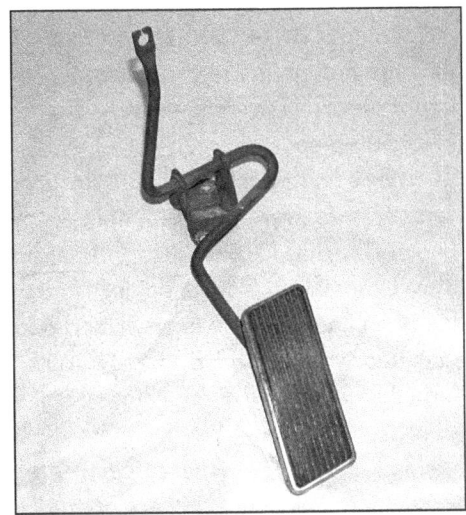

The 1969–1970 Mustang accelerator pedal is a good choice for conversions to cable-operated throttle bodies. It was the first year for the cable-operated carburetor and this pedal adapts well to other chassis.

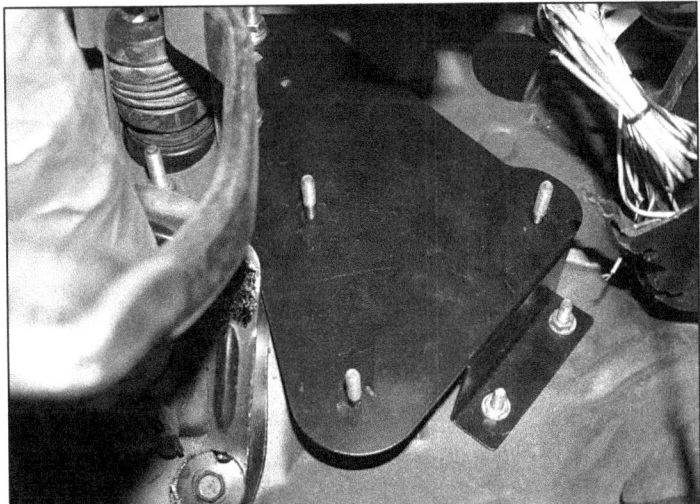

Mustangs to Fear sells an adapter plate to mount the throttle-by-wire in vintage Mustangs. It hangs the pedal at the correct height and angle, and a minimum amount of drilling is required to install it. This one is installed in a 1970 Mustang.

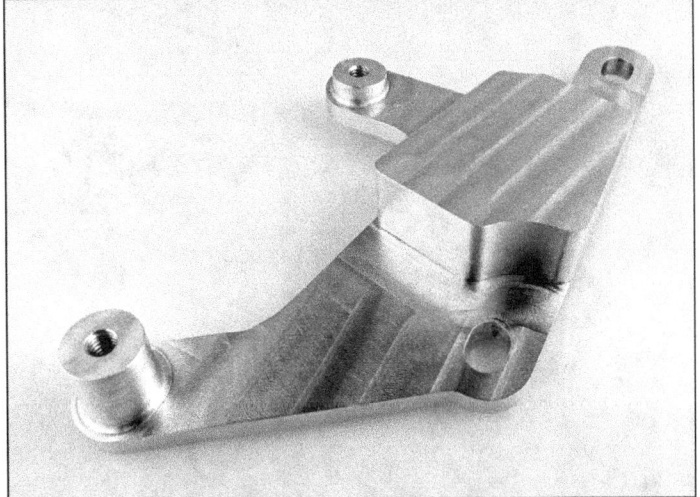

Scram Speed makes a billet aluminum adapter (PN SCM999) that adapts the throttle-by-wire pedal to the Fox-body Mustangs. It mounts the pedal at the correct angle and has additional material behind the pedal for a firm foundation in harsh use. (Photo Courtesy Scram Speed)

Swap Spotlight: Factory Five Cobra

Factory Five has never been a company to rest on its laurels. Before it entered the aftermarket roadster market, parts and kits for the aftermarket builders were kind of hit or miss, and based on technology that was slowly fading into the past. Factory Five hit the market with technology, commonsense, and modern design. Its Mk4 roadster is now the best-selling component car in the world, and Factory Five has no plans to slow down after 20 years.

In 2015, the company celebrated its 20th anniversary in the marketplace and decided to mark the occasion with a mark, Mk4, that is. This would be no ordinary roadster build: this Mk4 would be equipped with a full complement of custom items to denote the special car and would be limited to 20 units of production, which went quite quickly. With Factory Five's commitment to pushing technology for component car manufacturing, the logical choice for the engine in its car was the new Ford Performance 5.0 crate engine.

Along with the Coyote engine, Factory Five optioned out the anniversary cars with a long list of features, including special 20th anniversary badging, custom powder coating on the frame and footwells, polished stainless-steel side pipes and front and rear bumpers, and a custom chrome driver's rollbar with body grommets. The 2015 Mustang Mk4 was equipped with the new independent rear suspension. Its fully adjustable tubular front control arms are complemented by Koni custom coil-over shocks on all four corners. Massive Wilwood nickel-plated six-piston calipers up front and dual-piston calipers out back are used to stop the 13-inch drilled and slotted Wilwood rotors. Wheels are custom 18-inch Halibrands designed specifically for the car, with 18 x 11-inch out back and 18 x 9-inch up front. Special GPS speedometer gauges with the 20th anniversary logos were installed, and the kits were optioned with plenty of add-ons such as leather seats and padded dash and door panels.

The engine is a Ford Performance Crate Coyote 5.0 fitted with a Cobra Jet intake manifold and throttle body. A Ford control Pack computer is installed with HP tuners. This crate engine pushed 404 hp through the rear Halibrands. The transmission is a time-proven Tremec TKO 500 5-speed.

While the special-edition Mk4 anniversary cars were claimed right away, Factory Five has full parts lists and instructions for installing Coyote engines into its cars and has done the legwork and documented what you need to know to perform the conversion. Factory Five's online

Built to celebrate 20 years of successful component builds, the 20th Anniversary Factory Five Mk4 Roadster was a group effort between Factory Five and its suppliers. Ford Coyote power drives this car and its custom features. Sherwin Williams provided the one-off color scheme paint. Only 20 examples were built. (Photo Courtesy Factory Five Racing)

Component Recommendations

Here are some of the major components Factory Five recommends:

Ford Performance Parts

Part Number	Component
M-6007-M50	5.0 engine (or equivalent)
M-7003-R58C	TKO transmission
M-7771-A	Bellhousing bolt kit
M-7007-A	Transmission sandwich plate
M-6392-M46	Bellhousing
M-7560-T46	Clutch kit
M-7515-A	Clutch fork
M-6375-G46A	Flywheel (If not already on engine)
M-7548-A	Clutch release bearing for Ford engine F7ZZ.7548.AA
M-6397-A46	Clutch bolt kit
M-7600-B	Pilot bearing (If not already on engine)
M-4209ADPT-AC	Speed dial (speedo signal changer)
M-6017-A504VA	5.0 engine control pack with speed dial wires*
M-9680-M50	5.0 engine cover kit*
M-8600-M50BALT	5.0 alternator kit*

* These items are included on the Coyote Value Pack (M-6007-M50SVP), which also includes the M-11000-C50 starter. Factory Five recommends using a stock GT starter over the high-torque starter.

Other Components

Moroso low-profile oil pan (PN 20570) and pickup (PN 24570)
Aeromotive 13129 fuel bypass regulator
Walbro 392BX 255-lph fuel pump (or internal pump if you choose)
RC-5149 K&N air filter
Stock starter for a 2005 Ford Mustang GT or equivalent
Spectre tubing adapters, including 9741 reducer, 9771 hose coupling, 9799 90-degree tube, and 9705 mass air sensor adapter

forum is the place to go if you are looking to customize your build even further.

Factory Five lists specific parts you should look at that it has confirmed work with its kits. The instructions for its component cars are complete even down to individual hose fittings.

Although it is too late to get in on the 20th anniversary Mk4, there is sure to be another impressive build coming up for its next anniversary. Until then, Factory Five has done all the legwork for you, so you can have an amazing roadster with reliable, powerful modular engine technology under the hood.

The Coyote uses a throttle-by-wire accelerator pedal that has been shortened to work in the narrow pedal area of the roadster. Full instructions on this modification are included in the kit. Wilwood pedals are used for the clutch and brake systems.

The Ford Performance Parts Coyote crate engine powers the roadster to the tune of 404 hp and 348 rear-wheel torque pushed through the massive 18 x 11 Halibrand wheels. Factory Five topped off the Coyote crate engine with the Cobra Jet intake manifold (PN M-9424-M50) and Cobra Jet throttle body (PN M-9926-SCJ). Note that the taller intake manifold fits nicely under the low-slung hood and scoop. (Photo Courtesy Factory Five Racing)

The Tremec 5-speed is an excellent choice for the Mk4 roadster, as it can handle the power of the modular engine and it fits neatly in the transmission tunnel. One modification seen here is to remove the mounting boss that was located under the shifter to make clearance. Note that this transmission has the shifter in the forward mounting position in the middle of the transmission body.

The Coyote engine is fitted with the earlier SN-95 engine insulators, which drop in to the engine compartment mounts. Note that the insulators sit low on the engine mounts.

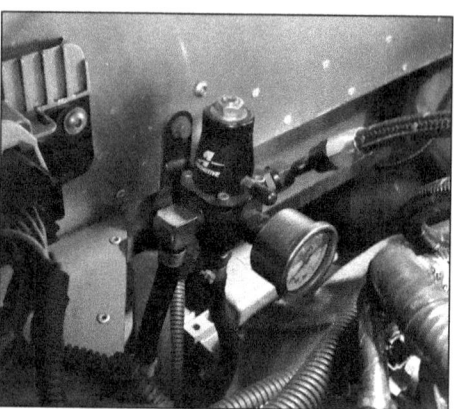

The Ford Performance Control Pack requires the use of a mechanical fuel pressure regulator, such as this Aeromotive unit. It mounts neatly on the firewall on the passenger's side of the engine compartment. The open port on top of the gauge is used for vacuum or boost to the gauge to correct the pressure delivery. If no port is available for intake manifold vacuum and no boost is being used, leave this port open to the atmosphere; don't cap it off.

Using a stainless-steel adapter and a remote radiator cap, the stock Coyote coolant hoses have been adapted to the Cobra radiator system. On the passenger-side apron is an overflow reservoir for the radiator. There is plenty of room between the front of the engine and the radiator for electric fan systems.

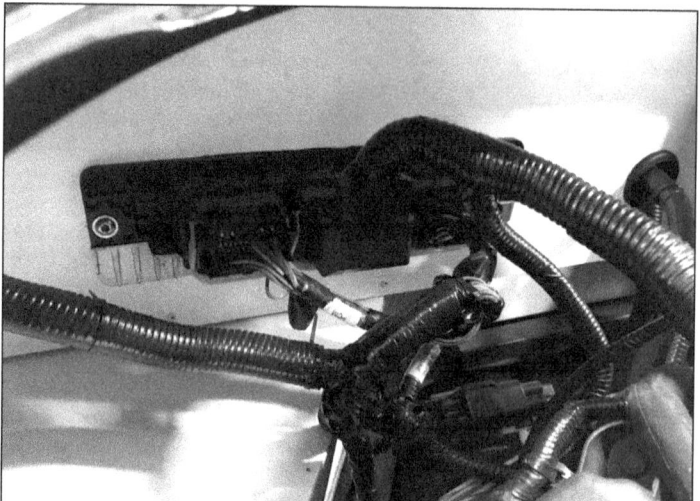

Two different mounting locations for the Coyote Control Pack PCM have been used. The earlier controls mounted up under the firewall on the passenger's side. The 2015–2016 version mounts under the passenger-side fender, shown here with the fender removed. Running the harness on the outside provides a cleaner installation.

CHAPTER 7

COOLING, IGNITION AND ENGINE SYSTEMS

This chapter discusses the systems external to the engine and should be considered when swapping a modular engine into any chassis. Items such as cooling, ignition, and gauges need to be designed to take advantage of some of the improvements of the modular engine over earlier V-8 designs.

Cooling System

The cooling system capacity must match the capacity of the engine. If the modular engine has been modified and puts out significantly more horsepower, it produces much more heat, and the cooling system must be upgraded to properly cool the engine.

The cooling system should be designed to bring the engine up to normal operating temperature and maintain the operating temperature. The engine is designed to run at a certain temperature: as an

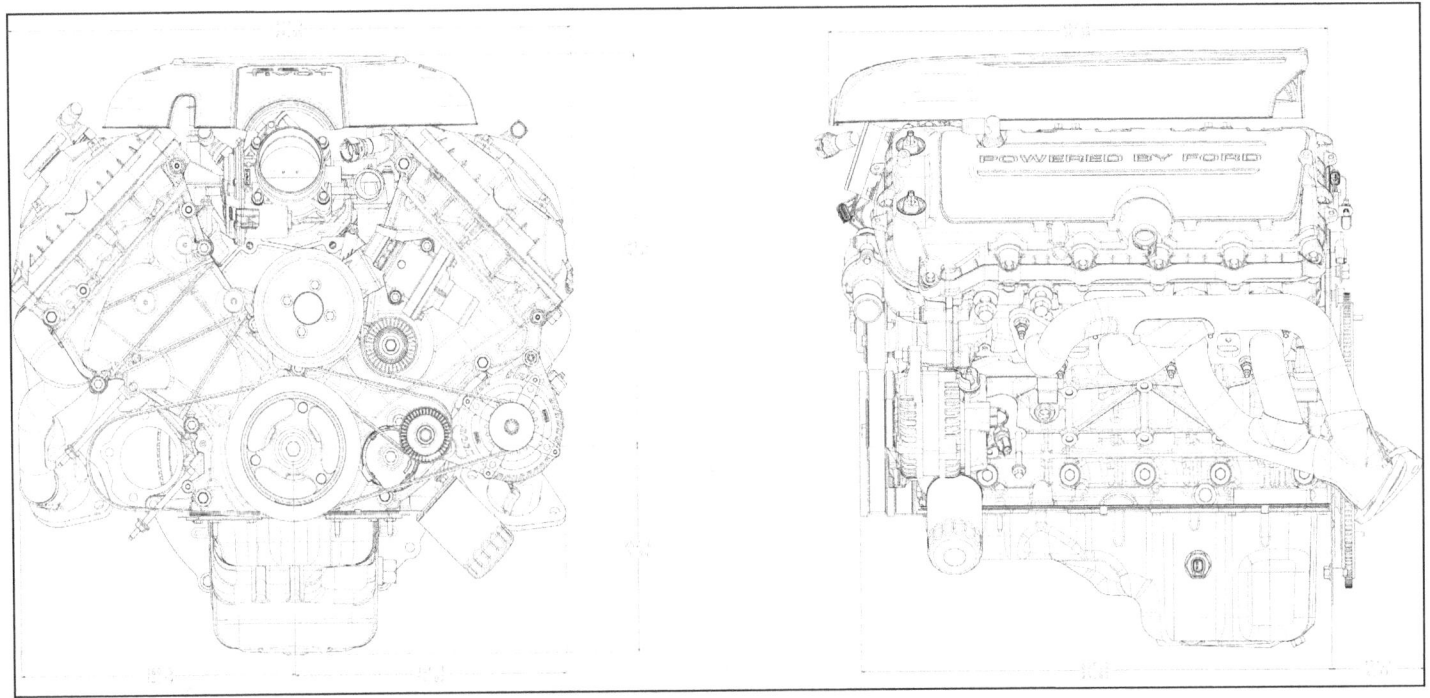

The 5.0 Coyote engine is excellent for swap projects, and it even looks beautiful in line art. Its good looks, support from Ford in terms of performance parts and computer controls, and the support of the aftermarket are making the Coyote conversion a more practical swap for many builders. (Photo Courtesy Ford Performance Parts)

HOW TO SWAP FORD MODULAR ENGINES INTO MUSTANGS, TORINOS AND MORE

engine warms up, the metals expand and seat properly. This is where the engine's tolerances are designed to work, and at normal operating temperature the engine experiences very little wear. Most engine wear occurs when the engine is cold (especially at start up).

The cooling system is designed to maintain the engine operating temperature, not to keep the engine as cool as possible. Although the internal combustion is creating the heat, the two factors that determine the temperature of the engine are the design of the cooling system and the load on the engine. The effectiveness of the cooling system is dependent on the size and efficiency of the radiator, how well the fan can draw air over the radiator at low speeds, and how well the coolant flows through the radiator.

Speed and volume of the coolant flow is important in the design of the cooling system. The cooling system should be designed to allow the coolant the proper length of time to operate at both the engine and the radiator ends. For example, the longer the coolant is in contact with the radiator tubes and fins, the more heat it can transfer: but the cost is that the coolant is also staying in the engine for an equally long time, and the coolant picks up more heat to dissipate. If the flow through the radiator is too high, it spends less time transferring heat to the fins, and the radiator won't be able to effectively cool the engine. Proper coolant flow is important to a good cooling system design; not too much and not too little.

Low-Temp Thermostat Requirement

No cooling occurs until the thermostat opens. The thermostat's primary job is to allow the engine to come up to operating temperature quickly, then regulate the engine temperature by opening and closing to allow the proper passage of coolant and maintain engine operating temperature.

On older modular engines, Ford used a 195-degree (90 Celsius) thermostat, and on later models some engines use a 180-degree thermostat (82 Celsius). As per Ford specification, the earlier thermostat doesn't fully open until 219 degrees (104 Celsius), above the normal operating temperature.

So does running a cooler thermostat help prevent overheating? Not really. If the cooling system is working properly and the thermostat opens too soon, the engine takes longer to get to its operating temperature (or never at all), and that can cause additional wear and lower performance. Engines that experience more load due to driving styles and performance upgrades may benefit from lower thermostat opening temperatures. However, if the engine is generating more heat from load or is experiencing poor cooling system operation, the thermostat could be running wide open and not regulating engine temperature anymore. If the engine is operated without a thermostat, a lot of load is required to bring the engine up to operating temperature, and if the car is not moving, and no air is flowing over the radiator, the engine eventually warms up because the radiator cannot transfer heat effectively without airflow.

A low-temperature thermostat does not make the engine run cooler. It begins the cooling process sooner, and causes the engine to work harder to get to operating temperature. Performance engines that experience more load may benefit from opening the thermostat sooner. If there is an issue with the engine overheating, there is a problem with the cooling system, not with the opening point of the thermostat.

Cylinder Head Temperature

The cylinder head temperature sensor may report a temperature about 10 to 15 degrees higher than the coolant temperature. This is normal because it is transferring that heat to the colder coolant.

Factory Cooling System

There are a few things you should know about the late-model cooling systems. First, Ford uses a de-gas setup, which includes a separate tank for filling and holding extra coolant without relying on vacuum to open and close the radiator cap. The separate tank allows more cooling fins to be used in the radiator, so there is no need for an expansion area in the radiator. On high-performance installations, Ford uses an oil cooler that takes coolant from the lower radiator hose and runs it through an oil cooler mounted to the block. All but the earliest engines used an electric cooling fan system.

Radiators

Although the radiator is fitted to the chassis and not to the engine, one quick note for first-generation Mustang builders: The SN-95 radiator fits between the frame rails of the first-generation Mustang and Cougar chassis with minor modifications. The 1965–1966 Mustang applications have the option of enlarging the radiator opening to take advantage of the wider radiator.

COOLING, IGNITION AND ENGINE SYSTEMS

For installations in early Mustangs, the SN-95 Mustang radiators fit between the frame rails. A simple set of lower mounting brackets and a bar to hold the top is all that is needed to make the late-model radiator work.

C&R Racing makes a custom conversion radiator for installing a Coyote engine into an early Mustang (PN 10-01067). It has an all-aluminum cross-flow design with 1½-inch inlets and outlets. A pair of Spal electric fans is custom mounted. (Photo Courtesy C&R Racing)

Electric Fans

Ford factory fans are high amperage, so caution needs to be taken when selecting a controller. Depending on the application, the fan system can be controlling a two-speed fan, a variable-speed fan, or multiple fans. Some aftermarket computers may have a difficult time controlling the factory fan, so conversion to a more traditional fan controller that works independent from the computer controls may be required.

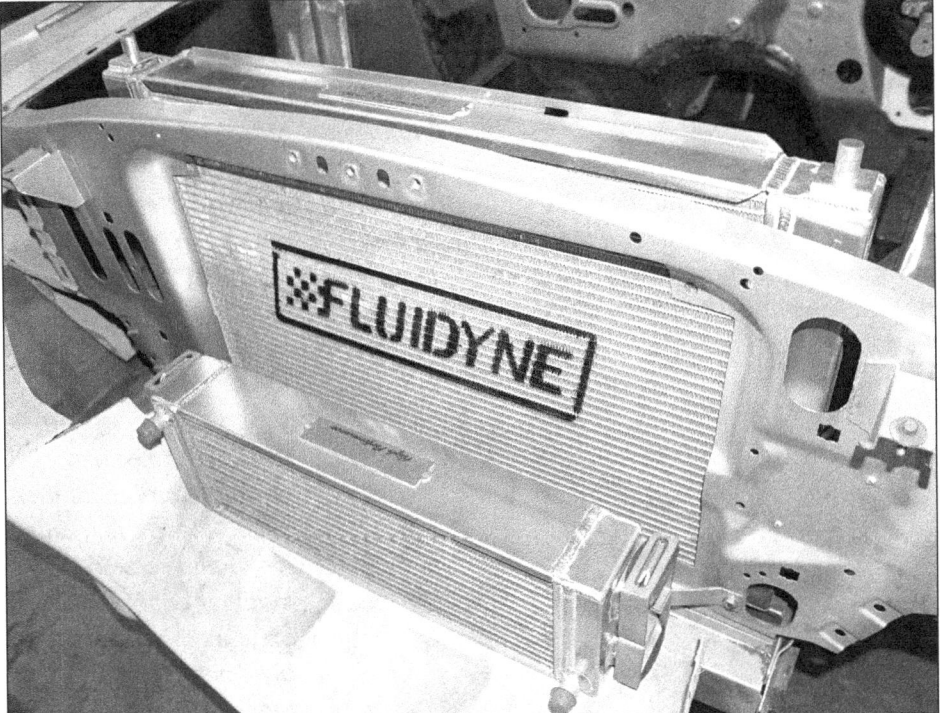

This Fluidyne radiator for a 2003 Cobra (PN FHP30-97MU) needs the top mount posts removed and the lower radiator drain moved from the side to the rear of the lower bowl. The Fluidyne intercooler is PN FHP35-COB-HX.

A typical modular engine electric fan. All but the very early engines used an electric fan setup. When using factory controls, make sure the fan matches the fan controller; some are single-speed, some are dual-speed, and some are variable.

CHAPTER 7

Spal makes a full range of electric fans including tight-fit units like this one (PN IX-30102049). It pulls 2,024 cfm, is 16 inches in diameter, and can be controlled with 30-amp fan controllers.

Derale sells a fan controller that can handle up to 65 amps and multiple fans (PN 16796). It uses pulse width technology, which means as it senses the temperature going up, it can ramp up the power to the fan incrementally. A high-amperage relay will turn all the power on at once instead. By sensing the temperature and adjusting the power to the fan, it can run the fan at a lower current rate at lower speed, lowering the noise of the fan. (Photo Courtesy Derale)

Ford Performance Control Pack includes this external relay controller (PN CM-14A006-A5LB). It controls the power to the PCM, fuel pump, and the engine fan. It is preferable to mount it somewhere in the passenger's compartment, but it can be mounted in a well-ventilated area under the hood if necessary. (Photo Courtesy Ford Performance Parts)

Thermostats and Housings

Thermostat location varies depending on the application. Some thermostats (for example, those on traditional Ford engines) are mounted on the engine, and some are mounted inline in a thermostat "pod," in either the upper or lower radiator hose. Modular engine thermostats have a bypass port built in, so a path needs to be provided for circulation through the bypass.

Here's a comparison between traditional thermostats and the modular engine version. The modular engine thermostat has the water pump bypass built into the bottom of the unit, allowing the water from the pump to circulate before the thermostat opens.

COOLING, IGNITION AND ENGINE SYSTEMS

This thermostat pod for a 2003 4V Mustang is mounted low on the inlet side of the radiator. A bypass hose comes from the top side of the coolant crossover and enters on the left. When the thermostat opens, it closes off the bypass and lets coolant flow from the radiator. The smaller outlet on the right is for the reservoir/de-gas tank fill.

De-Gas Coolant Tanks

The de-gas tank takes the expansion area out of the radiator and puts it outside and at the highest point on the coolant plumbing. A pressure port from the top of the radiator connects to the de-gas tank to vent gases trapped in the radiator. The tank is connected to the lower, or cold-side, radiator hose and acts like a reservoir, replacing coolant automatically and as needed. This eliminates the need for the radiator cap to build up pressure to open and act like a valve. Using a de-gas tank or overflow tank depends on the overall design of the cooling system.

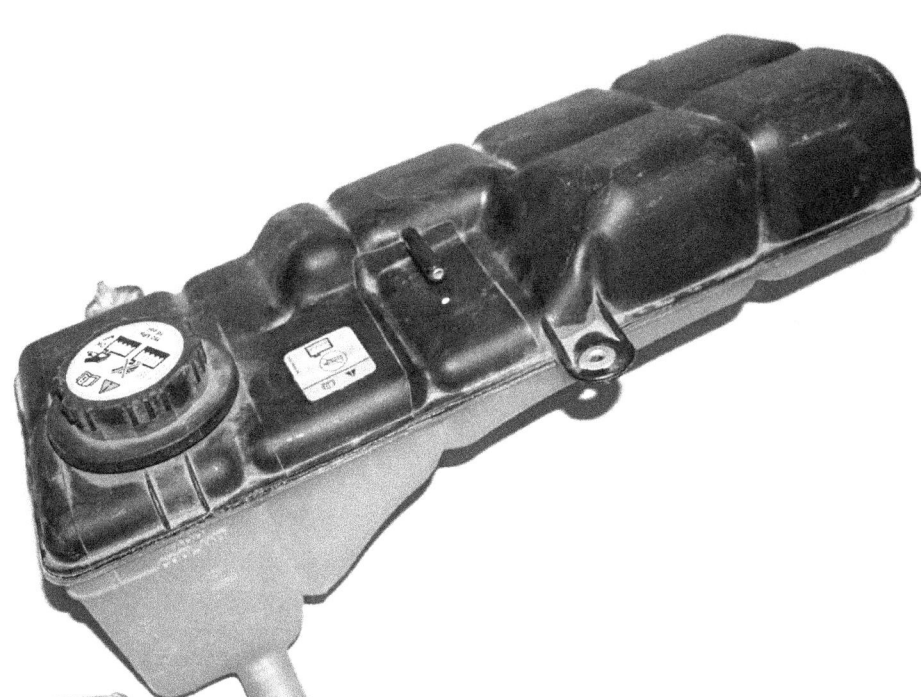

A typical de-gas bottle. This acts as the high point in the system and as the reservoir and fill point for the coolant.

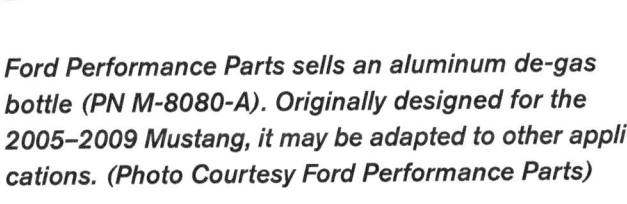

Ford Performance Parts sells an aluminum de-gas bottle (PN M-8080-A). Originally designed for the 2005–2009 Mustang, it may be adapted to other applications. (Photo Courtesy Ford Performance Parts)

Forte Parts manufactures a de-gas tank for use in custom-built roadsters and Factory Five vehicles. It is available with either straight or 45-degree inlet/outlets. (Photo Courtesy Forte Parts)

Ignition Coils and Coil Packs

Modular engines are distributorless and used a coil pack system up through 1998, then switched to coil-on plug ignition in 1999. Most COP applications work fine, but ultra-performance builders have reported that the Ford factory COP system may fail at high RPM.

Distributor Conversion

Several companies have developed a mechanical distributor conversion for a vintage look and for eliminating a computer to control the engine. The distributor connects to one of the drive gears of one of the camshafts and includes a new timing cover, valvecover, or conversion plate, depending on the application. Modular Motorsports Racing uses one of these conversions on its high-end dragsters (PN 400310), and it can be used with crank or camshaft pickup. Trick Flow Specialties has a unit (PN TFS-K52900801) that works on race-only 4.6 2V engines. Both systems use an MSD distributor as the base of their conversion. Dr. DOHC uses either an HEI-style distributor or a Vertex magneto for its distributor conversions. ∎

MSD PN 8241 direct replacement coil packs use its E-core coil efficiency and have a lower primary resistance than the stock coil pack. They work with the stock computer and with MSD ignition systems. (Photo Courtesy MSD Performance)

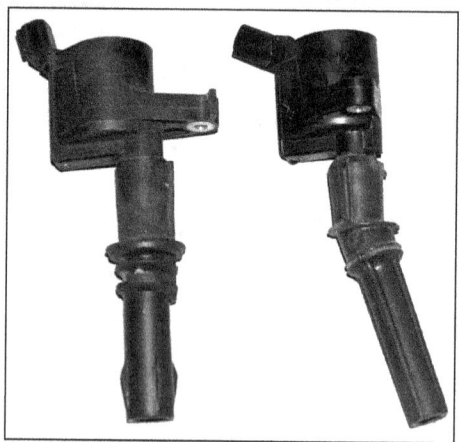

A comparison between stock coils for coil-on plug applications. On the left is a coil from a 5.4 truck, and on the right is a coil from a 4.6. The molded spark plug boot is straight on the truck, angled for the passenger car. Also note the angle of the connector plug.

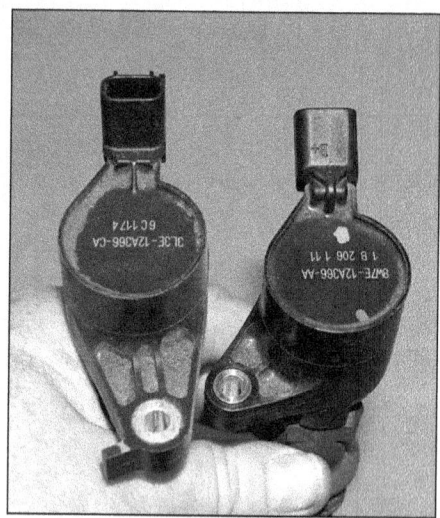

A top view of the two coils shows the different mounting points on the side of the coil. The truck coil was stuffed into the 4.6 before selling the engine; replacement was necessary.

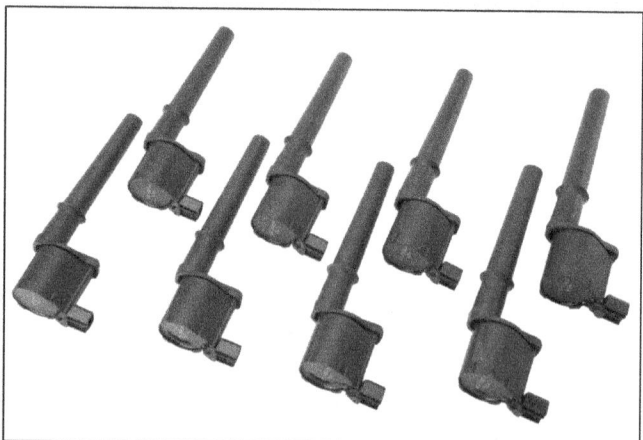

Ford Performance Parts sells these coils for 5.4 and 5.8 DOHC Shelby GT500 applications (PN M-12029-4V). It also has replacements for 4.6 3V and Coyote applications. (Photo Courtesy Ford Performance Parts)

COOLING, IGNITION AND ENGINE SYSTEMS

The MSD ignition controller (PN 6011) allows you to run your distributorless ignition system with a carburetor. It plugs directly in the coils and sensors and comes with PC-based Pro-Data+ software to control the timing curves, rev limiting, and vacuum advance. (Photo Courtesy MSD Performance)

FAST has a coil-on plug ignition controller that allows use of the stock COP system to work with the FAST XFI computer control system. It comes with a plug-and-play harness to allow the XIM control of the factory system. (Photo Courtesy Fuel Air Spark Technologies)

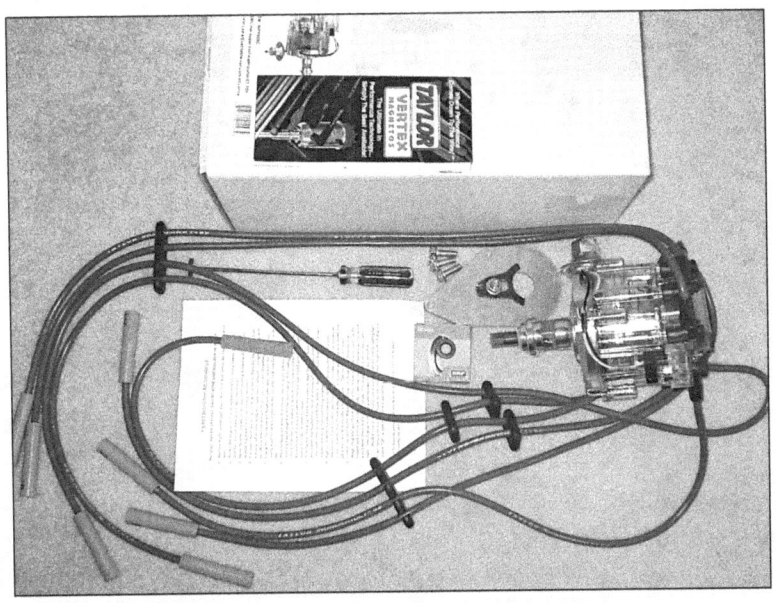

The Dr. DOHC conversion has the option of using the Vertex Magneto instead of a distributor, eliminating the need for an external coil system. (Photo Courtesy Dr. DOHC)

Sensors

The modular engine, like many other late-model engines, has many different sensors to monitor the current operating condition of the engine. Sensors must be integrated into the swap project so that you are fully aware of the engine's health and operating status. A quick definition of some of the sensors mounted on modular engines follows. Ford has added some sensors to the modular engines that don't appear on earlier V-8s.

Oil Pressure Sender

The modular engine still uses an oil pressure sensor with standard NPT threads. The late-model "indicator light" sensor works as all sensors have in the past: it is an on/off switch. An oil pressure sender for an oil pressure gauge needs to be matched to the gauge that will be used because different vendors use different methods to read the oil pressure. The late-model gauge is integrated into the instrument cluster.

Knock Sensor

Starting with 4V engines, the knock sensor was eventually added to the full line of modular engines. A knock sensor senses the shock wave that is generated when pre-detonation occurs in the engine. As the piston fights the compression, it creates a shockwave. The computer can use this information to adjust the timing or fuel delivery to prevent damage to the engine. Engines can have one or two knock sensors installed.

Cylinder Head Temperature Sensor

The cylinder head temperature (CHT) sensors work like coolant senders, but measure the temperature of the metal rather than the coolant drawing the heat of the metal. Part of the reason for using a CHT is to help with torque converter operations. It can also help the PCM if it senses an overheating condition to reduce engine overheating and avoid component damage (e.g., change timing and fuel mix).

Pulleys

Most of the forced induction vendors make pulley sets to match their systems. Pulley sets are available for stock engines to increase performance and improve appearance.

Alternators and Upgrades

Since the 1980s, Ford has used an internally regulated alternator with remote voltage sensing, and it's different from current aftermarket "one-wire" systems. The Ford alternator uses a remote sensing line that senses the voltage away from the alternator, having traveled through some of the wiring. Sensing at the

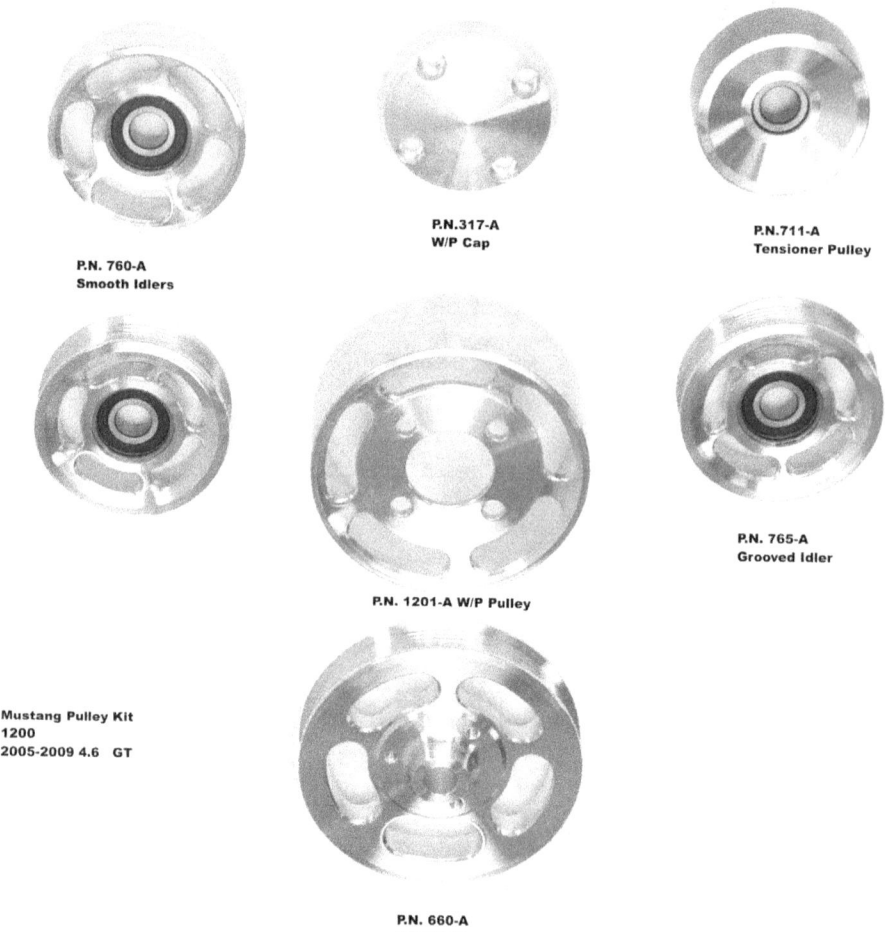

March Performance has several billet aluminum pulley sets for 4.6 applications. This one (PN 1200) is for 2005–2009 GT 3V engines. March also sells individual pulleys, SFI dampeners, and underdrive pulleys. (Photo Courtesy March Performance)

COOLING, IGNITION AND ENGINE SYSTEMS

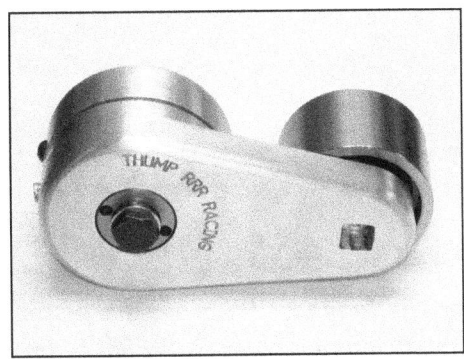

Thump Racing makes a line of billet belt tensioners to fit most modular engines, and they are recommended by Ford Performance. They can be used with 8- or 6-rib belts, are thicker than the originals, and come with a lifetime guarantee. (Photo Courtesy Thump Racing)

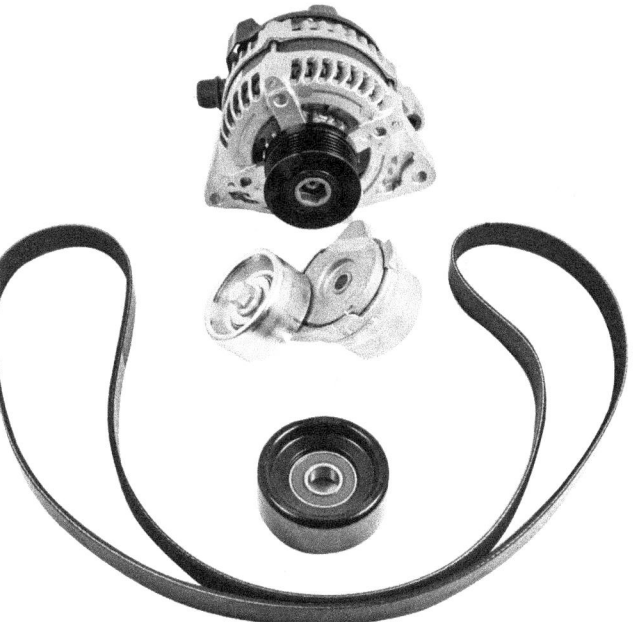

The Ford Performance Boss 302 alternator kit (PN M-8600-M50BALT) has a one-way clutch to prevent belt hop off during clutching that is designed for high-RPM use. It has a larger pulley to reduce rotation, horsepower loss, and parasitic drag and fits many of the Ford crate engines. (Photo Courtesy Ford Performance Parts)

Powermaster sells a line of one-wire alternators for the modular engine at outputs up to 200 amps. This one (PN 57781) is made for 4.6 applications and is available in natural, chrome, or polished finishes. It can be used with the original connector or in one-wire mode. (Photo Courtesy Powermaster Performance)

Sean Hyland Motorsport has developed an alternator relocation kit for the Coyote that moves the alternator to the passenger's side to get it away from the lower frame rail. The kit is available in 3-bolt or 4-bolt versions (PN SHM-212-3 and PN SHM-212-4) and it works with its A/C and power steering pump add-on kits. (Photo Courtesy Sean Hyland Motorsport)

alternator (true one-wire operation) reports only what is happening at the alternator. Sensing remotely can reveal voltage drops in the wiring and give a more accurate picture of the electrical load use on the electrical system. Some aftermarket wiring harness manufacturers run the remote line back around to the pin at the alternator, eliminating the remote sensing. I have installed many one-wire alternators with new wiring and have not experienced any problems. Keep in mind that you don't want to necessarily push more current through a poorly operating harness. That can make the electrical system unstable and unsafe as components tend to fry if overloaded. Prep your electrical system properly with good grounds, good wiring, and a proper voltage gauge that senses through a remote line. You should not have any problems with one-wire alternators.

PowerMaster has a full line of alternators for all the modular engine platforms, and most are one-wire installation. Tough Stuff also makes alternators for early modular engines, with some having the ability to work with a factory charge lamp.

Air Conditioning

The air-conditioning equipment frequently contributes to an engine fitment or packaging problem when modular engines are swapped into classic cars. In addition, the air-conditioning system adds weight, so some owners decide not to transplant the A/C system. Eliminating the air conditioning requires brackets similar to those used for pushrod-style conversions with serpentine belts. Custom brackets are now available for running a hydraulic power-steering pump with the A/C on Coyote engines (see Chapter 3).

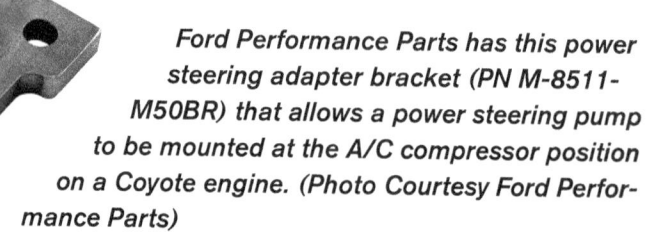

Ford Performance Parts has this power steering adapter bracket (PN M-8511-M50BR) that allows a power steering pump to be mounted at the A/C compressor position on a Coyote engine. (Photo Courtesy Ford Performance Parts)

Vintage Air sells a front runner accessory drive system (PN 174020) for the Coyote engine that combines the mounts for the air compressor and power steering pump all in one package. It uses a Sanden compressor pump and a Delphi-Saginaw power steering pump with a remote reservoir.

JMS sells a conversion bracket to mount an air conditioner compressor from a 1996–2001 Mustang GT onto a Coyote (PN AC9610W50). (Photo Courtesy JMS Performance)

COOLING, IGNITION AND ENGINE SYSTEMS

Instrumentation

Late-model Ford instrumentation is extremely integrated and is incorporated with the PATS system. While it is possible to run late-model gauge clusters in earlier vehicles, it is very costly compared to adapting original or converting to aftermarket. Depending upon the computer system selected, a light to denote check engine/error code should be mounted somewhere in the instrument cluster.

AutoMeter sells a tach adapter (PN 9117) that allows the tach signal from a distributorless ignition system to operate with a standard tachometer. It connects directly from the pulse signal of the crankshaft pickup and converts the signal into a standard square wave for your tach. (Photo Courtesy AutoMeter)

MSD sells a mini inductance pickup (PN 8918) that picks up the signal from one of the coils on the engine and converts it into a square wave pulse for the tachometer. This keeps you from having to splice into other signals for a tach pickup.

Aftermarket gauges may be the cheapest alternative in an engine swap; buying converters to make older gauges work or adapting the integrated instrument cluster can both be costly. Here's a full set of AutoMeter Pro-Comp gauges set up for a digital speedometer and standard tachometer. This aftermarket gauge cluster from Year One (PN APD697) allows for two additional gauges in a 1969–1970 Mustang and features a custom aluminum finish by Dave Stribling Restorations.

Swap Spotlight: 1952 International Pickup

Korek Design custom mixed the metallic cherry paint that adorns this 1952 International pickup, and it did one other thing to make this unconventional truck even more unconventional: It stepped away from the LS conversion crowd and gave this truck Coyote power under the hood. (Photo Courtesy Korek Design)

Most modular engines have been swapped into Ford vehicles. Chevy LS and small-block-based conversions have been the fashion for many decades, and it leaves a bad taste in the mouths of Ford purists. But that trend is going away. The LS swap is slowly losing ground to the modular engine swap for one really big reason: the modular engine looks so much better. This truck takes the good-looking modular engine swap to a whole different level, and it isn't a Ford chassis.

Korek Designs in New Berlin, Pennsylvania, built the 1952 International truck and highlights just how beautiful the engine compartment is with the right conversion. Ryan Korek and his crew have built everything from show-winning numbers-matching muscle cars to high-end NHRA dragsters, and its design and build efforts are phenomenal.

This 1952 showed up at the shop in pretty tired condition, so the group got to work massaging every panel on the car in preparation for installation on a full Art Morrison chassis conversion. The chassis came ready to roll and required only Strange Engineering coil-overs and massive Wilwood 13-inch brakes at all four corners. The fuel tank was custom fabricated out of aluminum, with a Tanks Inc. fuel pump mounted in the tank.

Head fabricator Joe Kahl fabricated the engine and transmission mounts and set the 5.0 Coyote down in the engine bay, then installed the cab and doghouse and began fitting the remaining parts. Engine mounts were made from flat steel, and a Trans-Dapt mount was modified to use with the new chassis. Joe reports that with the body chassis combination no real challenges to making it all work. However, it also custom fabricated everything in house, which makes things much easier.

The intake is a Boss 302 unit that has been heavily modified to match the styling cues under the hood. Both the intake and engine covers were custom reworked with an "International" flavor. The intake tube was also custom-made to fit the chassis. A Ford Control Pack computer was used to operate the engine. The engine is connected to a Magnum

With custom engine covers and matching paint scheme, the Coyote crate engine looks right at home in the bay of the truck. The intake is a Boss 302 and the intake tube was custom-built. (Photo Courtesy Korek Design)

T-56 6-speed transmission, which sends power back to the Strange Engineering 9-inch rear fitted with 31 spline axles and 4:11 gearing.

The interior of the truck is full custom, with the dash being lower by 1½ inches and made to flow into the doors. The instrument cluster is equipped with a full set of Dakota Digital gauges, and an ididit tilt steering column is topped off with a steering wheel from a 1965 Avanti. Tracey Weaver, with Recovery Room Hot Rod interiors in Plattesmouth, Nebraska, custom-made the console and built the interior.

Ryan also mixed a one-off PPG metallic cherry color for the outside and then adorned the truck with a set of Foose 20-inch rims in the rear and 18-inch rims up front. The exhaust exits out the sides of the rear bed, and the taillights were embedded in the rear bumper. There are simply too many custom touches on this car to list.

Above all is the stunning work done to the Coyote engine to set this engine compartment off from all the other conversions out there, and it demonstrates why the modular engine is beginning to overtake other conversions on the street rod scene. In the hands of Korek Designs, it is taken to a whole new level.

This early-phase design shows the engine mount made to use the Coyote vertical engine mounts. Note that the Coyote engine has an additional mounting hole on the side, and earlier modular engines are missing the lower back hole. (Photo Courtesy Korek Design)

Here's those beautiful engine panels being fabricated. The Boss intake gets a topper as well as a wraparound to cover the injectors. Little touches show everywhere on this build; note the International logo on the hood hinge far right. (Photo Courtesy Korek Design)

The custom-made T-56 transmission mount was installed, and this shot shows the mounting of the Wilwood brake cylinder under the cab. An Aeromotive fuel pressure regulator is mounted to the fully boxed frame, and a Mustang II suspension was used up front. (Photo Courtesy Korek Design)

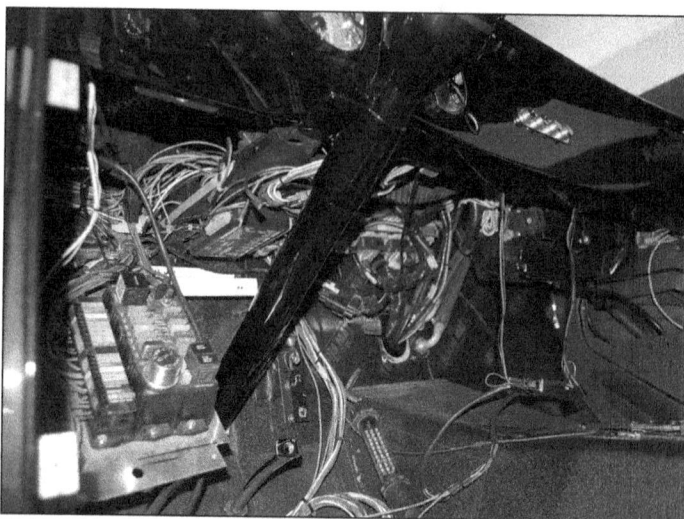

A Ford Control Pack computer was used to drive the crate engine, and this was integrated with the American Autowire Hot Rod wiring harness. (Photo Courtesy Korek Design)

This shot shows the cutback into the firewall necessary to fit the engine to the cab. The firewall was smoothed to match the engine compartment inner panels. A Ford 9-inch rounds out the suspension for this truck. (Photo Courtesy Korek Design)

The custom dash blends flawlessly with the doors, and the Recovery Room Hot Rod Interiors finished out the look of the inside to match the beast hiding under the hood. (Photo Courtesy Korek Design)

CHAPTER 8

TRANSMISSION AND DRIVETRAIN

The transmission is a major factor to consider when converting to modern drivetrain components. In particular, you must determine fitment in the transmission tunnel and shifter location. Modern transmissions, with their additional gears and capabilities, are considerably larger than their older counterparts, and there are many horror stories of chopped transmission tunnels to make the driveline fit.

The position of the engine is a big factor in determining the location and compatibility of the transmission. If an engine uses tall engine mounts, is pressed rearward, or is offset to clear components it will greatly affect the relationship of the transmission tunnel and the transmission. The bigger transmissions with extra gears do not want to fit in the early transmission tunnels.

The use of off-the-shelf components will limit your options for positioning the driveline to those designated by the vendor. With builds that start from scratch, the engine and transmission can be set for an optimum height and clearance in the tunnel.

Most street rod builders start with the chassis sitting on the correct wheels and tires, with the rear axle and front suspension set at the correct ride height. From there, the placement of the engine and transmission can be moved to clear the tunnel, as well as other components such as steering, suspension components, and ground clearance. Carbureted engines generally have a 3-degree drop at the back when installed. Looking at the carburetor flange on an old intake, the

The Tremec TR-3160 sits behind the Shelby GT350. It has been extensively modified to handle the 526 hp and 429 ft-lbs of torque from the 5.2 and massaged to work with the harmonics of the flat-plane crank. (Photo Courtesy Ford Performance Parts)

carburetor plate is machined so the carburetor is horizontal when the engine is sitting at 3 degrees. As a result, the engine is at the proper position for the ideal U-joint angles to the driveshaft. The U-joint should not operate in a straight line because the harmonics through the shaft may cause premature failure. The engine and rear-axle pinion angle need a couple of degrees offset to allow the joints to operate properly.

Many builders have claimed that the transmission tunnel on an early 1965–1970 Mustang requires modification to install big transmissions such as the T-56 6-speed. It may be possible, however, to fit the big transmissions by setting the proper ride height, pinion angle, and engine position.

On many Ford installations, the engine is offset to the passenger's side by about 2 inches. This is to allow for clearance on the driver's side for steering and other components. This may cause clearance issues on a chassis where the engine is designed to run down the middle. Four-wheel-drive adapters can also cause clearance issues.

Modern Ford cars offset the engine 2 inches to the passenger's side to aid in steering gear and shafts clearance. When the engine is placed down the middle of the tunnel, no modifications to the tunnel are needed for transmissions such as this 4R70W in a 1970 Mustang.

There is some good news. Because the modular engine bellhousing hasn't changed (with two very early exceptions; see Chapter 2), a full range of manuals and automatics are available for the conversion. Everything from modern 6-speeds to conversions to vintage 4-speeds and non-overdrive automatics are available. Yes, it is possible to mount a Ford Toploader behind a Coyote or even a race-prepped C4 small-block automatic.

Engine placement has a great influence on how the transmission fits into the tunnel. The engine here was placed against the firewall for supercharger snout clearance, so this Mustang's transmission tunnel reinforcement had to be trimmed for clearance of the T-56 6-speed. If the engine had been 1 inch forward no changes would have been needed.

Factory Manual Transmissions

Factory manual transmissions used behind the modular engine all have internal shift rails, as opposed to the external rods used on transmissions such as the Ford Toploader. Starting in 2005, the shifter used in Mustangs was a semi-external setup, eliminating the longer shifter rail. This can cause some difficulties with some conversions, as most aftermarket shifters are designed for the Mustang chassis.

In 1999 Ford started using a Vehicle Speed Sensor (VSS), sometimes referred to as the Output Speed Sensor (OSS) in place of a mechanical speedometer cable and gear to measure the speed of the vehicle. The speed sensor information is sent to the PCM and then is sent to the gauge cluster and the speed control servo.

On some Tremec 6-speeds, an electronic reverse lockout was used to prevent shifting into reverse, depending on the shift pattern. The reverse lockout is controlled by the

TRANSMISSION AND DRIVETRAIN

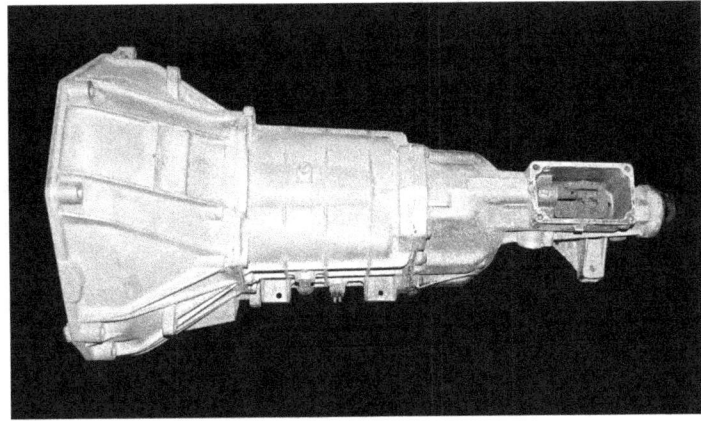

The first 5-speed to be installed in a Mustang was the Tremec T-45. The T-45 was not very durable and suffered from several recalls for gears and fork issues.

The Tremec T-3650 replaced the T-45 in 2001 and was a good transmission behind the 2005–2009 3V GT engine and the earlier non-supercharged 2V and 4V Mustangs. It is easily identified by its boxier shape compared to the T-45.

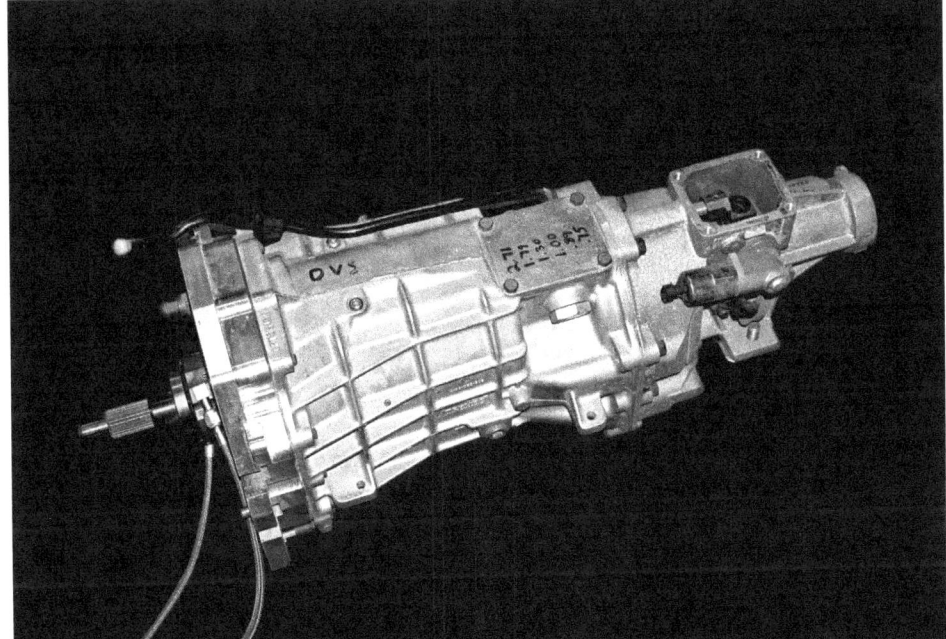

The T-56 first saw use in the 2000 Cobra R and was standard in the 2003–2004 Cobras. The T-56 is a very strong transmission and can be built to handle enormous horsepower. The cylinder mounted on the side of the shifter box is the reverse lockout solenoid.

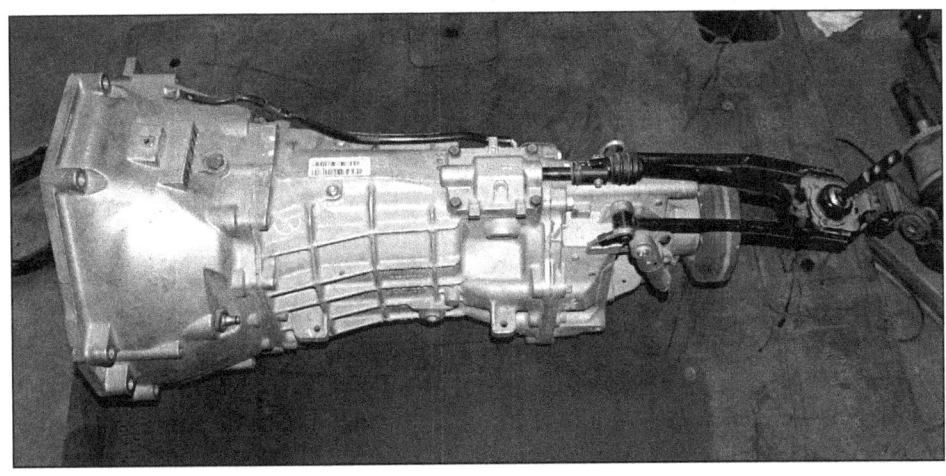

Ford used the T-6060 behind the Shelby GT500 supercharged engines. The 6060 used T-56 technology with improved internals. Note the external shifter and rod to fit the 2005–2010 chassis. This transmission is also set up for a hydraulic throw-out bearing.

CHAPTER 8

PCM, and if the computer senses that the car is in motion, it locks out the ability to place the transmission in reverse. The MT-82 reverted back to a mechanical reverse lockout system.

Most pre-2011 transmissions have the same length input shaft. The MT-82 has a different length shaft, but the bellhousing arrangement makes them interchangeable.

Aftermarket Manual Transmissions

Yes, it is possible to install a Ford Toploader behind a modular engine, and if you have no need for the overdrive or are doing a nostalgic build it might be the right choice. The newest transmissions from Tremec can handle enormous amounts of power and torque, are comparable in weight (aluminum versus cast-iron housings), and have overdrive capabilities. The much narrower Toploader may fit in certain tunnels without major modifications, but also has external shifter linkage that can cause an obstruction. It can be done, but you need to weigh all the factors before deciding. If you decide to install a classic transmission with your build, you need to determine your application and performance target. Also note that this same bellhousing is also used to install Muncie- and Richmond-style racing transmissions, so if your racing class calls for one of these transmissions, it can happen. If you have decided on a Toploader, you need to refer to the bellhousing section to see how to mate the transmission to the modern engine. One of the advantages to using an aftermarket transmission is the multiple mounting locations for the shifter, allowing the transmission to be adapted to the chassis.

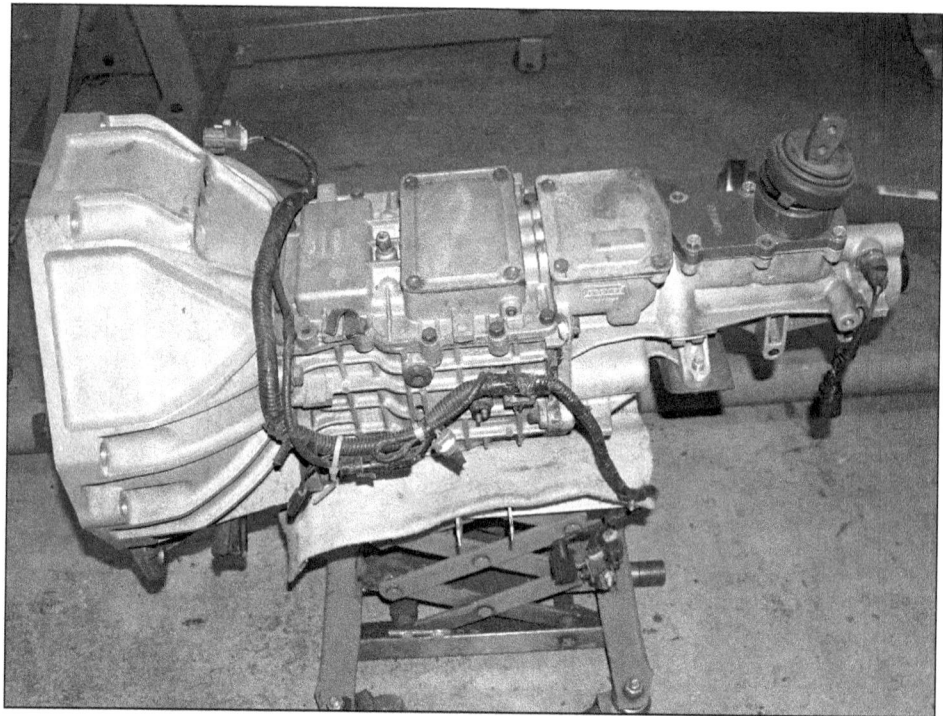

The Tremec 3550 and TKO 5-speeds are still an excellent choice for a transmission swap due to their compact size and ability to handle large power numbers. They are frequently used in cars such as the Factory Five roadsters where space is a premium.

Most owners opt for a Tremec T-56 or T-56 Magnum conversion because these are durable and have an overall excellent design. Modern Driveline sells the Tremec transmission in a variety of arrangements, tailshaft outputs, and shifter positions, and it has T-56 kits to fit almost any chassis.

TRANSMISSION AND DRIVETRAIN

Factory Automatic Transmissions

All automatic transmissions on modular engines are overdrive, and most are electronically controlled. Through the years, Ford has improved the shifting and torque converters to improve mileage and performance. As with the manual transmissions, Ford began using an electronic pickup rather than a speedometer cable in 1999.

Ford overdrive transmissions allow turning off the overdrive circuit in the transmission. Most systems use a normally open on-off switch to disengage the overdrive circuit. When running an older AOD, there is no provision for the TV cable used in the older transmission to adjust the pressure. When using a drive-by-wire engine setup, it is better to use a computer-controlled pressure system.

The AOD, AODE, and 4R40W transmissions were derived from the FMX transmission and have been developed to be reliable automatics with a minimum footprint. The AOD was a popular conversion before the modular engine, so parts to install it in many chassis already exist. The 4R70W is a sturdy platform in stock form. (Photo Courtesy Sean Hyland Motorsport)

Aftermarket Automatic Transmissions

The aftermarket has vast experience with some of the older automatic overdrives used behind the modular engine. The AOD and 4R70W 4-speed automatics have been very popular with not only the early modular engine drag racers, but really found a base following with the last of the pushrod Mustang racers. Companies such as Lentech and TCI have developed the 4R70W to handle drag racing amounts of horsepower, and its smaller size over the 5- and 6-speed automatics make it a good choice when tunnel space is at a premium. It is also possible to run a C4 non-overdrive automatic, as the components have been developed by Performance Automatic. While losing the advantages of the overdrive

The 5R55E used until 2010 was developed from the 4R series and adds an extra gear. The case became larger as more gears were added. This one is from a 2008 Mustang 4 3V.

for a street car, it is a compact unit that, built correctly, will last forever.

Transmission Crossmembers and Designs

The transmission mount hasn't changed much over the years. In fact, the original rubber bushing from the 1960s Mustangs and other Ford cars still bolts to many of the modern transmissions. The crossmember has changed considerably, depending on model and year of the vehicle. For the more popular conversions there are off-the-shelf

HOW TO SWAP FORD MODULAR ENGINES INTO MUSTANGS, TORINOS AND MORE

Performance Automatics has a full line of Ford automatics with improved clutches and bands, and hydraulic circuit modifications to make these transmissions drive better and handle serious horsepower. Deep pans and other options are available. Shown is the 5R55S 5-speed (PN PA27101). (Photo Courtesy Performance Automatic)

If you are looking for a super compact transmission that can be built to high-horsepower for drag race or similar application, Performance Automatics has its Street Smart C4 conversion kit for Coyote applications (PN PASS26107 for street, PASS26108 for drag trim). This company has been building C4s for more than 35 years; these transmissions can handle big power. (Photo Courtesy Performance Automatics)

LenTech Automatics is one of the early pioneers to make AOD/AODE/4R70W automatic 4-speeds that are track and street capable. It has since developed a line of parts to take these transmissions to trouble-free heights. The example shown here (PN 7000-4R70-STR) is rated to 1,500 hp and includes the custom-made valve body. (Photo Courtesy LenTech Automatics)

TCI now offers a performance version of the 6R80 6-speed transmission (PN 271701P7). It includes the 6-speed transmission, the TCI-EZ TCU transmission controller, a cooler, and a flexplate for 8-bolt applications. Note also the transmission comes with a genuine dipstick to check the fluid. (Photo Courtesy TCI Automotive)

Automatic Transmission Controls

Considerable credit for the increase in fuel efficiency in newer cars can be attributed to the newer automatic transmissions and how the computer controls the operation of the transmission. Here are a few of the acronyms used with the newer automatics (not all are used in every automatic):

Digital Transmission Range (DTR)

Tells the PCM and transmission which gear is selected and provides signal for the reverse lamps and safety neutral switch.

Electronic Pressure Control (EPC)

Adjusts the pressure in the transmission under load conditions so pressure moves through the transmission more effectively.

Intermediate Shaft Sensor (ISS)

Starting with the 5R55 5-speed, the ISS is used to aid the PCM in adjusting the pressure inside the transmission.

Line Pressure Control (LPC)

This solenoid adjusts the pressure to the main regulator valve.

Shift Solenoid (SSA through E, or SS1 through 5)

Depending on the gear, the PCM engages the solenoids to shift the transmission. As many as five shift solenoids are used, depending on the transmission. The solenoids are marked with a letter or a number.

Torque Converter Clutch (TCC)

This solenoid controls the pressure to the torque converter clutch. It controls when the clutch locks up and slipping (or stall).

Transmission Fluid Temperature (TFT)

This is a resistor-style sensor that measures the temperature of the fluid. The computer uses this data to adjust the TCC and other systems when the fluid is cold and monitors if the fluid gets too hot.

TR1, 2, 3A and 4

These signal lines tell the PCM which gear has been selected (through the DTR). 3A is an analog signal, not digital. The analog signal allows the PCM to detect if a fault occurs in either the DTR switch or the signal line to the DTR.

Turbine Shaft Speed (TSS)

This sensor monitors the forward clutches to help determine which gear to select, shifting points, and converter operations.

solutions for the crossmember. Dave Stribling Restorations sells a universal crossmember that adjusts up to 6 inches in three axis for installation into 1967–1970 Mustangs. Ron Morris Performance manufactures a crossmember that takes advantage of the inner frame rail extensions and is fully adjustable for T-56 installations in the early cars. Stifflers makes a bolt-in crossmember for conversions into Fox-body platforms, and Schrader Performance has a crossmember to mount the 6R80 transmission in earlier vehicles.

Aftermarket Controllers

Except for the very first transmissions, the PCM controls all automatics and the circuit used is called the TCU (Transmission Control Unit). If the engine computer cannot control the transmission, or the engine doesn't use a computer at all (carburetor), several transmission controllers are available to operate the transmission.

If there is a mismatch of speedometer output devices (mechanical speedometer and a digital VSS, or the inverse), converters are available to make the parts work together.

Shifters

Manual transmissions are all shifted internally and automatics are all cable-operated. The semi-external

Stifflers Chassis and Suspension has a full line of transmission crossmembers to mount late-model transmissions into the Fox-body Mustang. This example (PN TCB-M02) mounts the T-45, T-56, T-56 Magnum, TR-3650, or TH-400 into the 1982–1993 Fox-body Mustangs. (Photo Courtesy Stifflers Chassis and Suspension)

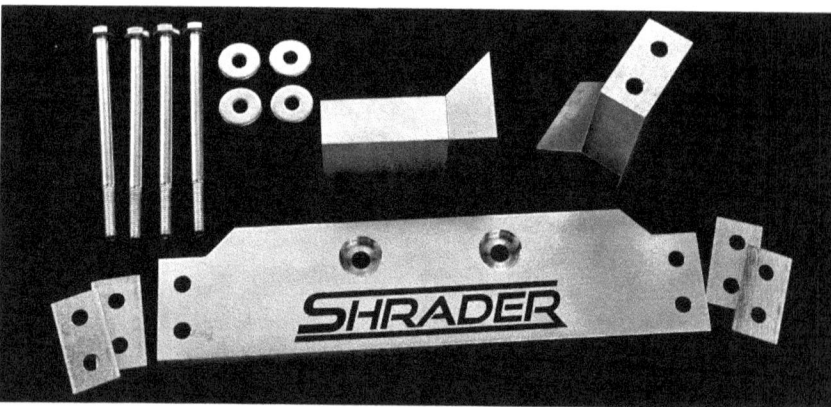

Shrader Performance sells a transmission crossmember to install the 6R80 and Getrag MT82 6-speeds into the 1999–2004 SN-95 Mustangs, but its modular design may allow it to be modified to fit other chassis. It uses the 2011–2014 3-bolt isolator and its narrow design may help with some X-pipe installations. (Photo Courtesy Shrader Performance)

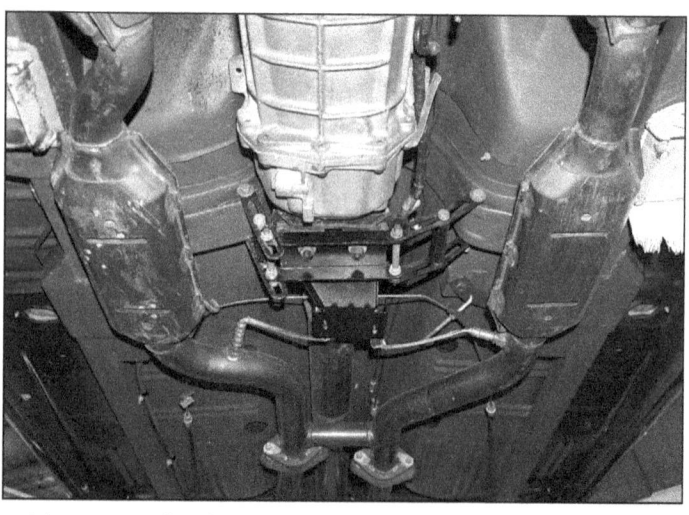

Dave Stribling Restorations has a fully adjustable crossmember to fit 1967–1970 Mustangs and Cougars, and it can be modified to work in 1965–1966 Mustangs. The UTC crossmember fits most transmissions that used the old-style rubber mounting bushing. Fully adjustable in three axis by up to 6 inches, it can help when setting the proper drivetrain angle and making room for exhaust.

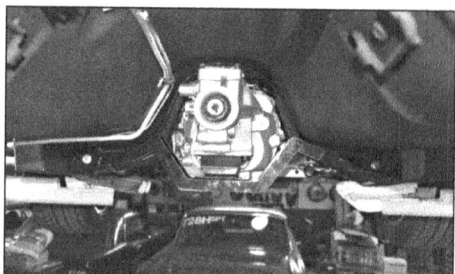

Ron Morris Performance makes a T-56 transmission crossmember for 1965–1973 Mustangs that is fully adjustable and mounts to the inner frame rail extensions, and it is custom designed for maximum exhaust clearance. (Photo Courtesy Ron Morris Performance)

TRANSMISSION AND DRIVETRAIN

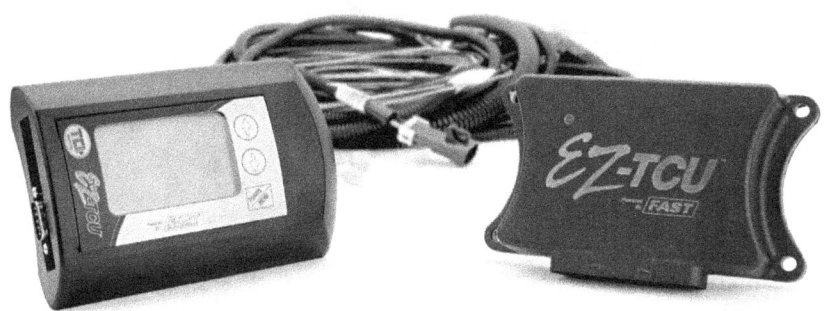

TCI now makes its EC-TCU transmission controller available to work with the 6-speed Ford transmissions. It comes ready to go right out of the box with no setup required and is self-contained and fully programmable through the handheld control unit. (Photo Courtesy TCI Automotive)

shifters on the 2005-and-newer Mustang make conversion difficult, but many shifters are available for all the modern transmissions.

Flywheels, Clutches and Pilot Bearings

All modular engines use a zero-balance flywheel or flexplate from the factory as well as 164-tooth ring gears. Depending on the assembly plant, the flywheel has either a 6-bolt (Windsor) or 8-bolt (Romeo)

Dakota digital has a converter to convert an electronic speedometer output signal back to a mechanical speedometer signal. ECD-100 works with Ford and GM cables and uses a remotely mounted switch to calibrate the speedometer using industry standard "measured mile" and GPS calibration methods. (Photo Courtesy Dakota Digital)

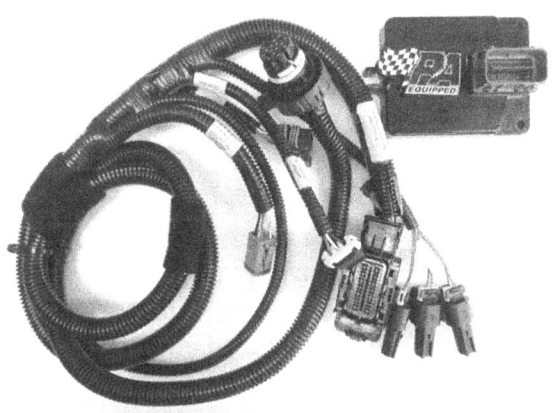

Performance Automatic makes a transmission controller including one for the 2011–2014 6R80 6-speed automatic for Coyote applications (PN PA99142). It comes complete with a harness, and the Street Smart controller requires no computer connection to make adjustments. (Photo Courtesy Performance Automatic)

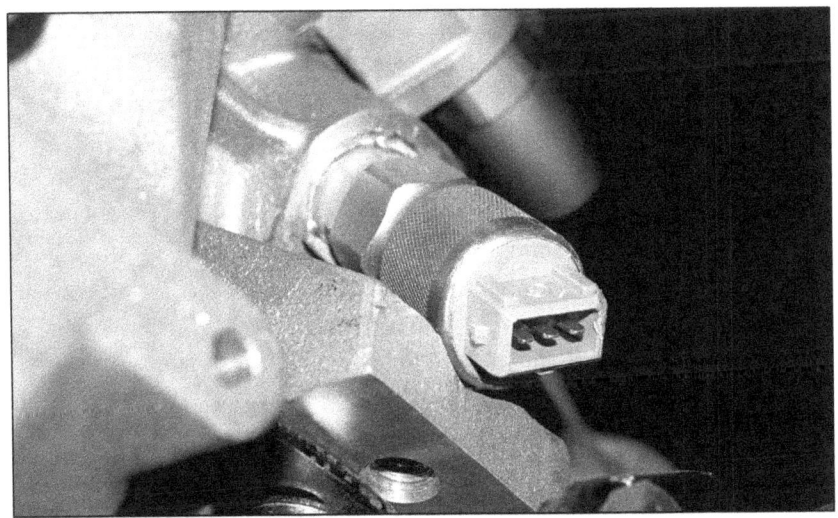

Several styles of pulse generators are available for converting mechanical speedometer motion into a digital signal for electronic speedometers. This Classic Industries example (PN SN16) generates a clean pulse from most newer Ford transmissions.

HOW TO SWAP FORD MODULAR ENGINES INTO MUSTANGS, TORINOS AND MORE   115

bolt pattern. Ford factory clutches came in either 10.5 inch or 11 inch, depending on the application.

Since the Y-block days, or Stone Age in manufacturing time, Ford has used a .67-inch pilot shaft on the Ford transmissions (with the exception of some early 6- and 4-cylinder applications). Ford originally used an oillight bronze bushing, then went to a needle bearing system, and the new heavy-duty bearings are once again a bushing (aids with some minor imperfections with corroded input shafts that might damage roller bearings).

Modern Driveline also offers this offset solution for the Tremec transmission. The offset shifter brings the shifter to the driver's side of the transmission and can be mounted in either the front position (shown) or the rear to fit your chassis. (Photo Courtesy Modern Driveline)

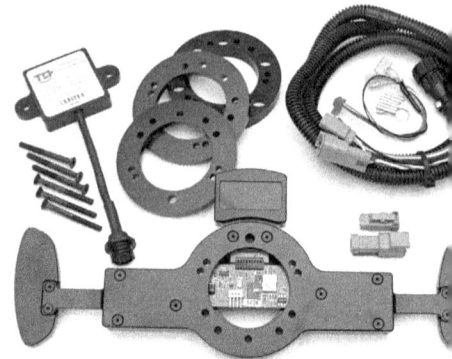

With electronic controls of the transmissions, cool, tech-like paddle shifters are now available for custom installations. This is the TCI paddle shifter (PN 301442) that works directly with the EZ-TCU transmission controller. The display shows the current gear and it works with aftermarket 5- or 6-bolt steering wheels. (Photo Courtesy TCI Automotive)

Modern Driveline has shifter solutions from stock-looking to modern, and it has a full line of shifters that adapt to many different chassis combinations. This Quick Stik shifter (PN MD-83-421-204-02) fits the TKO 5-speeds and allows the shifter to be mounted in either the front or the rear position of the shifter box. A 1-inch offset allows fine tuning of the final shifter position to the chassis shifter opening. (Photo Courtesy Modern Driveline)

Bellhousing and Adapters

Because all modular engines have the same bellhousing bolt pattern (except for the very first AOD and front-wheel-drive models, see Chapter 3), the supply of bellhousings available to mount just about any transmission available is surprisingly nice. The biggest and most popular conversion is for a T-56 6-speed. QuickTime makes a bellhousing (PN RM-8080) that works with the factory fork or with a hydraulic throw-out bearing and fits all modular engine platforms. Next would be for the Tremec TKO transmissions, for their

TCI's Outlaw Blackout shifter is available for most Ford transmissions, including the new 6-speed. It is NHRA/IHRA approved for reverse lockout function and can be fitted with optional handle-mounted buttons to control items such as line locks, trans brakes, or nitrous. (Photo Courtesy TCI Automotive)

TRANSMISSION AND DRIVETRAIN

Ford Performance Parts offers multiple flywheels for modular engines made of aluminum, billet steel, and nodular iron. This is a billet-steel flywheel for 8-bolt applications on 4.6 and 5.0 engines (PN M-6375-M50). (Photo Courtesy Ford Performance Parts)

Clutch assemblies for the modular engines abound, so you should be able to find the clutch/pressure plate combination you need. This Centerforce Dual Friction clutch kit is for a 2003 Cobra Terminator (PN DF-148075).

durability and ability to take abuse. QuickTime sells bellhousings with and without a clutch fork provision. Although the 4R70W is plentiful for the modular engine, a conversion kit is available from Performance Automatics, LenTech, and QuickTime.

Clutch Actuation

Ford has used both cable and hydraulics to operate the throw-out bearing on the late-model manual transmissions. Some of the later-model transmissions do not have provisions for a clutch fork. In fact, Ford dropped the clutch fork in 2005 and went to a hydraulic throw-out bearing in the Mustang. A cable-style clutch was installed in the SN-95 Mustangs and a large eccentric mounted under the dash that can conflict with other components in a conversion. Modern Driveline has solutions for both hydraulic and cable actuation of the clutch.

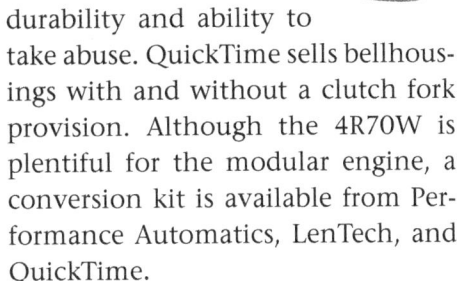

QuickTime bellhousings has a full line of bellhousings for both manual and automatic conversions. It has solutions for new and old transmission, such as this bellhousing for a modular engine equipped with a T-56 6-speed (PN RM-8080). (Photo Courtesy QuickTime)

The GM TH-350 automatic remains a popular racing transmission, and yes, you can install one behind a modular engine. J.W. Performance Transmissions sells a version (PN 92462-46TH) designed to install behind a modular engine. It is made from cast aluminum and is five times stronger than the original. (Photo Courtesy J.W. Performance Transmissions)

This lightweight, aluminum Centerforce flywheel has a steel insert and for use with 11-inch clutches installed behind 4.6 DOHC engines. The flywheel (PN 900205) weighs only 12.7 pounds and is for 8-bolt applications.

HOW TO SWAP FORD MODULAR ENGINES INTO MUSTANGS, TORINOS AND MORE

CHAPTER 8

Older Toploaders have the same mount pattern as the Tremec TKO, so you could use a QuickTime bellhousing (PN RM-6080) for these transmissions to fit the Toploader. You would probably need to use a hydraulic throwout bearing because the clutch fork arrangement is different. A bellhousing for Muncie/Jerico transmissions is also available (PN RM-6082). (Photo Courtesy QuickTime)

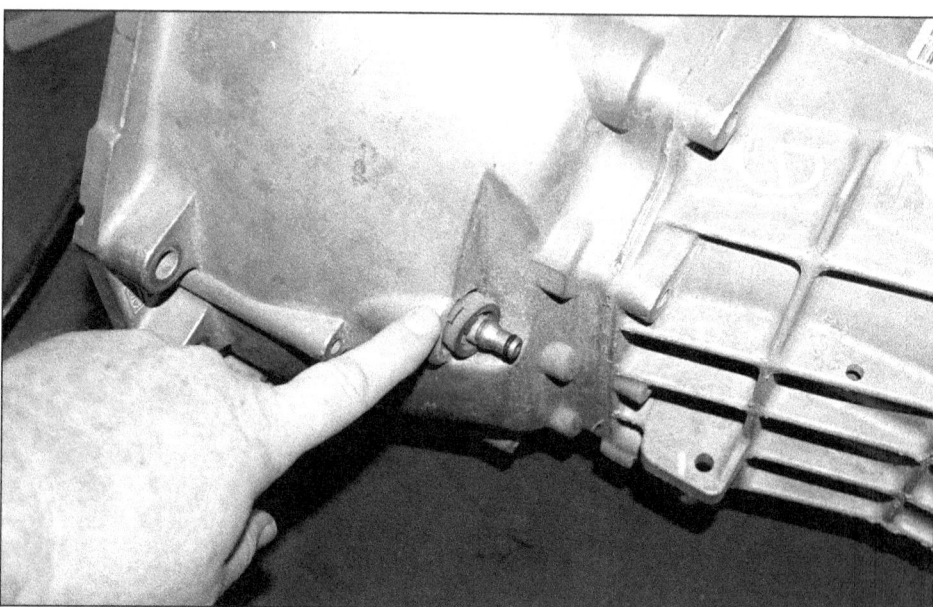

The hydraulic throwout bearing, which Ford began using in 2005, allowed Ford to close off the bellhousing and run a hydraulic fitting to the driver's side of the bellhousing. This setup is from a T-6060 transmission.

Converting to a hydraulic throw-out bearing eliminates under-dash clutter and line-of-sight issues with cable and additional slaves cylinders. A throw-out bearing such as Modern Drivelines part MD-900-2506 for the T-56 is fully self-adjusting and with line extensions can get around header clearance issues without affecting performance. Consider eliminating all the mechanical clutch release designs and look at installing a hydraulic throw-out bearing used since 2005.

Driveshafts

Ford installed a two-piece driveshaft in many applications, such as Super Duty trucks and full-size vans prior to 2005, but in 2005, it

Modern Driveline makes a full line of hydraulic conversion components for your project. This kit (PN MD-910-1002) bolts to the side of a T-5 or TKO aluminum bellhousing and allows for a conversion of the original clutch fork over to hydraulic actuation.

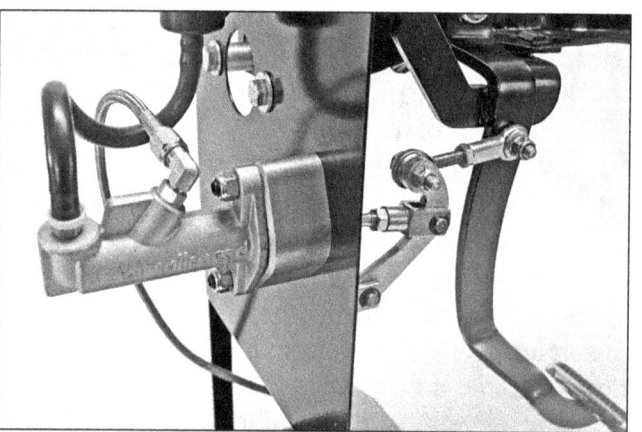

Modern Driveline's LF series of hydraulic clutch conversions is available for early Mustangs, Cougars, Falcons, Comets, Fairlanes, Mavericks, Granadas, 60s, F-100 pickups, and Fox-body Mustangs. The pedal adapter has been engineered to provide the exact ratio needed for the clutch master cylinder. This is kit MD-910-0002 for 1965–1966 Mustangs. (Photo Courtesy Modern Driveline)

began installing two-piece driveshafts in Mustangs for resonance compliance. These two-piece driveshafts allow for high-RPM stability and eliminate resonance that can destroy the driveshaft. This style of driveshaft has a central bearing and uses CV joints instead of a U-joint on the rear-axle side. At the rear-axle end, a damper is installed to absorb axle vibration and attenuation. Most modular engine conversions use a one-piece driveshaft due to cost, and your late-model engine doesn't require the two-piece unit.

Primary materials for the driveshaft are steel, aluminum, and carbon fiber. Steel DOM driveshafts are the most common and the lowest cost. Aluminum driveshafts are now used in most factory installations due to their light weight and reduction in reciprocating weight. Carbon fiber is the lightweight king and is very strong, but is the most expensive to build. Companies such as the Driveshaft Shop and Dynotech Engineering can help you design the right shaft for your project. Most local shops can build you a nice driveshaft with off-the-shelf parts for most projects, but as you get into higher horsepower and exotic materials, it is better to seek out companies that have real experience making these shafts. Building a shaft out of carbon fiber is completely different from welding up DOM, and I have seen a lot of shaft failures because of inexperience. Seek out a reliable builder for the more exotic shafts.

McLeod Racing sells hydraulic throwout bearings for all popular Ford transmissions and offers complete kits for some conversions. This is the 1300-series bearing (PN 1302) for T-5 and T-56 applications in a bolt-on style. (Photo Courtesy McLeod Racing)

Modern Driveline uses race-proven Tilton throwout bearings in its conversion kits. This example (PN MD-900-2506) for Magnum T-56 applications is a slip-on design with a centering bolt to connect to the input shaft collar. (Photo Courtesy Modern Driveline)

This typical late-model two-piece driveshaft shows the center bearing. The center bearing helps to improve high-speed vibration issues with solid rear axles. Most applications don't require this center bearing.

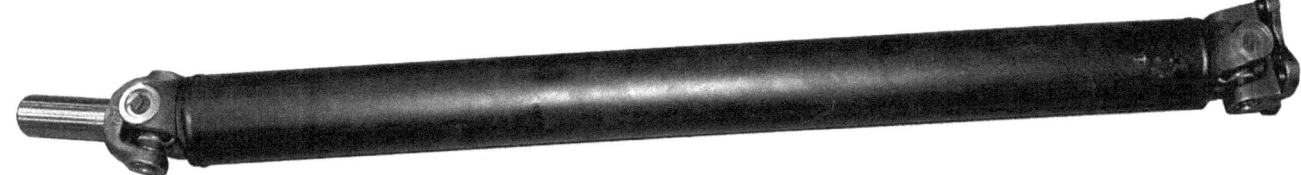

This driveshaft was made by a local fabricator to fit an early truck with a Magnum T-56 mated to a 2003 Cobra IRS conversion. It was made with DOM steel, and all the parts to build it were off the shelf.

CHAPTER 8

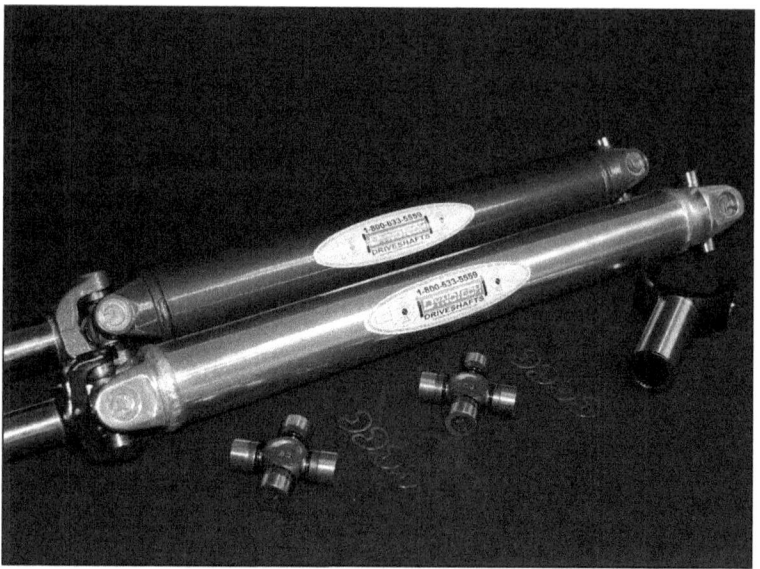

Dynotech custom fabricates any driveshaft from steel, DOM steel, aluminum, or carbon fiber to any specified length. It can also make two-piece driveshafts with a center bearing if your project requires one.

Ford uses three primary U-joints: 1310 (left), 1330 (right), and 1350 (not shown). Most applications call for a 1310 or 1330, with trucks and high-performance applications using the bigger joint. Note that the 1330 joint has a grease fitting and the 1310 does not. The grease fitting has been known to crack under heavy load, so it is recommended to use joints without the fitting in performance applications.

How to Measure for a Driveshaft

Most drivetrain swaps require a custom-length driveshaft. The variation of the driveshaft design in late-model vehicles has made the measuring process a little difficult. Here is what the driveshaft builder needs to know to fabricate the correct driveshaft. Remember that you may have a driveshaft with a combination of different ends, and note that this procedure is for one-piece driveshafts. If the build requires a two-piece driveshaft similar to late models, you need to provide information on the position and size of the center bearing.

The first step in the procedure is to make sure the vehicle is at ride height. The suspension should be fully loaded with the weight of the car. If the car is not finished, the alignment of the engine/transmission and rear suspension must be as if the car is complete and sitting on all fours. Next, you need to measure the overall length of the driveshaft. If the transmission uses an input yoke and not a flange, measure from the end of the transmission case. Take this measurement from the very end of the transmission extension housing, not the rubber seal. If the transmission has a flange on the output shaft, measure from the face of the flange.

If the input shaft to the rear axle is a yoke style, measure from the gap in the flat area of the saddle. If the rear axle uses a flange, measure from the front face of the flange.

If the transmission uses a flange that is bolted to the end of the output shaft, measure from the face of the flange.

At this stage, you need to measure the transmission output shaft. If the output shaft has a splined shaft that protrudes from the transmission extension housing, use a tape measure and measure this distance. It may be necessary to push back the rubber seal to expose the shaft. Count the number of splines on the shaft. Finally, note if the shaft has been machined for a thread on the end of the shaft.

For transmissions equipped with a flange, measure the diameter of the bolt-mounting holes, and note how many mounting holes are in the flange. Measure the diameter of the pilot centering hole or shoulder.

Then, you need to measure the rear-axle input shaft. If the rear axle uses a yoke-style pinion, check to see if there are locating tabs to hold the U-joint in place. If there are tabs, measure the distance between the tabs. If the input pinion uses U-bolts and does not have locating tabs, measure the distance between the U-joint saddles. Measure the width of the U-joint saddle mount at the flat of the saddle.

If the rear pinion uses a flange, measure the mounting bolt circle diameter and note the number of mounting holes in the flange. Measure the pilot hole or shoulder, if equipped.

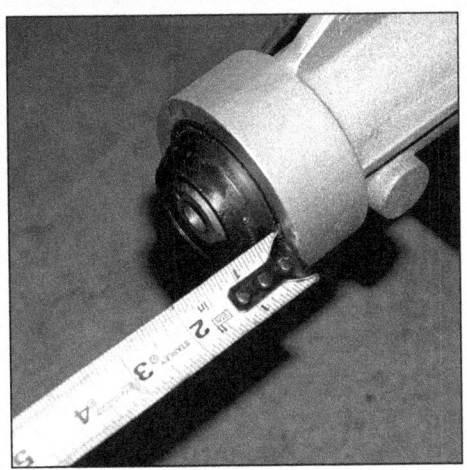

If the transmission has a splined output shaft, overall measurement should be made from the end of the transmission case.

If the transmission has a flanged output shaft, measure from the face of the flange.

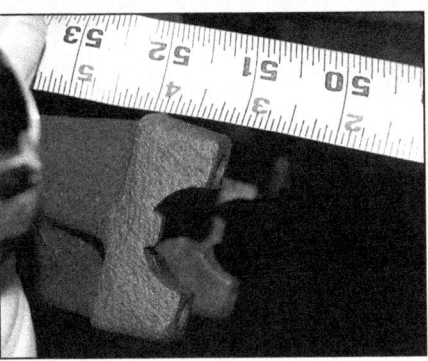

If the rear axle yoke connects directly to the U-joint, measure overall length from the flat in the saddle.

Flange-style rear-axle yokes are measured from the face of the flange.

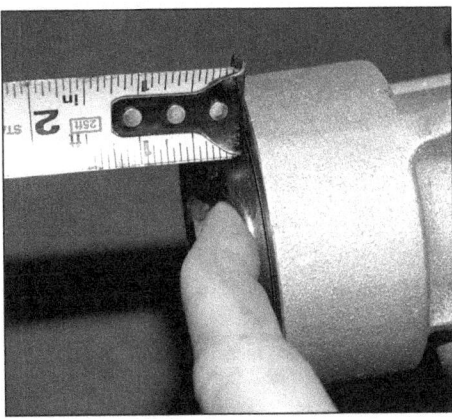

If necessary, pull back the rubber seal to measure the distance from the end of the tailshaft housing to the output shaft on splined outputs.

Note the number of holes and the diameter of the bolt pattern on the flange. If the flange has an alignment shoulder, note the diameter.

The width of the U-joint is measured between the saddle tabs, if equipped.

If no tabs are used, measure the inside distance of the saddles.

As with a front flange face, measure the bolt circle diameter, note the number of holes and measure any shoulder diameter if present.

CHAPTER 8

How to Measure for a Driveshaft

Driveshaft Measurement Worksheet

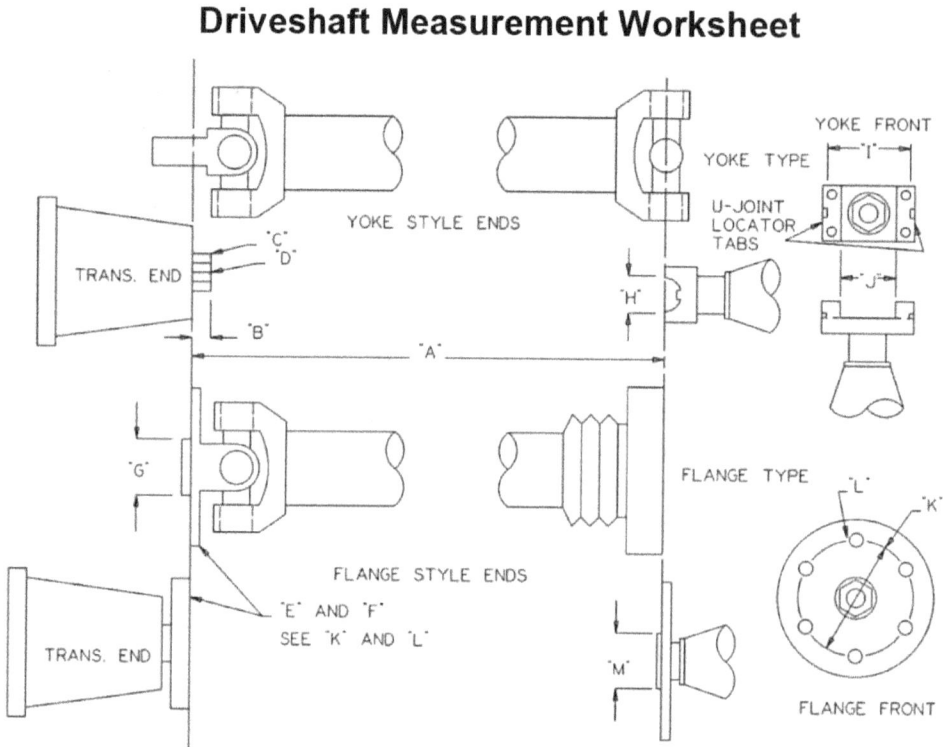

ALL MEASUREMENTs SHOULD BE TAKEN WITH VEHICLE AT RIDE HEIGHT

Base Information

Type of transmission _____ Output shaft type Yoke ☐   Flange ☐

Type of rear axle _____ Input shaft type   Yoke ☐   Flange ☐

Horsepower estimate _____

Driveshaft material: Seamed Steel ☐   DOM Steel ☐   Aluminum ☐   Carbon Fiber ☐   Other _____

Driveshaft Diameter _____   Horsepower estimate _____

Driveshaft Measurements

"A" - Overall length _____

Output Shaft Measurements

Yoke   "B" transmission housing to output shaft _____
       "C" output shaft splines _____
       "D" shaft drilled and tapped?   Yes ☐   No ☐

Flange "E" diameter mounting bolt circle _____
       "F" number of mounting bolt holes _____
       "G" diameter of pilot hole or shoulder _____

Axle Input Shaft Measurements

Yoke   "H" U-Joint saddle flat _____
       "I" between U-joint locating tabs (if app.) _____
       "J" between saddles w/o tabs (if applicable) _____

Flange "K" diameter of mounting bolt circle _____
       "L" number of mounting bolt holes _____
       "M" diameter of pilot hole or shoulder _____

Use this worksheet to get the measurements for your driveshaft builder. He may have additional questions, but this should give them the basics for building your driveshaft.

Swap Spotlight: Coyote Swap into a Fox-Body Mustang

Skyler Hardy's 1992 Mustang LX is finished in its original Wild Strawberry paint. Mickey Thompson radials, 26 x 6 in front and 26 x 10 drag radials in the rear, are mounted on 17 x 4.5 and 15 x 10 SVE drag rims. These are the big clues to the real secret that lies under the hood.

The Fox-body Mustangs of 1979–1993 are only second in swap popularity to the first-generation Mustangs. Indeed, there are so many Fox conversions now that the specific parts available to do this conversion outweigh those for the first-generation cars.

We didn't need to look far to find a quality conversion. Skyler Hardy of Avon, Indiana, is the proud owner of this 1992 Wild Strawberry Mustang LX. This car began life as a 5.0 5-speed. A nice ride for sure, but Skyler just wasn't satisfied with the performance from the original pushrod 5.0, so he opted for a 5.0 with dual overhead camshafts, in the form of a 2013 sealed crate engine.

After pulling the pushrod engine, Skyler got to work cleaning up the engine compartment for a much cleaner install. Scott Rod panels were used to smooth out the interior, and all the wiring would be hidden on the back side of the aprons as much as possible. A UPR Fox-body tubular K-member was used that was already adorned with modular engine mounts, and the UPR coil-overs were used with 10-way Strange adjustable shocks and struts. Maximum Motorsports caster camber plates were installed along with a Steeda bumpsteer kit and a Flaming River manual rack-and-pinion steering system. The rear suspension has all Team Z parts with relocated upper control arms and dual adjustable lower arms.

A Tremec 3550 5-speed with an 11-inch clutch and stock Ford adjustable clutch cable were used. Scram Speed made the throttle-by-wire pedal adapter, Stifflers made the transmission crossmember, and the whole conversion is a bolt-in affair. An aluminum driveshaft came straight from Ford Performance and ties to the 8.8 rear axle with 3.73 gearing.

The sealed crate engine didn't need too much tweaking, but the computer was reprogrammed with a Coyote tune via Palm Beach Dyno. The Ford Control Pack computer system is mounted behind the front engine apron out of sight. American Racing Headers makes a Coyote-specific full-length conversion header, and JLT provided the cold air intake. The return system already installed in the Fox body was upgraded with an Aeromotive fuel pressure regulator attached to the stock lines. The cooling system was a generic Fox-body radiator that Skyler just had "laying around." They had to cut off the outlet and relocate it, but it works just fine.

Skyler reports that fitting the engine was a straightforward job, and the most difficult part of the swap was routing and securing the wiring and cables. There was a small clearance issue with the number-2 header tube, so a set of spacer plates was made to raise the engine enough to clear the header tube. A set of custom heater crossover tubes was fabricated to complete the flow of coolant through the engine, and the

Skyler swapped out the 5.0-liter pushrod engine for a 5.0-liter DOHC Coyote engine via Ford Performance. This sealed crate engine has been unsealed and is now pushing 430 hp and 398 ft-lbs of torque courtesy of a new Palm Beach Dyno tune, JLT intake, and ARH headers.

After a clean-up of the original wiring harnesses and a fresh coat of paint, the Fox Mustang was fitted with a UPR tubular K-member pre-engineered for installing the Coyote engine using earlier SN-95 engine mounts.

A Ford Performance Parts adjustable clutch cable was used to handle clutch duties, and an Aerospace Components master cylinder makes room for the Coyote engine in the bay. A Hurst line lock mounted by the hood hinge gives you a clue about the potential use of the car when completed.

The mounting position of the engine in this chassis gives you an idea of the room at the front of the engine bay for turbo or supercharger applications. The radiator is a universal, generic-fit unit.

mass air meter connections were lengthened to fit.

The 1992 Mustang LX is finished in its original Wild Strawberry paint. Mickey Thompson 26 x 6–inch radials were installed in front while 26 x 10–inch drag radials are mounted in the rear on 17 x 4.5– and 15 x 10–inch SVE drag rims. The clean lines on the outside give only a small hint to what has occurred under the hood.

Take a look at Skyler's award-winning ride and get a feel for how a Coyote engine would look in your Fox-body platform. You can see why the Fox body crowd has been re-energized.

The UPR K-member is already set up for the Coyote engine in the Fox chassis. A manual rack and pinion was installed because the crate engine doesn't have provisions for a power steering pump.

A Ford Control Pack and computer were used with this conversion, and the computer was tucked away under the passenger-side fender. The wiring was run through the firewall and then through the side of the engine compartment under the passenger-side hood hinge for a cleaner install.

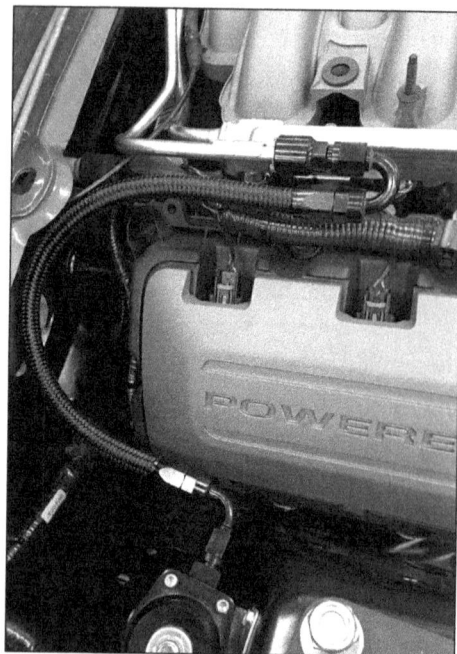

The Fox-body fuel system has a return line for the pushrod engine, so hooking up the Coyote was a snap using an Aeromotive fuel regulator. The Ford Control Pack requires the conversion back to a mechanical fuel return system. The inlet from the late-model setup was reversed via a 180-degree AN fitting and Ford fuel line adapter.

CHAPTER 9

Exhaust System

With most modular engine swaps, space restrictions under the hood of the swap vehicle will affect the exhaust system. Often, components can contact and interfere with the routing of the header tubs or exhaust manifold castings. When building a high-performance car, owners often opt for headers to allow the engine to breathe well and produce optimal horsepower for the application. Owners can either buy off-the-shelf headers or have custom headers fabricated for their project car. Proper planning and positioning of the engine should allow you to use off-the-shelf headers in most cases, but in some special applications and certain vehicles you may have to have headers fabricated. You must trial fit the headers to the engine and chassis to verify if there's any contact between the headers and the brake booster, steering rod, suspension parts, or any other component. If you find a clearance problem, you need to consider all the options and select the best one for the project.

Factory Exhaust Manifolds

Because exhaust ports have changed frequently on modular engines, aftermarket solutions for conversions have been few and difficult to find. Depending on the chassis, modifications to an existing design may be required to

Ford's 2016 flat-plane-crank 5.2 engine comes with a set of free-flowing tubular headers. Because of the left and right bank firing order, there is no oddball firing order and the pipes are pressurized evenly. It does not require a crossover tube in the exhaust to equalize the pressure of the two exhaust pipes. Ford installed one anyway. (Photo Courtesy Ford Performance Parts)

HOW TO SWAP FORD MODULAR ENGINES INTO MUSTANGS, TORINOS AND MORE

CHAPTER 9

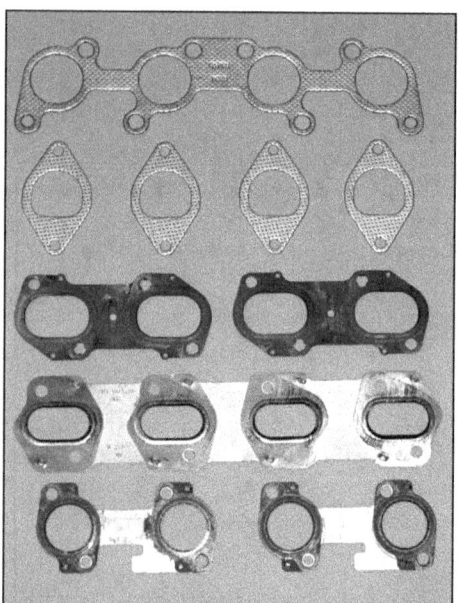

This picture of the exhaust manifold gaskets shows you the evolution of the exhaust port design for the modular engine and why care needs to be taken when selecting exhaust manifolds or headers. Bottom to top: the 4.6 SOHC round port head, the 4.6 DOHC oval port, the slightly larger 5.4 DOHC oval port, the D-shaped 4.6 three-valve SOHC, and the 5.0 Coyote round port. Note that the first and last shared the same port design, albeit much larger and freer flowing for the Coyote. Also note that the bolt mounting pattern changed from a back slash pattern, to vertical bolts, to bolts angling in to the middle.

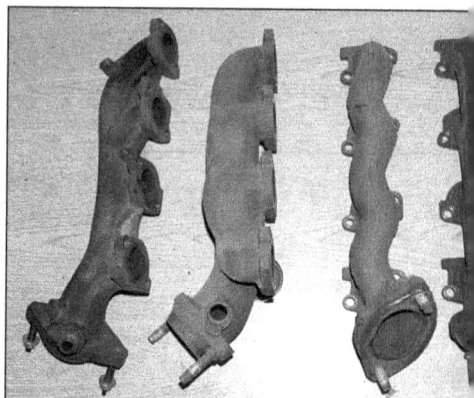

The inner pair of 4.6 SOHC exhaust manifolds are a set from a 1997 Mustang GT while the outer set are from a later-model Crown Victoria. Both pair come straight out from the block, rather than angling down as with earlier pushrod engine designs. The GT manifolds have a funny "squiggler" in the middle that looks odd until you see how it works. The direction and size of the output port is different between the two sets.

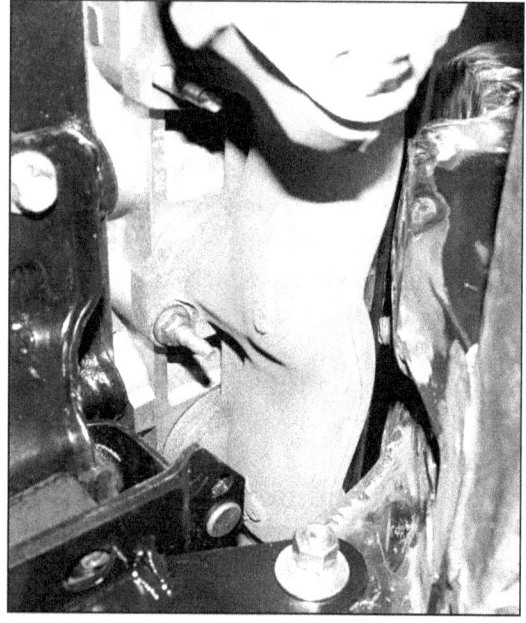

That funny little squiggle works amazingly when placed at the angle of the cylinder head. The Crown Victoria manifolds touched the cut-back shock towers of this 1970 Mustang (see Chapter 3), but the GT manifolds fit right in and clear the cut-back towers.

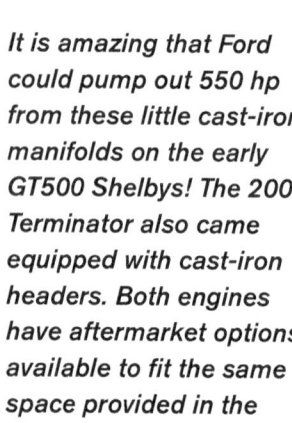

It is amazing that Ford could pump out 550 hp from these little cast-iron manifolds on the early GT500 Shelbys! The 2003 Terminator also came equipped with cast-iron headers. Both engines have aftermarket options available to fit the same space provided in the original cast-iron version.

With the 5.0 Coyote I finally had a set of factory tubular headers. They are made from 409 stainless to fit the late-model chassis, but the up and over design may fit other engine bays. Much like the original Tri-Y headers from the 1960s, they feature a two-into-one and two pipes into the collector design. (Photo Courtesy Brenspeed)

properly fit the exhaust system. The Coyote platform has become very popular, so some good conversion systems have come out in support of the 5.0.

Aftermarket Exhaust Manifolds and Headers

The aftermarket offers cast-iron manifolds, shorty headers, mid-length headers, and long tube headers. The choice between these manifolds depends largely on the exhaust-port design of the engine and the available engine compartment space. The cast-iron manifolds provide the greatest amount of room for tight engine compartments. Shorty headers have two advantages over cast-iron manifolds: they generally flow a little better, and they can be modified if necessary.

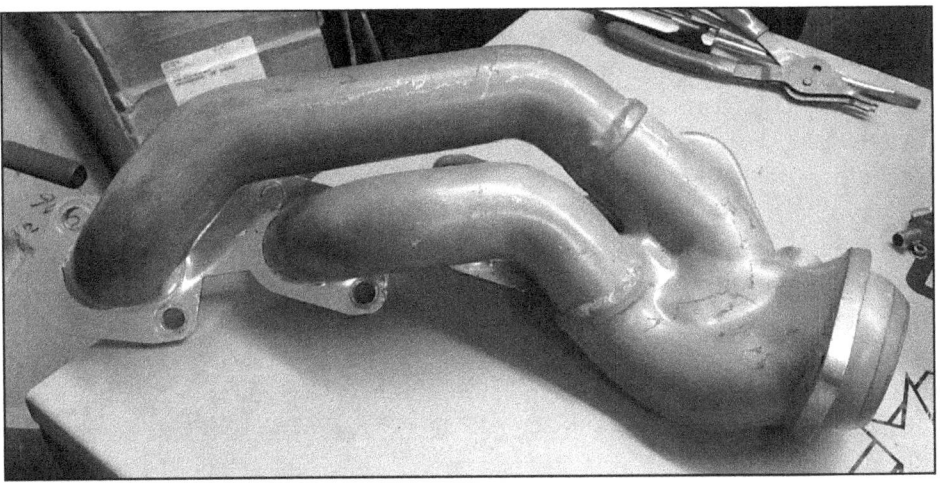
These early Ford Performance tubular headers are actually 2000 Cobra R versions made for that specific rare car. They are made from 409 stainless, which gives them the brownish color once they start to rust. They last much longer than straight steel headers and fit the original space where the cast-iron Cobra manifolds resided. The 409 stainless is bendable and you can weld on it, so if you need to make a slight tweak to a set of these manifolds (for example, change the angle of the outlet just slightly), you can do it with ease. (Photo Courtesy Alexandros Varvounis)

JBA makes a universal shorty header for all the modular engine exhaust ports. This one (PN 1625S-7JT) is for a 4.6 4V. They use JBA's exclusive fire-cone design and are titanium ceramic coated (shown, also available in silver ceramic or bare stainless steel). They are designed for maximum clearance of steering components. Note the high mounting of the outlet flange. (Photo Courtesy JBA)

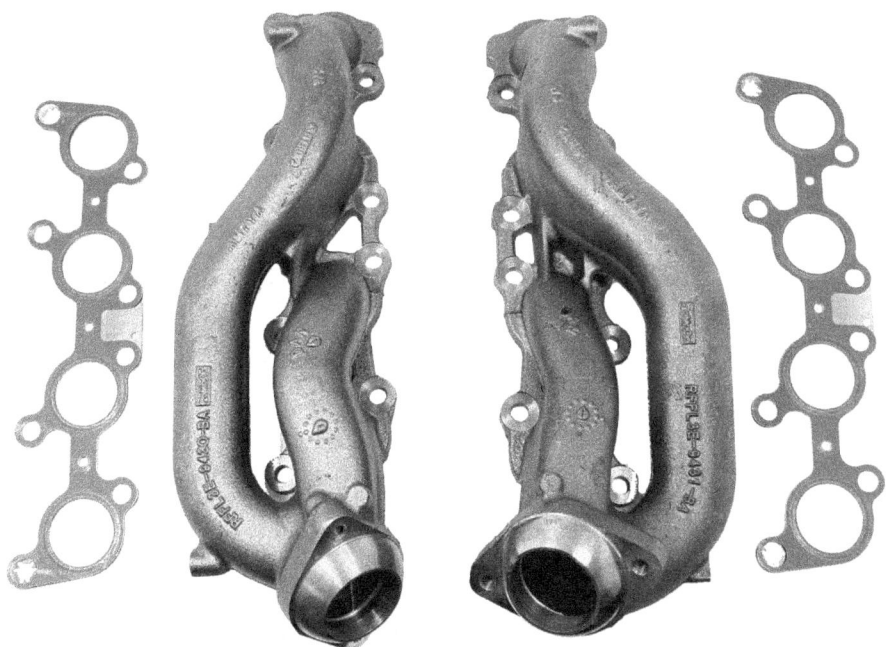
Ford Performance Parts has a set of low-profile cast-iron headers (PN M-9430-SR50A) to fit the Coyote engines that are found on later Ford F-150 trucks. They hug the block and run up and over for tight spaces. (Photo Courtesy Ford Performance Parts)

CHAPTER 9

Mid-length headers are designed to follow along the top of the exhaust line and then drop down to run under the body. In the 1960s, headers were designed to have the pipes drop down almost immediately, but this conflicts with many of the modern steering systems, including rack-and-pinion conversions. Where most shorty headers are designed to exit at the same location as stock manifolds (and thereby use stock exhaust outlets if needed), the mid-length headers pull the outlet to the back of the engine a little farther and may provide clearance in some chassis configurations.

Full-length headers are available, but they are often purpose-built for specific applications. Like the mid-length headers, most new

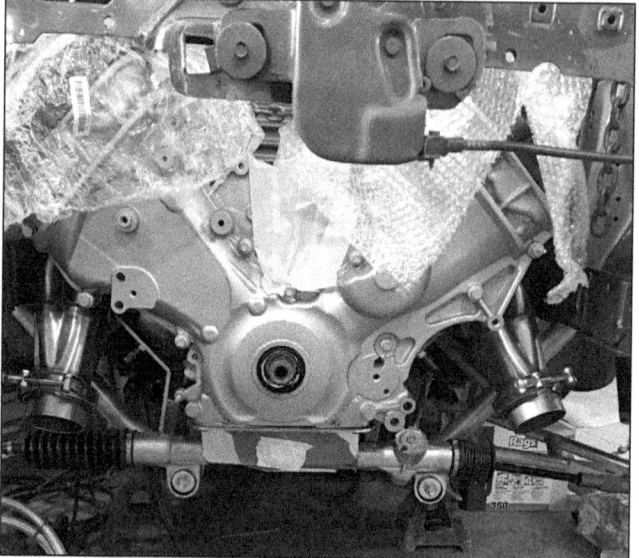

Krona Performance has designed a set of forward outlet headers for 5.0 Coyote swaps in Fox-body applications using single or dual turbochargers. They are made from 304 stainless and feature a 3-inch V-band for connecting to your turbo piping. The 1¾-inch tubing clears most rack-and-pinion systems. (Photo Courtesy Krona Performance)

Sanderson has taken its expertise in tight-fit headers for street rods and applied it to the 4.6 2V, 3V, and 4V as well as the Coyote 5.0. Rather than come straight down like traditional "hugger"-style headers, they come back first to clear the engine mounts. The design clears most popular steering designs and comes in bare steel or aluminized coatings. They feature a special leak-free design that requires no gasket. (Photo Courtesy Sanderson Headers)

Doug's Headers makes chassis specific long-tube headers for clearance with most of the available modular engines. This set (PN D-6652) is made for a Coyote engine in an early 1964–1973 Mustang, 1960–1965 Falcon, or 1966–1967 Fairlane. They are made from raw steel so you can powder-coat them with your choice of coatings. (Photo Courtesy Doug's Headers)

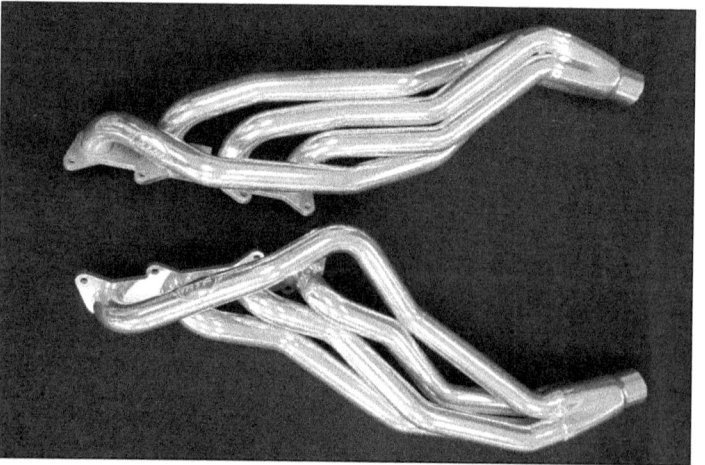

Full-length stainless headers for Coyote, 5.4, and 5.8 engines are available from Mustangs to Fear. They are made to fit 1964–1973 Mustangs, 1967–1968 Cougars, 1960–1965 Falcons, and 1966–1967 Fairlanes. They feature stainless-steel construction with 1¾-inch primaries and 2½-inch collectors. (Photo Courtesy Mustangs to Fear)

EXHAUST SYSTEM

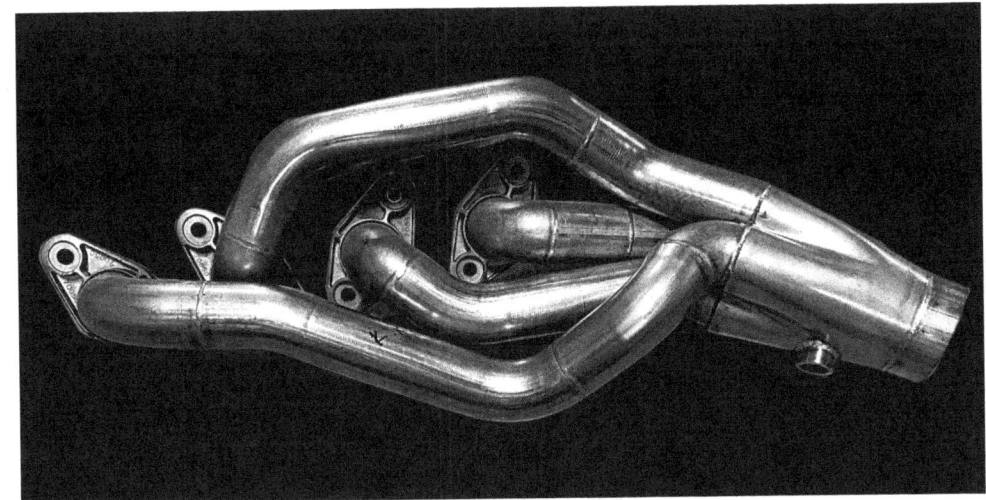

Revology cars use Ultimate Headers in all their custom Coyote conversion Mustangs. These mid-length rear dump headers keep the collector and primaries away from steering shafts and frame rails. Designed for early Mustang installations, they may fit other chassis with tight spaces. They are made from 321 stainless steel with individual header flanges. They come complete with their patented Cometic Ultra Seal gaskets and ARP bolts. (Photo Courtesy Ultimate Headers)

designs go up and back rather than straight down and back. This helps with clearing steering and engine-mounting components. Unless your application has specific headers made for the conversion, fitting the headers may be trial and error, as most header companies don't publish dimensions.

Stainless Steel Works not only has a full line of pre-made full-length headers (it partners with Trick Flow on its stainless exhaust systems), it can sell you the components to make your own headers for a one-off or uncommon installation. It has every exhaust flange outlet available (stainless flanges for a 2003–2004 Cobra, PN HF-4.6, shown), and can provide collectors, pre-bent tubing, and can even work with you to custom-build headers. (Photo Courtesy Stainless Steel Works)

Conversion Headers and Header Components

Several companies are now offering headers specifically designed for engine and chassis combinations, and this list continues to grow as conversions become more popular. Doug's Headers, Detroit Speed, and Mustangs to Fear offer full-length headers for 1964½–1973 Mustangs. Several companies, including American Racing Headers, BBK, and Kooks, now make Coyote conversion headers for the Fox body. Because the early Mustang frame is narrow, these headers may fit other narrow chassis.

If a sufficient exhaust header can't be found, companies are now providing the components for your header builder to build you a set from scratch. Stainless Steel Works sells a complete line of stainless-steel flanges and pre-bent tubing that can be used to fabricate your own headers. Dynatech and Kooks also sell its flanges separately so you can build your own exhaust.

Catalytic Converters

Ford has installed two types of catalytic converters on its vehicles. Two of the converters are a three-way type while two other converters are

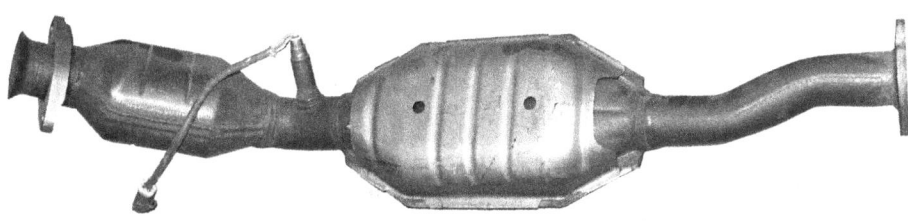

A typical Ford catalytic converter setup contains two different converters, which remove different exhaust gases depending on the catalyst. When choosing an aftermarket converter, take care that you choose one that allows you to pass your regulations. California and New York have stricter regulations than other regions.

HOW TO SWAP FORD MODULAR ENGINES INTO MUSTANGS, TORINOS AND MORE

CHAPTER 9

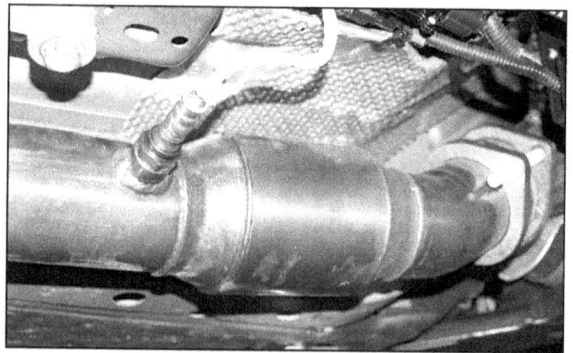

Kooks Headers makes a "green" catalytic converter (PN GE-90140) that is certified by the EPA to meet emissions with integrated catalytic converters. It is made of 304 stainless and good for engines up to 800 hp. It can withstand 1,500 degrees and work with naturally aspirated or forced induction engines.

Flowmaster sells a full line of converters to meet federal, California, and New York regulations. It has vehicle-specific replacements as well as universal-fit units, and its converters can be used with many of its full exhaust kits.

conventional. They use different honeycomb internals to scrub hydrocarbons, carbon monoxide, and nitrogen oxides from the exhaust gases.

Catalytic converters are mandatory for most regions, and unless the car is for off-road duty they need to be installed. Due to the function of the cat system, it is difficult to replace the converters and not affect emissions output.

Because the exhaust flows over the ceramic surface inside the converter, smaller is not necessarily better. A smaller converter has less surface area and won't support larger engines and output.

By law, factory catalytic converters are required to last 80,000 miles, so they are generally built well to last the warranty period. In general, aftermarket converters must last 5 years or 50,000 miles, so most of your aftermarket units are made to the same standards. Laws apply to converter installations that do not meet OEM specifications, so check the local laws before selecting your converter.

Because of the conversion process, catalytic converters generate a lot of heat. Factory-style converters are wrapped in a stainless-steel shield, and some aftermarket units do not use the shield to save space. This should be taken into consideration when designing the exhaust layout. Also, single converters may not perform as well as the original system due to the different honeycomb internal makeup of the two style converters.

Choosing the right converter has a lot to do with the laws in your area. Some exhaust manufacturers will make exhausts only from the catalytic converter back because dealing with the regulations is difficult. Magnaflow and Flowmaster both sell universal converters and may be the best choice when designing your exhaust system. They are knowledgeable on the laws in your area and can help you build the correct system. Kooks also makes a universal converter, but be sure to check your local regulations first. It may be best to choose your converter as a complete system rather than as a universal product.

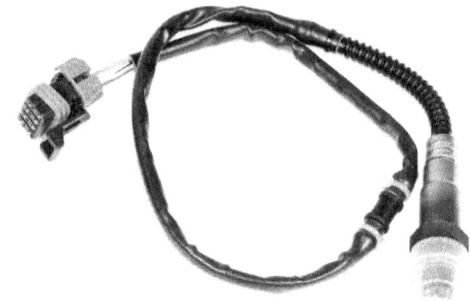

Holley sells both wide-band and narrow-band oxygen sensors for both NTK and Bosch applications. This wide-band sensor (PN 554-101) is for NTK applications. (Photo Courtesy Holley)

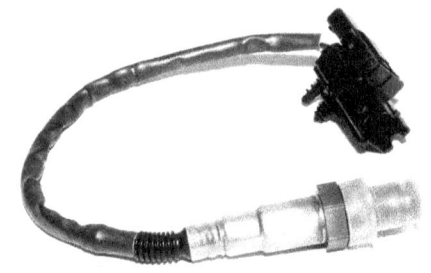

FAST also sells a replacement wide-band oxygen sensor (PN 170408) that can read between 10:1 and 16:1 and works with the FAST EZ-EFI or the FAST air/fuel meters. (Photo Courtesy Fuel Air Spark Technology)

Oxygen Sensors

Ford uses four oxygen sensors from the factory. Two are mounted before the converter and two after, so the fuel/air ratio is measured as well as the efficiency of the catalytic converter. The computer can measure the exhaust gases after they have run through the converter and adjust the fuel/air output to improve emissions. Some early systems used two heated and two non-heated oxygen sensors, but eventually Ford changed to four heated sensors. The oxygen sensor is designed to work in the exhaust-gas temperature range, and heating them brings them into this range faster and makes them more efficient.

Oxygen sensors have become more and more sophisticated over the course of the modular engine run. Early sensors had two wires, and the newer ones can have five wires or more. Typically, the more wires coming out of the sensor, the more complex they are to test. When selecting oxygen sensors, make sure they work properly with your engine computer. Some aftermarket engine computers require you to run a specific oxygen sensor.

Wide-band and narrow-band oxygen sensors are offered to regulate air/fuel ratios. The very first oxygen sensors were designed to tell the computer if the air/fuel ratio varied from the ideal ratio of 14.7:1. That ratio means that there is sufficient air to burn all the fuel, and this ratio is referred to as the *stoichiometric mixture*, or stoic mix. If the mixture has too much air the mixture is considered lean, and the burn is hotter and can damage components. If the mixture has less air it is considered rich, and the burn is cooler and less efficient.

Narrow-band oxygen sensors tell the computer if the mixture is stoic, lean, or rich, so the computer can adjust the mixture to try to correct the ratio. However, the sensors can't communicate the specific lean-ness or richness to the computer; rather, these sensors communicate just lean or rich condition.

Wide-band oxygen sensors measure fuel/air ratios wider than the stoic mix, and this information can help the computer and tuner better tune the engine. Some narrow band sensors are still used behind the catalytic converters, but most oxygen sensors (and ones used in performance applications) are the wide band variety.

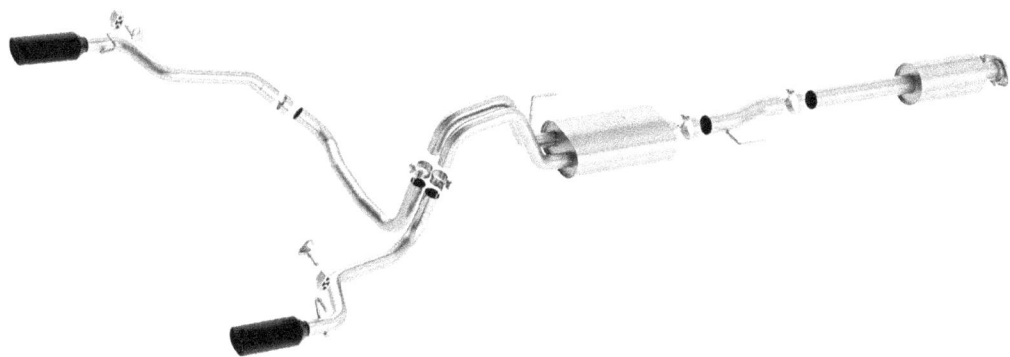

Some pre-bent exhaust may be close enough to work on your project with a small amount of finesse. Ford Performance Parts teamed up with Bassani to provide stainless exhaust kits for newer Ford cars and trucks that are 49-state legal. This F-150 exhaust (M-5200-F1550DSB) is made from mandrel-bent 304 stainless steel and features black chrome exhaust tips. (Photo Courtesy Ford Performance Parts)

Cat-Back Exhaust

"Cat-back" is a simple way of saying everything after the catalytic converter. Here, manufacturers have a little more leeway with design than with the converters. Some areas have strict noise regulations that penalize any change to the mufflers from OEM. Be sure to check local regulations prior to selecting an exhaust system.

As with getting air into the engine, bigger isn't always better on the exhaust system. The larger the pipes, the slower the exhaust gases flow through them, and the more the engine works to push those gases out of the exhaust. With less pressure, exhaust gases can begin to swirl around and disrupt the flow and cool. When the exhaust gases cool, they become denser, and the engine has to work harder to force the denser gases out. Most exhaust systems in stock form suffer from undersized exhaust manifolds and headers, which forces the engine to fight against the restriction. Err on the side of larger pipes.

Ford has used 409 Stainless in its exhaust for most of the modular engine run. 409 stainless is a combination of mild steel and stainless steel, and it has some of the qualities of both metals. It bends easier than stainless, and does not rust out nearly as fast as mild steel. It typically turns brown rather than rusts. Mild steel is easy to work with but rusts over time, and stainless exhaust systems are made from pre-bent tubing that is usually welded together. Some of the larger exhaust companies offer fully bent one-piece exhaust systems.

Swap Spotlight: 1968 Torino

This 1968 Torino is all home built and done on a meager budget. Craig Wood and Jeremy Keller of Windsor, Canada, decided to build a pair of 1968 Torino GT fastbacks: one with conventional vintage iron and one as a modern, updated powerplant. Just because the build was low-budget doesn't mean these guys didn't do the job well. The amount of engineering involved to create their car is extraordinary. Turns out Craig and Jeremy work in the automotive field as engineers, so they were fully aware of what it would take to make the project a success. And the results are amazing.

The Torino is equipped with a 4.6 SOHC pulled from a 2001 Mustang GT, but it certainly isn't stock. A modified Roush Stage 3 supercharger and 73-mm pulley kit give it a serious boost in performance, and Torino is infused with a lot of parts from the 2004 SVT Cobra. The front suspension uses a K-member and towers grafted to the original Torino frame rails, and the engine compartment panels were adapted to the new strut towers. From there, the stock SN-95 spindles were fitted with 14-inch Alcon rotors and calipers. The 2004 Cobra rack-and-pinion is mated to the original steering shaft with a modified F-150/Lincoln Navigator steering shaft. Braking to all four corners is handled by a 2004 Cobra hydroboost system.

The transmission was sourced from a 2004 Cobra in the form of a T-56 6-speed. The clutch is a cable release design and a Steeda Tri-ax shifter is used

This 1968 Ford Torino GT hails from Ontario, Canada, and is the engineering marvel of two honest-to-goodness automotive engineers, Craig Wood and Jeremy Keller. Rather than just buy a bunch of off-the-shelf parts and slap the car together, the duo decided to make this a cost-conscience build and make use of their talents to build a mix of old and new. (Photo Courtesy Craig Wood)

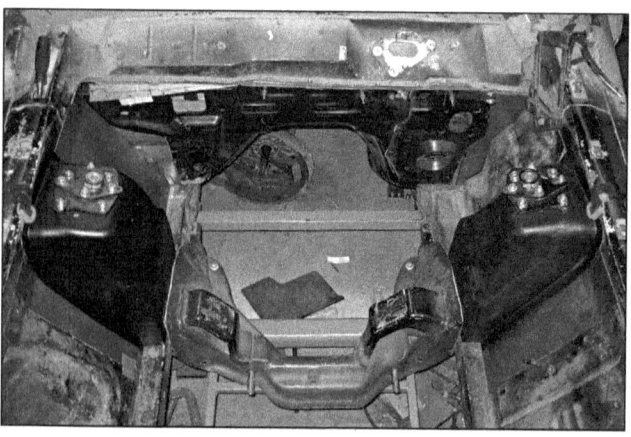

This is the fabrication required to make the SN-95 front suspension work in the Torino chassis. The engine side aprons were remade to fit to the new strut towers, and the K-member was modified to fit directly to the frame rails. Maximum Motorsports 4-bolt caster camber plates are used. Modifications are heavy to the firewall as parts from the Mustang were grafted to the Torino firewall to allow the use of the SN-95 heating and A/C under-dash unit. (Photo Courtesy Craig Wood)

The stock transmission "hump" was removed and a new version was fabricated to fit the Steeda Tri-ax shifter mounted to the T-56 6-speed transmission. For this build the transmission tunnel was modified and raised to make more room for the large T-56. (Photo Courtesy Craig Wood)

in a modified tunnel conversion cover. An aluminum driveshaft from a Crown Victoria police car fit perfect with the setup and drives the power through a 2004 Cobra independent rear suspension fitted with 3.55 gearing.

The computer is a factory EEC-V system with a 2004 Roush tune and stock SN-95 Mustang wiring harnesses. This allowed for the use of all the SN-95 components on the Torino frame. Some of the real engineering in this build happens under the dash. The complete HVAC system from the 2004 Cobra was grafted to the Torino firewall, and then the controls were grafted to the original Torino control unit. The gauges are modern and based off the 2004 dash and electronics. The boys used an in-dash ignition switch from a Ford Thunderbird, and then custom grafted the Mustang electronics to fit the Torino gauge cluster compartment. The result is an instrument panel that can take full advantage of the Ford PATS system, cruise control, keyless entry, late model speedometer, and intermittent wiper system.

A 2004 Cobra dual fuel pump was custom grafted into a stock Torino fuel tank and baffles were added to assist the pump. A Moroso road racing oil pan was used for the extra capacity, and oil is cooled through an Earls oil cooler. A Magnaflow exhaust and X-pipe were used along with a Magnaflow outlet pipe made for a Cobra IRS, with custom exhaust tips added to fit the Torino chassis.

The GT rides on a set of Roush 18-inch forged chrome-plated aluminum wheels originally used on the 2009 Roush P51B edition Mustangs. Michelin Pilot Sport tires ride on all four corners with 18 x 9-inch rims with 275/35/18 tires up front, and 18 x 10-inch wheels with 315/30/18 tires at the rear.

The Torino is currently finish in a stealthy flat black, which may be changed in the future. And don't think this car is for show only, one of the first trips out for this beast was Gingerman Raceway in South Haven, Michigan, where it performed quite nicely, thank you very much.

Craig and Jeremy's 1968 Torino GT is a testament to the fact that you can build a car on a budget and do an amazing job. With patience, seeking out the right knowledge, and finding the right parts at the right price, you, too, can build something no one else has and make it turn heads wherever it goes.

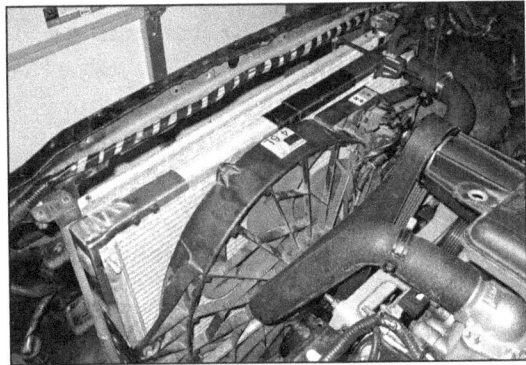

Cooling comes from an extra-wide 36-mm-thick aluminum radiator and a 2004 Cobra electric 2-speed fan system. Note the routing of the Cobra wiring harness up and under the lip of the radiator shroud. (Photo Courtesy Craig Wood)

A 2004 Cobra dual fuel pump was grafted to the Torino fuel tank using a baffle and mounting ring acquired from the local junkyard. The fuel system is returnless and all custom stainless lines were bent for the Torino chassis. (Phot Courtesy Craig Wood)

The duo was able to graft the modern printed circuit board instrument cluster to the Torino three-pod gauge cluster. This allows for use of the engine warning light, electronic speedometer, and all the function of the 2004 system. (Photo Courtesy Craig Wood)

Here's the front of the gauge pod. Note the fourth pod, which was fabricated from a second gauge pod and fitted with additional gauges. The gauges are LED backlit and the gauge faces were all handmade. The 160-mph speedometer also reads in kilometers per hour for Canadian roads. (Photo Courtesy Craig Wood)

CHAPTER 10

STARTUP TIPS FOR SUCCESS

Below are a few miscellaneous final tips to get the projects out and on the road. Proper handling, proper startup, and proper run-out are all important and these pointers will help you avoid costly mistakes.

Engine Handling

Some factory assemblies weren't installed using lift hooks; they were installed from underneath because the engine was attached to the K-member prior to installation. Clearance issues in some chassis also dictate raising the body and removing the engine with the front suspension K-member (if equipped). Gone are the days of pulling the carburetor and bolting a plate to the intake manifold. Grabbing a modular engine at the plastic intake manifold is not the way to go. Handling a Ford modular engine requires grabbing it from the proper threaded points, which means a set of lifting hooks that bend out far enough to clear the valvecovers. Try to avoid flexible straps when lifting the engine, they can damage the valvecovers.

Ford has a special tool that allows the engine to be tilted from the center mounted alternator mount point. This plate can be used once the engine is in place to tilt the engine backward for ease of installation of items such as the exhaust manifolds.

Engine Priming

Because the modular engine does not use a distributor, there is no oil pump driveshaft to connect to and prime the oil pump. Ford recommends priming the engine with a pressure tank connected to the oil pressure sender outlet. Proper priming of the bearings and chain tensioners is important to the survival of the engine. The Ford-recommended version looks like a steel garden sprayer, and that is what many builders have retrofitted to prime its engines. A good pressure sprayer with a fitting to fit the sender outlet and hoses strong enough to handle the pressure needed to feed oil to the engine works like a champ. Ironically, when I was checking with most of the dealerships in my area, none of them had a priming system to prime modular engines (and they gave me a curious look when I asked). It should be done with a new engine or an engine that has been sitting for a long while.

Bleeding the Coolant System

On some systems the coolant crossover tube is the highest point of the coolant system, which can trap air pockets. Ford sometimes runs vacuum lines to the high points of the cooling system to the de-gas tank, and sometimes they provide a port that you can open to bleed air out of the system. Most Ford official manuals do not tell you to bleed the

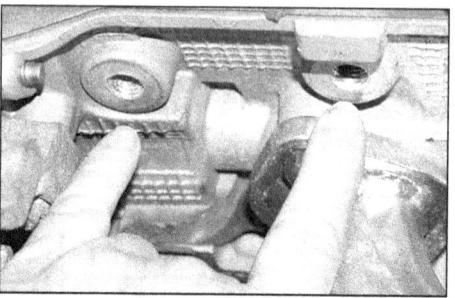

Lifting a modular engine by the plastic intake is a no-no. Ford has cast lift threads in the front of the driver- and the rear of the passenger-side heads to mount engine lift hooks. The hooks need to curve around the larger valvecovers to avoid scratching or denting the covers. These holes are 18 mm x 1.75 pitch, and one is raised higher than the other, so when fabricating lift hooks, a spacer or an offset mount needs to be made to fit the lift hook properly.

STARTUP TIPS FOR SUCCESS

cooling system at this port, but it helps to perform this task. You can bleed the system by one of several methods; most are a variation of the official Ford recommendation, which is several cycles of filling the de-gas tank, running the system until the thermostat opens (but not too hot), allowing the system to completely cool, and topping off the coolant level. Filling the coolant at the crossover tube when the system is cold can help get coolant into the upper part of the engine and remove air bubbles. Proceed with caution anytime you are dealing with the cooling system.

Power Steering Priming

The power steering pump needs a vacuum drawn on the reserve to assist pulling all the air out of the system. This can be done with a rubber stopper and a handheld vacuum pump. The procedure varies, depending on the application, but before you run the steering back and forth as usual, you need to run the engine and draw a vacuum to pull excess air out of the system. Then running the steering to lock can purge the system. Be careful to not hold the steering at the limit lock for more than 3 to 5 seconds or damage can occur to the pump.

Fuel Pressure

Some fuel systems have a Schrader-style valve mounted to the fuel rails for reading the fuel rail pressure to the injectors. When Ford went to the fuel rail pressure transducer, it removed the valve because the pressure could be checked through the PCM.

The Schrader valve can be used to depressurize the system, but be careful. Spraying hot fuel on the engine is very dangerous. The simpler method is to pull the fuel pump relay or fuse and turn the engine over for a couple of seconds; this releases the fuel pressure.

Mac's Custom Tie Downs makes an adapter for the PIVOT engine lifting system that works with all Ford modular engine platform 2V, 3V, and 4V and Coyotes. The adapter holds close to the engine for tight compartments and the PIVOT system can adjust up to 35 degrees. The adapter plate mounts to the existing PIVOT carburetor plate. (Photo Courtesy Mac's Custom Tie Downs)

Ford factory lift hooks are cast out of steel and curve to allow clearance for the big valvecovers. These are for 4-cam applications. They can sometimes cause problems with clearance as they stick out farther behind the engine when installed, and for tight engine compartments may conflict with the firewall.

Ford sells a stamped-steel engine lift hook set that was also installed on some Ford crate engines, so it may be available used. Ford sells them under several different part numbers: 303-D074 (D91P-6001-A) is an early-engine lift-hook set; or they are sold individually as 303-D087 (D93P-6001-A1) RH bracket and 303-D088 (D93P-6001-A2) LH bracket. Ford also sells a special lift bracket (PN 303-639) that mounts in place of the alternator and assists in tilting the engine backward for installing items such as the exhaust manifold. (Photo Courtesy Alexandros Varvounis)

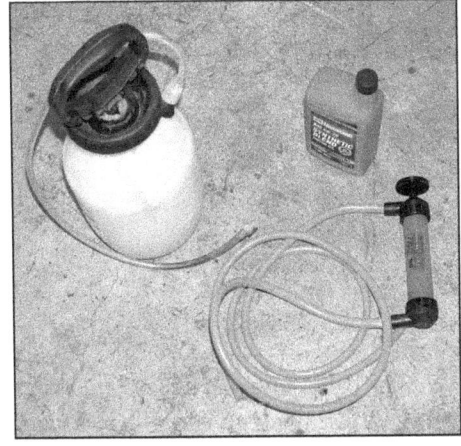

A garden sprayer with a 1/4-inch pipe fitting can be adapted to prime the engine before startup. A hand pump adapted to the pipe fitting can be used to draw oil directly out of the bottle and connect to the oil pressure sender port.

Electronic Checks/Startup Program

A tuner can provide you with a startup tune to initially tune the engine based on the information you provided about your build. If you have a tuner/programmer, now is a good time to run through some of the built-in PIDs if you are running a Ford computer or your PCM allows you to run individual tests. You should check items such as the electronic fan to see if they turn on and off. Check the sensors to make sure they are reading in range. This also helps find circuits that may have been missed and not connected.

Maximizing Dyno Time

Getting your project up and running is not the end of the build. Before regular use, you need to invest in some calibration and data gathering, which usually means a trip to the chassis dynamometer. So much information about the engine setup can be gleaned on the dyno (and you are not supposed to be running at WOT on the street, and at the track is too late). This information may save your engine, help you to conform to emissions requirements, establish maximum horsepower, and make sure all the components are working properly.

Before you go and strap the project down to a dyno, you need to be aware of some important items to prevent you from wasting time and money.

Evaluation Run versus Data Collection and Analysis

You have probably been to a bigger car show where someone has pulled in a chassis dyno and is strapping down cars for runs. These runs tell you the power levels at the time of the pull, but not much else. There is a time and place for this data and it is fun, but it doesn't tell you what is happening in the drivetrain; it is just giving you the end results. Unless someone is collecting data and using that data to calibrate the drivetrain, it is just horsepower numbers.

Real drivetrain analysis involves time to collect data and calibrate the data to match the drivetrain to the type of driving desired with the vehicle. To do that you need to find a tuner who will work with you on not only setting up the computer, but also on making sure the components selected work properly together.

I took a field trip to Brenspeed in Pierceton, Indiana, and talked directly with Brent White, who has been tuning modular engines for almost as long as there have been modular engines. Here are his recommendations on how to prepare and what to expect at the dyno.

Your dyno time is going to involve much more than just strapping your car down and doing a few pulls. You need to be prepared to take your modifications to the best level, and that means lots of data collection. The test subject for the day at the dyno is a 2016 Supercharged Roush RS3. This car off the shelf would be in the 650-hp range, but with proper tuning and data collection, the engineers at Brenspeed are pushing an extra 100 hp more.

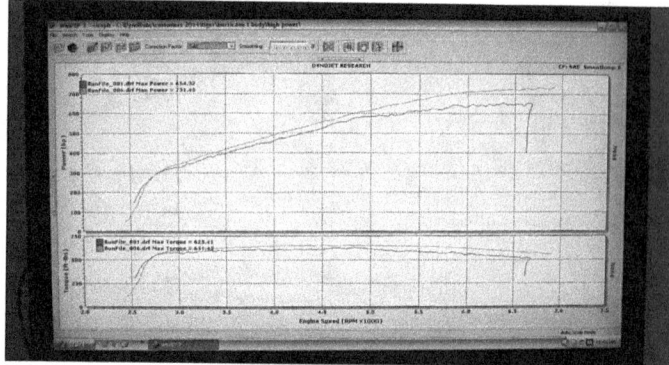

The typical horsepower and torque curves everyone wants to see after the dyno pull. On a hot, sticky day this car made impressive horsepower; note that the environment affects horsepower output, and you won't always be in ideal conditions. Brenspeed prefers to use the SAE standard for power correction, as opposed to the STD. These two formulas are how the computer determines the horsepower at the rear wheels, and STD sometimes shows a higher number. Brenspeed prefers to use the SAE because it is the industry standard.

STARTUP TIPS FOR SUCCESS

Preparation

The worst thing you can do in a project build is to *not* take advantage of the database of knowledge a top tuner might have. You need to find a good tuner and work with him/her during the build; a good tuner has tested many different combinations and generally can steer you in the right direction. If you have someone else build the engine, make sure your tuner is in the loop, as they may have found certain combinations that look good on paper but don't perform well in practice.

It is also important to share with the tuner what you intend to do with your vehicle. Ford has to put a tune on its vehicle that passes emissions and is suitable for a wide range of potential uses such as city driving, track time, and road running, and makes decent mileage. You don't tune a dragster the same way you tune a road racing car, even if they have some of the same components installed. Work with your tuner and tell them how you plan to use the car.

It is also important that you share all the information about the build (e.g., what type of air filter you are using, what kind of cams, did you lock the cam phasers down). A friend of mine had a supercharger installed on his Mustang and the cam selection and other items installed made it so the Ford dealer couldn't do anything with the engine once the tune was changed. The tuner needs to know exactly what you have done. No two cars work exactly the same because of variations in components and how power moves through the drivetrain. Most top tuners have built up a sizable library on different components to help them understand what is happening in the engine.

One important thing to keep in mind: the more custom your build, the longer it takes at the dyno to calibrate everything properly. As stated above, most of the bigger tuning shops have built up a considerable library of data on specific off-the-shelf components. Sticking with off-the-shelf helps them evaluate the data received. Any kind of custom part (e.g., custom-made intake tubing) is essentially a "new" piece and will require new data to form a baseline. A build that uses a Ford crate engine and off-the-shelf components may be a one-day tune; the more custom the application, the more time and resources you need to commit to the tuning.

As discussed in Chapter 4, some tuners won't give you a start-up tune if they are not familiar with the project. All too often something is left out and the tune is blamed for the problem (e.g., an engine with radical cams that didn't have the cam phasers locked down can advance too far and destroy itself). The tuner also has no control over items such as wiring, so some may not be willing to assist with some builds.

Use caution when it comes to picking a tuner. Some top tuning shops have a full-time staff member who does nothing but calibrations. Although all tuning shops have to start somewhere, be cautious of the shop that says "yeah, bring it in, we can tune it." Unless this shop understands exactly what you have done, and doesn't ask you a lot of questions first, you may want to steer clear. Tuning blind gets you perhaps 75 percent of what you need. Just because a tuner doesn't have a good database doesn't make them a bad tuning shop, but a good tuning shop will understand that unknowns mean data analysis and that means more than just a standard tune. If you call your doctor and tell him or her your elbow hurts, he or she probably won't recommend anything without seeing your elbow; it may be tendonitis or it may be a pit bull clamped on your elbow. Choose wisely.

Pre-Dyno To-Do List

- Make sure the car is ready for the dyno. Getting to the dyno and not being prepared is time consuming and expensive. Using your start-up program, run the engine through a heat cycle. Make sure all the oil leaks, hose clamps, and other items associated with a new installation have been checked. Running your engine to WOT and blowing a hose doesn't just make a mess, it costs you money and valuable time. Make sure your vehicle is ready for the pulls.
- Check for vacuum leaks twice. Vacuum leaks can cause all kinds of problems on the dyno, especially those after the throttle body.
- If you can, run some of your PIDs before you get to the dyno. Here again, chasing down an unplugged oxygen sensor or the electric fan not kicking on can cause delays at the dyno. Although your tuner can run these tests, if you have a programmer that allows you to run tests prior to strapping the car down, run them in advance.
- Make sure that dyno tuning time is part of your project build costs. And the more you do custom, the more you need to plan for tuning.

So what happens after your car is strapped down? Usually there are two connections to the vehicle: the dyno computer is connected to the DLC and a tach wire is connected to one of the coils to get proper tachometer readings. They typically check items such as air pressure in the tires because race cars may not carry the same air pressure as street cars. The dyno operator should know how you intend to run your vehicle.

Maximizing Dyno Time continued

Although the display screen can be customized to show all kinds of data, the three things that Brent starts with are the air/fuel ratio, the engine RPM, and the speedometer setting. If the engine leans out during a pull it can cause serious damage, so he usually starts with a fairly rich setting to evaluate items such as the injectors and fuel pump, to make sure they are up to the task for the engine capabilities. Running rich can have its own set of issues, but running lean can severely damage an engine.

After getting the fuel/air ratio set the next step is timing; again, Brent starts out very conservatively, working the timing up is where big changes occur.

Having the speedometer setting on the main screen helps Brent establish the accuracy of the speedometer after changes have been made. With the newer engines and computers, the speedometer can be calibrated with the computer tune.

Then the look at the data begins. The car may have made a certain horsepower level, but it may be stressing certain components to get there (see Chapter 7 on injectors running at 100-percent duty cycle). If there are unfamiliar components or custom parts on the engine, the new data baseline can be started and built up for the new combination. The process continues until the desired result is achieved, or a change is needed to get the desired results (this injector not working well with that intake).

A successful dyno session is the completion of your build.

This chassis dyno allows the user to display whatever information desired during the pull. Most important is engine RPM and air/fuel ratio. The tuner monitors the air/fuel ratio to make sure the engine doesn't lean out during a pull. The bottom shows the current environment (humidity, temperature, and barometric pressure), and in the corner is the actual MPH being read by the dyno, which helps to calibrate the speedometer.

Swap Spotlight: 1976 Ford F-100

Chris and Steve Donaldson of Knoxville, Tennessee, hand-built almost everything on this 1976 Ford F-100 themselves. The added kicker is that the truck was purchased brand new in 1976 by Chris' grandfather, George Donaldson. The 8½-year labor of love also blazed some new trails, as the duo decided that a little overhead cam action was a perfect fit under the hood of the project.

This F-100 started out life as a 300-inline 6-cylinder with a manual 3-speed column shift. The first upgrade to the truck was a 460 big-block transplant, but Chris wanted something with looks and better mileage than the 460 was offering. The duo acquired a 1998 Lincoln MK VIII and 4R70w automatic transmission for the conversion project, and they were on their way.

This third-gen 1976 F-100 retains its original body lines but is highlighted by the shaved door handles, drip rails, mirrors, and marker lights. It was lowered onto Coys knock-off rims. (Photo Courtesy Chris Donaldson)

Chris reports that the DOHC engine fits the truck chassis better than the 460 does: while the heads are wider, the bottom end is the same as other Ford small-blocks, so fitment was a breeze. They mounted the engine back toward the firewall, and because of the engine placement there were no modifications needed to fit the overdrive transmission. The engine remains stock, and parts that were needed or design enhancements were taken from the 2003 Mustang Mach I platform, because it is one of the few performance platforms that use an automatic transmission. The engine remains stock except for the custom intake fabricated from leftover parts from a previous 4-inch intake project. The air filter is mounted under the fender and pulls air through one of the original openings in the truck chassis, making it a true cold-air setup. The computer is the stock Lincoln EEC-V and wiring harness, custom shortened and modified by Chris. One of the few processes performed by outsiders is the re-programming of the computer to bypass the PATS system.

The front suspension and steering is courtesy of a Fatman Fabrications Mustang II independent front suspension and rack-and-pinion steering. The rear suspension is a custom four-bar setup attached to a Ford 9-inch rear with 3.90 gears. Braking is via a four-wheel-disc setup with MII front rotors and oversize GM-style calipers, and the rear has a custom-mounted kit taken from a 2001 Mustang. The polished master cylinder is a Corvette-style unit attached to a firewall-mounted vacuum booster. The brake pedal is in the stock position and did not require moving to clear the four-cam heads.

A stock truck fuel tank was used in conjunction with a Walbro 255-lph fuel pump mounted with a custom 3-inch mount. The original tank pickup was modified to work as the return line from the engine. The filler neck for the tank was installed behind the rear taillight for a cleaner look. Many trips to the auto parts store were required to get just the right combination of hoses to make the cooling system work. The power steering uses custom stainless lines to route the fluid from the stock 1998 pump down to the new rack. Topping off the engine is a Powermaster 200-amp one-wire alternator, which has been given a custom finish.

Because the design took a lot of cues from the 2003 Mach I, a set of Patriot full-length headers were used and fit perfectly in the truck chassis. Chris reports that the headers for Cobras had

The stock-style fuel tank now has a Walbro 255 lph in-tank pump, mounted in a custom 3-inch mount with built-in slosh baffle. The fuel inlet pipe was relocated to fit behind the rear tailight, and the return line is the original sending unit pickup.

some clearance issues, but the headers for the automatic cars work just fine. A custom 2½-inch exhaust flows into a set of two-chamber Flowmaster mufflers.

The cab and bed were finished in 1996 Ford Bright Tangerine and the paint cues were added to the engine and apron areas. Chris laid down all the paint.

Chris and Steve's efforts have paid off big time, and although it was an 8½-year project, it was well worth the effort. I hope that this three-generation build will serve as an inspiration to all those father/son projects that are still languishing out in the garage.

The 1996 Bright Tangerine paint scheme makes its way onto the valvecovers and engine compartment of the F-100 conversion. The engine is a mostly stock Lincoln DOHC with the early dual-port intake manifold. The intake tubing and inner fender panels were hand fabricated. (Photo Courtesy Chris Donaldson)

Chris and Steve custom bent the exhaust and mated it to a pair of Flowmaster two-chamber mufflers. The 4R70W transmission fits with room to spare and the custom mounts tie in to the boxed frame.

GLOSSARY

The following is a list of some of the more common terms used when you are sorting through your engine project. Don't let the acronyms confuse you; they are simple to understand once you know what they do.

Accelerator Pedal Position Sensor: The electronic sensor that tells the computer how far you have pushed the gas pedal; this signal is used to operate the throttle-by-wire engine mounted to the throttle body.

ACT (Air Charge Temperature Sensor): When you compress the air by supercharging or turbocharging, it raises the temperature of the air charge. After air is run through an intercooler you need to know the temperature of the air charge, as it has changed from measuring it out at the air filter and IAT. This gives the computer more information about the air going into the cylinders, and allows the computer to adjust the fuel flow.

Battery Junction Box/Bussed Electrical Center: This is the big current box, usually under the hood. This contains the high current fuses and circuit breakers and sends power to the central junction box.

CCRM (Constant Control Relay Module): This provides power to some of the components controlled by the PCM, including the A/C clutch and the fuel pump.

Central Junction Box: The fuse block.

CKP (Crankshaft Position Sensor): The modular engine uses a magnetic sensor and a wheel with cogs that pass through a magnetic field to trigger the sensor. By counting the number of sensor pulses the computer can determine where the crankshaft is and how fast the engine is turning.

CMP (Camshaft Position Sensor): Like the crank position sensor, this tells the computer where the camshafts are in the rotation of the engine. During start up, the computer needs to know where the cams are in relation to the crank (compression or exhaust), and it has to work with the variable cam timing.

COP (Coil On Plug): With an individual coil on each spark plug, the charge to the plug can be much greater than with coil packs, and gives the computer better control on triggering the individual cylinders.

CHT (Cylinder Head Temperature Sensor): Some engines use this instead of an ECT; some use both. It is located in the cylinder head, not in the coolant passage and is used to determine the temperature of the engine. A simple way to think of it: It measures how efficiently the coolant is working, rather than how hot the coolant is.

DLC (Data Link Connector): This is the D-shaped plug used to talk to the computer, using a code reader or a programmer.

DTR (Digital Transmission Range Sensor): In cars using an automatic transmission, this sensor is used to tell the computer what gear you are in; it also works as the safety/neutral switch. The computer uses this information along with the other sensors to determine how to operate the transmission (e.g., passing, kick down, hauling large loads)

ECT (Engine Coolant Temperature Sensor): A fancy way to say "water temperature sender."

EEC (Electronic Engine Control System): This is what Ford named its computer system. The Roman numeral identifies the basic revision of the computer.

EGR (Exhaust Gas Recirculator): Takes a portion of the exhaust gases and sends them back through the engine to be re-burned, lowering emissions.

ETC (Electronic Throttle Control Motor): In throttle-by-wire systems this is the engine that opens and closes the throttle plate based on the signal coming from the accelerator pedal controls.

EDIS (Electronic Distributorless Ignition System): Modular engines don't use distributors; the computer determines when to fire the coils.

EVAP (Evaporative Emissions Control): The EVAP system takes fuel vapors that used to be vented out to the air and draws them into the engine where they can be burned.

FRPS (Fuel Rail Pressure Sensor): On a returnless fuel system this sensor measures the pressure of the fuel at the rails, and the computer can increase or decrease the voltage to the fuel pump to maintain pressure. This eliminates the need for a mechanical pressure regulator and return line back to the fuel tank.

FTP (Fuel Tank Pressure Sensor): You want the fuel vapors to go through the EVAP system, and by measuring the pressure in the fuel tank, the computer can detect leaks and keep the EVAP system working properly. This is the guy that throws the error code when you leave the gas cap off or loose.

GEM (Generic Electronic Module): This box controls the power to some of the auxiliary controls, including the power windows,

GLOSSARY

and monitors some of the safety features such as the "door ajar" circuit.

HO2S and O2S (Heated Oxygen Sensor or Oxygen Sensor): Exhaust sensors only start to work when they reach the proper temperature, and by heating them before the exhaust can bring them up to temperature they can start providing information to the computer faster.

IAC (Idle Air Control Valve): When the throttle plate is closed, this solenoid allows a small amount of air to bypass the throttle plate so the engine doesn't shut down at idle.

IAT (Intake Air Temperature Sensor): This sensor measures the temperature of the air entering the engine. The cooler the air, the denser the charge into the cylinder. The computer uses this information to determine optimum air/fuel ratio.

IFS (Inertia Fuel Switch): If the vehicle is jostled severely (as in a wreck), this switch trips and shuts off power to the fuel pump, preventing fuel from being sprayed at fuel injection pressures.

IMRC and CMCV (Intake Manifold Runner Control and Charge Motion Control Valve): This is a throttle plate system that blocks off the dual port runners on the intake at low RPM and idle. This helps with low-end torque and acceleration at low RPM.

ISS (Intermediate Shaft Speed Sensor): Used with automatic transmissions to help the computer know when to best shift the transmission.

Knock Sensor: These are generally mounted in the inner intake area of the engine and detect when per-detonation is occurring. When this occurs the computer adjusts the timing or air/fuel mix to prevent damage.

MAF (Mass Airflow Meter): This device measures the amount of air flowing into the engines and then the PCM can adjust the fuel/air ratio to the engine.

Multiplex Communication Network or Module Communications Network: This is the data channel that the computer uses to talk to different items such as the anti-lock brakes, GEM module, the gauges, airbags, and other equipment. It also is how you talk to the computer via the DLC.

OBDII (OnBoard Diagnostics II): This is the standardized set of error codes that all manufacturers use to tell the outside world what is happening to the vehicle; it has been used since 1994. Some codes are manufacturer specific.

OSS (Output Speed Sensor): A magnetic pickup that replaces the traditional speedometer gear. The computer counts the number of pulses and sends this information to the electronic speedometer.

PCM (Powertrain Control Module): Fancy name for the computer.

PCV (Positive Crankcase Ventilation Valve): Most of you know what this is, but some of you may not know that some of the newer ones are heated, because in cold weather moisture can be drawn into the valve and cause it to freeze, causing blowby and potential damage to the engine. This valve opens and allows oil vapors to be drawn into the intake and burned, and relieves the pressure being built up in the crankcase.

SJB (Smart Junction Box): An intermediate connection point where Ford brings different circuits together; it also has some fused circuits mounted in it.

TPS (Throttle Position Sensor): This sensor tells the computer the angle of the throttle blade so it can make adjustments to the fuel/air mix; it senses when you open or close the throttle plate to adjust the timing.

TSS (Turbine Shaft Speed Sensor): Used with automatic transmissions, this sensor reads the speed of the transmission input shaft. The information is used by the PCM to determine when to shift the transmission.

VCT and TI-VCT (Variable Camshaft Timing and Twin Independent Variable Camshaft Timing): The later engines can advance or retard the camshaft timing to improve performance on the intake timing and improve emissions on the exhaust timing.

Source Guide

Accufab
1326 E Francis St.
Ontario, CA 91761
909-930-1751
accufabracing.com

AEM Performance Electronics
2205 W 126th St., Unit A
Hawthorne, CA 90250
310-484-2322
aemelectronics.com

Aeromotive
7805 Barton St.
Lenexa, KS 66214
913-647-7300
aeromotiveinc.com

ATI ProCharger
14801 W 114th Terr.
Lenexa, KS 66215
913-338-2886
procharger.com

AutoMeter Products
413 W Elm St.
Sycamore, IL 60178
866-248-6356
autometer.com

Aviaid Competition Oil Systems
10041 Canoga Ave.
Chatsworth, CA 91311-3004
818-998-8991
aviaid.com

Baumann Electronic Controls
207 Mistr Ln.
Pickens, SC 29671
864-646-8920
becontrols.com

BBK Performance
27440 Bostik Ct.
Temecula, CA 92590
951-296-1771
bbkperformance.com

Brenspeed
8088 E 400 N
Pierceton, IN 46562
574-594-9559
brenspeed.com

BORLA Performance Industries (Induction)
500 Borla Dr.
Johnson City, TN 37604
877-462-6752
805-986-8600
borlainduction.com

BORLA Exhaust
701 Arcturus Ave.
Oxnard, CA 93033
877-462-6752
805-986-8600
borla.com

Canton Racing Products
232 Branford Rd.
North Branford, CT 06471
203-481-9460
cantonracingproducts.com

Centerforce (Midway Industries)
2266 Crosswind Dr.
Prescott, AZ 86301
928-771-8422
centerforce.com

C&R Racing
6950 Guion Rd.
Indianapolis, IN 46268
317-293-4100
crracing.com

Dakota Digital
4510 W 61st St. N
Sioux Falls, SD 57107
800-593-4160
dakotadigital.com

Dave Stribling Restorations
2110 Indianapolis Rd.
Crawfordsville, Indiana 47933
765-362-1967
davestriblingrestorations.com

Derale Performance
3901 Medford St.
Los Angeles, CA 90063
323-266-3850
derale.com

Detroit Speed
185 McKenzie Rd.
Mooresville, NC 28115
704-662-3272
detroitspeed.com

Diablosport
1790 E Airport Blvd.
Sanford, FL 32773
561-908-0040
diablosport.com

Doug's Headers (Pertronix Performance Products)
440 E Arrow Hwy.
San Dimas, CA 91773
909-599-5955
pertronix.com

Dr. DOHC
702-285-7177
drdohc@cox.net
drdohc.com

Edelbrock
2700 California St.
Torrance, CA 90503
310-781-2222
edelbrock.com

EFI Hardware Australia
7 Monomeeth Dr.
Mitcham, VC
Australia 3132
03-9873-5400
efihardware.com

Engineered Components
PO Box 841
Vernon, CT 06066
860-872-7046
ecihotrodbrakes.com

EPAS Performance
941-504-8686
epasperformance.com

Factory Five Racing
9 Tow Rd.
Wareham, MA 02571
508-291-3443
factoryfive.com

Fatman Fabrications
8621-C Fairview Rd., Hwy. 218
Mint Hill, NC 28227
704-545-0369
fatmanfab.com

Flowmaster Mufflers
707-544-4761
flowmastermufflers.com

Fluidyne
202 Raceway Dr.
Mooresville, NC 28117
704-662-8119
fluidyne.com

Ford Performance Parts
PO Box 490
Dearborn, MI 48121
800-367-3788
performanceparts.ford.com

Forte's Parts Connection
40 Pearl St.
Framingham, MA 01702
508-875-0016
forteparts.com

Fuel Air Spark Technology (FAST)
3400 Democrat Rd.
Memphis, TN 38118
877-334-8355
fuelairspark.com

Fuel Safe Systems
1550 NE Kingwood Ave.
Redmond, OR 97756
800-433-6524
fuelsafe.com

Gateway Classic Mustang
10461 N Service Rd.
Bourbon, MO 65441
800-396-6488
gatewayclassicmustang.com

SOURCE GUIDE

Griggs Racing Products
707-939-2244
griggsracing.com

Gordon Tronson Hot Rods
Las Vegas, NV
gordontronson.com
doubletroublehotrod.com

Haltech USA
157 Venture Ct., Ste. 12
Lexington, KY 40511
760-598-1941
haltech.com

Heidts Automotive
800 Oakwood Rd.
Lake Zurich, IL 60047
800-841-8188
heidts.com

Hellion Power Systems
2735 Della Rd.
Albuquerque, NM 87105
505-873-4670
hellionpowersystems.com

Helm
47911 Halyard Dr.
Plymouth, MI 48170
800-782-4356
helminc.com

Hogan's Racing Manifolds
303 N Russell Ave.
Santa Maria, CA 93458
805-928-8483
hogansracingmanifolds.com

Holley Performance
    Products
1801 Russellville Rd.
Bowling Green, KY 42101
270-782-2900
holley.com

Hot Wire Auto
256 Polk Rd. 43
Mena, AR 71953
479-243-9115
hotwireauto.com

HP Tuners
701 Dartmouth Ln.
Buffalo Grove, IL 60089
hptuners.com

Injector Dynamics
214-607-9022
injectordynamics.com

JBA Headers
440 E Arrow Hwy.
San Dimas, CA 91773
909-599-5955
jbaheaders.com

JLT Performance
1008 Executive Blvd.
Chesapeake, VA 23320
757-335-1940
jlttruecoldair.com

JMS Chip and Performance
3247 Hwy. 63 S
Lucedale, MS 39452
601-766-9424
jmschip.com

Justin's Performance Center
    (JPC)
301 Serendipity Dr.
Millersville, MD 21108
410-729-0005
jpcracing.com

JW Performance
1826 Baldwin St.
Rockledge, FL 32955
321-632-6205
racewithjw.com

Kenne Bell
10743 Bell Ct.
Rancho Cucamonga, CA
    91730
909-941-6646
kennebell.net

Kinsler Fuel Injection
1834 Thunderbird St.
Troy, MI 48084
248-362-1145
kinsler.com

K&N Engineering
PO Box 1329
Riverside, CA 92502
800-858-3333
951-826-4000
knfilters.com

Kooks Headers & Exhaust
141 Advantage Pl.
Statesville, NC 28677
1-866-586-KOOK (5665)
kooksheaders.com

Korek Designs
1030 New Berlin Mountain
    Rd.
New Berlin, PA 17855
570-966-3100
korekdesigns.com

KRC Power Steering
2115 Barrett Park Dr.
Kennesaw, GA 30144
800-451-1074
770-422-5135
krcpower.com

Krona Performance
kronaperformance.com

Lentech Automatics
3835 McBean St., Unit 2
Richmond, ON
Canada K0A 2Z0
613-838-5390
lentechautomatics.com

Lokar Performance Products
2545 Quality Ln.
Knoxville, TN 37931
865-824-9767
lokar.com

Mac's Custom Tie-Downs
PO Box 1140
Sagle, ID 83860
800-666-1586
macscustomtiedowns.com

March Performance Pulleys
16160 Performance Way
Naples, FL 34110
888-729-9070
marchperformance.com

Modern Driveline
25308 Arroyo Ct.
Caldwell, ID 83607
208-453-9800
moderndriveline.com

Modular Motorsports Racing
816 Calle Plano
Camarillo, CA 93012
805-383-4130
modularmotorsportsracing.
    com

Moroso Performance
    Products
80 Carter Dr.
Guilford, CT 06437
203-453-6571
moroso.com

MR2 Performance
722 W Pearl St.
Lebanon, Indiana 46052
765-483-9371
mr2performance.com

MSD Performance
1490 Henry Brennan Dr.
El Paso, TX 79936
888-258-3835
915-857-5200
msdperformance.com

Mustang Don's Garage
5711-C Greendale Rd.
Richmond, VA 23228
804-397-9745
mustangdon.com

Mustang Steve
1123 Bales
Cleburne, TX 76033
972-345-5466
mustangsteve.com

Mustangs To Fear
2123 Southway 31
Rochester, IN 46975
877-899-9021
574-223-9021
mustangstofear.com

Performance Automatic
5119 Pegasus Ct., Ste. F
Frederick, MD 21704
240-439-4650
performanceautomatic.com

Powermaster Motorsports
1833 Downs Dr.
West Chicago, IL 60185
630-849-7754
powermastermotorsports.
    com

Randall's Rack and Pinion
877-500-RACK (7225)
randallsrack.com

SOURCE GUIDE

The Roadster Shop
28775 N Rte. 83
Mundelein, IL 60060
847-949-RODS (7637)
roadstershop.com

Rockstar Ridez
2528 Main St., Ste. C
Chula Vista, CA 91911
619-816-8158
rockstarridez.com

Ron Morris Performance
1001 Reno Ave., Ste. 2F
Modesto, CA 95351
ronmorrisperformance.com

Russell Performance
501 Ampola Ave.
Torrance, CA 90501
310-781-2222
russellperformance.com

Sanderson Headers
517 Railroad Ave.
South San Francisco, CA 94080
800-669-2430
650-583-6617
sandersonheaders.com

Schrader Performance
3200 Lowell Rd., Ste. A
Gastonia, NC 28054
704-674-6979
schraderperformance.com

Scram Speed
4102 H Colleen Dr.
Champaign, IL 61822
866-936-9610
scramspeed.com

SCT Tuners
4150 Church St., Ste. 1024
Sanford, FL 32771
407-774-2447
sctflash.com

Sean Hyland Motorsport
691 Jack Ross Ave.
Woodstock, ON
Canada N4V 1B7
888-282-2566
519-421-2291
seanhylandmotorsport.com

SPAL Automotive USA
1731 SE Oralabor Rd.
Ankeny, IA 50021-9412
800-345-0327
spalusa.com

Specialty Car Solutions
4804 NW Bethany Blvd.
Ste. I-2, Box 261
Portland, OR 97229
800-930-7568
503-974-8552
specialtycarsolutions.com

Stainless Works
9899 E Washington St.
Chagrin Falls, OH 44023
800-878-3635
stainlessworks.net

Stifflers
(Innovative Performance
  Technologies)
660 Andico Rd., Ste. A
Plainfield, IN 46168
317-837-2444
buystifflers.com

Sullivan Performance Products
639 Pueblo Blvd.
Henderson, NV 89015
866-216-5067
702-566-1390
sullivanperformance.com

Tanks
260 Welter Dr. at Hot Rod Ln.
Monticello, IA 52310
877-596-3842
tanksinc.com

TCI Automotive
151 Industrial Dr.
Ashland, Mississippi 38603
888-776-9824
662-224-8972
tciauto.com

Thump RRR Racing
1275 Bloomfield Ave. #8-63
Fairfield, NJ 07004
862-210-8512
thumpracing.com

Tinman Fabrications
21461 Aberdeen St. NE
East Bethel, MN 55011
877-866-2338
763-753-4265
tinmanfabrication.com

Trick Flow Specialties
285 West Ave.
Tallmadge, OH 44278
330-630-1555
888-841-6556
trickflow.com

Total Control Products
A Chris Alston's Chassisworks Brand
8661 Younger Creek Dr.
Sacramento, CA 95828
888-388-0298
916-388-0288
totalcontrolproducts.com

QuickTime Bellhousings
(Holley Performance Products)
1801 Russellville Rd.
Bowling Green, KY 42101
270-782-2900
holley.com

Ultimate Headers
682 W Bagley Rd., Unit 21
Berea, OH 44017
440-234-9600
ultimateheaders.com

Vintage Air
18865 Goll St.
San Antonio, TX 78266
800-862-6658
210-654-7171
vintageair.com

VMP Performance
Deltona FL 32738
321-206-9369
vmpperformance.com

Western Motorsports
223114 Range Rd. 285
Rocky View, AB
Canada T1X 07J
403-243-6205
wmsracing.com

www.ingramcontent.com/pod-product-compliance
Lightning Source LLC
Chambersburg PA
CBHW081451070526
44586CB00019B/2308